Christmas 1988

Christmas 1988

Washtenaw County

"Partners in Progress"
by Margo MacInnes and Joan Kmenta

Produced in cooperation with the Washtenaw
County Historical Society

Windsor Publications, Inc.
Northridge, California

Washtenaw County
AN ILLUSTRATED HISTORY BY RUTH BORDIN

For Lewis G. Vander Velde and F. Clever Bald,
who understood the true importance of local history

Windsor Publications, Inc.—History Books Division
Vice-President/Publishing: Hal Silverman
Edtorial Director: Teri Davis Greenberg
Director, Corporate Biographies: Karen Story
Design Director: Alexander D'Anca

Staff for *Washtenaw County: An Illustrated History*
Photo Editor: Lynne Ferguson Chapman
Assistant Director, Corporate Biographies: Phyllis Gray
Editor, Corporate Biographies: Brenda Berryhill
Production Editor, Corporate Biographies: Thelma Fleischer
Proofreader: Susan J. Muhler
Editorial Assistants: Didier Beauvoir, Michael Nugwynne, Kathy M.B. Peyser, Pat Pittman
Sales Representative, Corporate Biographies: Greg Gavrilides
Layout Artist, Corporate Biographies: Mari Catherine Preimesberger

Designer: Christina McKibbin Rosepapa

Library of Congress Cataloging-in-Publication Data
Bordin, Ruth Birgitta Anderson, 1917-
 Washtenaw County: an illustrated history.
 Bibliography: p.172
 Includes index.
 1. Washtenaw County (Mich.)—History.
2. Washtenaw County (Mich.)—Description and travel—
Views. 3. Washtenaw County (Mich.)—Industries.
I. Washtenaw County Historical Society. II. Title.
F572.W3B67   1988   977.4'35   87-29825
ISBN 0-89781-234-4

Previous page: This winter scene captures the tranquility of Washtenaw County's countryside.
Photo by Dick Pietrzyk

Facing page: Downtown Ypsilanti in 1907 had a brick-paved street, interurban tracks that led to Ann Arbor, a single automobile, and several horse-drawn cabs and buggies. The street was first laid with bricks in 1899, and the original wooden awnings were removed that same year by order of the mayor, who wanted to modernize the city. Courtesy, Ypsilanti Historical Museum

CONTENTS

PREFACE   6

INTRODUCTION   8

CHAPTER I
A PLACE OF RIVER AND FOREST   11

CHAPTER II
A PLACE OF BOOK AND PLOUGH   29

CHAPTER III
A PLACE OF LEARNING, PRODUCE, AND
MANUFACTORY   49

CHAPTER IV
A PLACE OF STRENGTH AND QUEST   69

CHAPTER V
PARTNERS IN PROGRESS   113

BIBLIOGRAPHY   172

INDEX   174

PREFACE

Courage is the primary requisite for attempting to write a history of the county where one has lived for nearly 40 years. Every Washtenawian has strong feelings about his personal heritage and ethnic roots, his sense of place, and her sense of the "history" that preceded her. If every person is his own historian, almost everyone feels truly competent to interpret the history of his immediate environs. No one quakes at being an expert on her county. Everyone knows something unique to contribute to such a tale.

Only a mildly mad and heedlessly fearless social historian would undertake the task I have assumed. Every one of you will find some occasion to say, "But how could you write a history of Washtenaw County without . . ." But I have striven for balance, fairness, and as much completeness as very limited space allowed. So although the concerns of no single one of you receive all the attention and scope they deserve, hopefully all of you will find something that enlightens, reminds, or commemorates some part of that community we all share.

Washtenaw County is especially fortunate in the professionalism and completeness with which its records have been preserved. This has made my task considerably easier, as has the work of dozens of others who earlier have written on some phase of Washtenaw County. But this good fortune has also created a host of obligations. Many people have contributed their talents and knowledge to this volume. The Bentley Historical Library's collections, staff, and former staff members have been my chief research and picture resource. I am indebted to everyone on its roster of employees from director to page. But other repositories in the county have also assisted in invaluable ways. The county's public libraries—Ann Arbor, Ypsilanti, Dexter, Chelsea, Saline, and Manchester—have all answered queries and supplied source material. The archives of Eastern Michigan University, Concordia College, and Washtenaw Community College have been generous with pictures and staff time. The Ypsilanti and Dexter historical museums have provided splendid early photographs. The Ann Arbor Conference and Visitors Bureau has been a willing source of recent pictures. I owe to each of these preservers of the county's history some special debt.

And, of course, a salute to our forebears who provided us with such a meaningful and colorful past is in order.

Facing page: This charming engraving of the University of Michigan campus, made just before the Civil War, shows the medical building at the far left, the law building dominating the center, and the two wings of University Hall, the original classroom and dormitory building, at the right. Courtesy, Bentley Historical Library, University of Michigan

INTRODUCTION

What we now know as Washtenaw County changed direction some 160 years ago when it began to shed its ancient garb of open forest, unleashed streams, and well-worn footpaths for agricultural settlements, mills, roads, and dams. The first American settlers followed the rivers as far as they were navigable and then made their way along Indian trails. Settlement was steady in the 1820s and 1830s and subsistence agriculture was the economic mainstay. Most of the products of local farms and saw- and gristmills were consumed locally. The coming of the railroad in 1838 accelerated settlement and made new markets accessible. But the opening of the University of Michigan and Michigan Normal School were even more important, changing the fundamental character of the new community almost overnight.

Agriculture continued to flourish, especially in the southern townships, and eventually eastern and parts of western Washtenaw became part of the greater Detroit industrial complex. But research and learning, laboratories and classrooms, scientists and scholars have given Washtenaw County its essential character. The values, tastes, aspirations, recreational activities, and occupations of the county's people reflect the influence of two large centers for higher education in their midst.

Local business has been tied to library, hospital, and laboratory as frequently as to factory and engine works. It is no accident that producers of highly specialized books, the nation's largest microfilm publisher, and a major surgical instrument maker have run worldwide enterprises from within Washtenaw's borders, and that drug manufacturers and laser developers have flourished near its academic centers. Few in the county have gone untouched by higher education's presence. Ann Arbor's State Street entrepreneurs cater to the fashions of the late adolescent. The Manchester farmer has learned to satisfy exotic palates from around the world through the goods he brought to the farmers' outdoor markets. And at long last, late in the 20th century, the restaurant scene reflects the cosmopolitan taste of its patrons.

Men and women also made a difference. If Samuel Dexter, John Allen, James Kingsley, and others of Washtenaw's early developers had not been extraordinarily well-educated men—attracting others of their kind—perhaps the state's first university might not have been lured to Ann Arbor, followed in less than a decade by the nation's first teacher-training institution west of the Alleghenies. Henry Tappan and James B. Angell's visions of a national university on this side of the mountains ensured that the University of Michigan would be able to call itself a world-class institution in the later decades of the 20th century, just as John D. Pierce's and Alpheus Felch's understanding of the importance of training professional public school teachers provided the base on which Eastern Michigan University's commitment to undergraduate education could build.

Road building was still primitive and required much hand labor when the paving of trunk lines began in 1914. This stretch of M-17 was two miles east of Ypsilanti. Courtesy, Ypsilanti Historical Museum

Stands of tall pine such as this one can still be seen in some of the less populous regions of Washtenaw County. Photo by Dick Pietrzyk

I

A

PLACE OF

RIVER AND

FOREST

THE LAND ITSELF

All early travelers in what became Washtenaw County commented on its quiet beauty, sparkling streams, crystal clear lakes, and vast trees in a parklike forest with luxuriant grass and herds of graceful deer. More than one observer compared the land to an English country estate, a carefully kept bucolic paradise for strolling and hunting.

The physical features of Washtenaw County as its first settlers saw them were the product of the great glacial epochs that receded nearly 15,000 years ago. As the glaciers moved southwestward from Canada across the Great Lakes Basin, they carried with them boulders or small stones in either a clay or sand matrix and built moraines in spots where the ice held a constant position for long periods. These moraines—long, low-lying ridges—can be seen along the north bank of the Huron River or the eastern shore of Whitmore Lake. Water, escaping from the melting ice at the moraines, formed sandy plains, an example of which is found on the south

shore of Whitmore. Of Washtenaw's total area about a third is tillable clay, one-quarter is fertile, sandy soil, and one-seventh is gravelly loam. The rest of the land does not lend itself to agriculture, largely because of lakes or swamps.

The glaciers also created Washtenaw County's lakes. In the western part of the county Portage, Base, and Strawberry lakes occupy parts of an elongated pit formed by the last ice invasion. There are more than 80 other lakes more than a mile in diameter within the county's borders.

Four major rivers intersect the county. The largest is the Huron with a drainage basin of over 1,000 square miles. It traverses 90 miles before reaching Lake Erie. The Raisin, with a slightly smaller drainage basin, is actually a longer river—130 miles in length—but it crosses only Washtenaw's southern townships of Sharon, Manchester, and Bridgewater.

The east branch of the Grand River, which eventually makes its way to Lake Michigan, rises in the highlands in the western part of the county. The Saline River, which joins the Raisin before it empties into Lake Erie, forms the fourth member of the county's riparian quartet.

While the rivers made their major contribution to agriculturally based small industry, they were first used by advancing settlers as highways. Although Elisha Rumsey and John Allen, Ann Arbor's first settlers, arrived by one-horse sleigh through the snow-covered forest, many of Washtenaw's first American inhabitants poled or rowed their way just east of Ypsilanti to Rawsonville, site of the first substantial rapid water on the Huron.

Although there are no true waterfalls on Washtenaw's rivers, there are many rapids. The fall on the Huron River between Dexter and Ypsilanti is 124 feet,

Above: Although Washtenaw County's first settlers arrived overland, most of the people making their way up the Huron River Valley in the 1820s came by steamboat to Detroit. On the "Walk-in-the-Water," the first steamboat on the Great Lakes, the cost of passage ranged from seven to eighteen dollars. After 1825 a number of ships made the trip from Buffalo. Courtesy, Bentley Historical Library, University of Michigan

8 feet to the mile. The Raisin is equally well-endowed, and the economic consequences of this natural bounty were profound. The Huron River provided mill sites almost every mile, and as settlement advanced most of them were occupied at one time or another. Waterpower, augmented by crude dams, turned the wheels of the county's gristmills, sawed its lumber, and eventually drove the engines that powered its woolen mills.

The completion of the Erie Canal in 1825, linking the Hudson River with Lake Erie, facilitated travel to Michigan from the East. But the flood of water-borne immigrants began even earlier. The *Walk-in-the-Water,* the first steamboat to ply Lake Erie between Buffalo and Detroit, began service in 1818. By 1830 boats left daily from Detroit for Buffalo. Indian trails provided the second highway for settlers heading west.

Much of the land that these rivers and trails crossed was not the usual forest with heavy underbrush. Dense forest did grow along the southern border of the territory, but much of Washtenaw was parklike, carpeted with meadow grass under towering oaks. Prairie fires swept through the oak openings spring and fall, both natural fires kindled by lightning and contrived fires set by the Indians to eliminate the underbrush and facilitate hunting. The heavy corklike bark of the burr oak could withstand the fire's heat and the trees were not harmed. Maple, ash, elm, beech, and oak grew in Washtenaw County. There was so much maple that Indians had made sugar for centuries. Black walnut was also prevalent. One tree cut in Webster Township in the winter of 1827 to 1828 had a base diameter of 7 feet and was sawed into eight 12-foot logs.

The open woods with their abundant grass served as pasture for deer and scores of wild turkey. Deer and wolf were the largest animals, but red and gray fox and racoons were common in the woods, and otter frequented the banks of the Huron. Wolves still ran in packs in the Huron Valley in the 1820s, living off the deer herds and later, of course, the settlers' cattle and sheep.

Despite its abundant natural gifts, Michigan for years was dubbed "the Great Swamp" and bypassed by settlers for states further south. U.S. Surveyor General Edward Tiffin had reported in 1815, when he was charged with finding land for War of 1812 veterans, that not more than one Michigan acre out of 100 was cultivatable.

THE NATIVE AMERICANS

The inhabitants of Michigan before white settlement began were Algonquin-speaking Ottawa, Chippewa, and Potawatomi. By the time settlers arrived, the Indians had already responded to the presence of Europeans by being on the move, and few Indians actually lived in Washtenaw. Still, a good many Indians

This sketch of a male Potawatomi Indian was made about 1820. The Potawatomi lived in the territory that is now Washtenaw County, on land that was officially ceded to them by the federal government in an 1807 treaty. As a result of this treaty, Michigan settlers and the Potawatomi did not contest the territory. Ironically, the Potawatomi later agreed to go west and find new homes across the Mississippi. Courtesy, Charles Weissert Papers, Bentley Historical Library, University of Michigan

The sylvan quality of the Huron River and its economic assets have dominated Washtenaw County from its beginning. The river looks little different in this photograph from the way it looked when the first settlers arrived. Photo by Dick Pietrzyk

traversed Lima township, at least periodically, even after settlement began. They crossed from the southwest, sometimes in bands as large as a hundred, using the St. Joseph Trail on their way to Malden, Ontario, where they collected bounties for assisting the British in the War of 1812. Other transients passed near Woodruff's Grove on the Great Sauk Trail.

Earlier the Potawatomi had made their homes on Washtenaw's streams. The remains of their cornfields were long evident near the mouth of Honey Creek in Scio Township. Washtenaw's native people possessed a well-defined culture with its own teleology, rules of conduct, and political system. Their primary social unit was the clan, and their economy was nourished by a plentiful supply of fish, small game, and deer, supplemented by agriculture and gathering. They raised not only corn, but also pumpkins, squash, and beans. They ate wild plants—sunflower seeds, milkweed roots, lily bulbs, berries, wild rice, and edible nuts. They dried berries, pumpkin, and squash for the winter.

Indian claims to the part of Michigan that includes Washtenaw were officially relinquished by treaty in 1807. So-called chiefs of the Ottawa, Chippewa, Potawatomi, and Huron tribes were assembled in Detroit. They signed there a treaty with Territorial Governor William Hull, ceding to the United States a large area in southern Michigan. In return they received $10,000 in cash, some merchandise, and the promise of $2,400 annually.

BEGINNINGS OF SETTLEMENT

When the first permanent white settlers arrived in Washtenaw in 1823, Europeans had been living in the county for a dozen years and had been around sporadically much longer. After Detroit was settled in 1701, fur traders and Jesuits visited the area while the French fleur-de-lis flew over southeastern Michigan. During the Seven Years War the French were replaced by the British, who continued to occupy the area until 1796, when the United States finally took possession of territory ceded in the Peace of Paris (1783), which ended the Revolutionary War. The British, however, burned Detroit during the War of 1812, and it was not until 1815 that American control was truly secure.

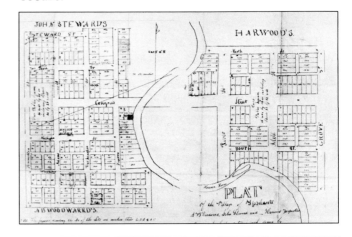

Above: In 1918 a Potawatomi tepee was erected on Michigan Normal's campus. Julia Pokagon, granddaughter of a Potawatomi chief, attended the dedication ceremonies with her husband and children. The wigwam had originally been erected at Chicago's Columbian Exposition of 1893. Courtesy, Eastern Michigan University Archives

Above right: In 1825 this plat of the village of Ypsilanti was entered by proprietors Augustus Woodward, John Stewart, and William Harwood at the United States government land office in Detroit. The proprietors arranged for the Huron River, then unbridged, to divide the new settlement almost equally, an arrangement that led to future difficulties. Note the provision for two public squares, assuring land for common use. Courtesy, Bentley Historical Library, University of Michigan

No photographs could have been taken of the first settlers of Woodruff's Grove. However, this couple with ox cart, oxen, and driver, restaging the first settlement for the 1923 centennial, probably looked remarkably like the original residents. Courtesy, Ypsilanti Historical Museum

YPSILANTI

VILLAGE LOTS AT AUCTION.

On Friday, the 8th day of June next.

THE subscriber, one of the proprietors of the village of YPSILANTI, in the county of Washtenaw, will offer for sale at the time and place of the sale of the Contracts on the Chicago Road, the part of said village owned by him, consisting of about one hundred lots. Payment to be made by instalments, and terms easy. Particulars on the day of sale.

Of the local advantages, and prospects of Ypsilanti, to those who are acquainted with it, and with other parts of the peninsula, it is unnecessary to say any thing. To those who are not acquainted with it, the subscriber would say, situated as it is, upon a navigable stream, and that one of the finest in the Territory, with the advantages of water power to any extent, surrounded by a pleasant, healthy and fertile country, and watered by numerous crystal springs of the clearest and purest water, with the great road from Detroit to Chicago passing directly through it, Ypsilanti cannot fail of becoming, at no very distant period, one of the most important towns in Michigan.

YPSILANTI has an elevated and uncommonly healthy and agreeable situation, on the banks of the River Huron, in the flourishing county of Washtenaw. It is 30 miles from Detroit; 33 from Pontiac; 8 1-2 from Ann Arbour; 17 from Dexter; 1 from Woodruff's Grove; 25 from Monroe; and 25 from Tecumseh.

The surrounding country, though mostly open, affords an abundance of the best of timber for boards and the frames of buildings. There are several *Saw Mills* in the neighborhood, and one in the immediate vicinity of the Village. There is also a *Grist Mill* in operation, on the River, about a mile below. Lime, of the best quality, is made in abundance near by, and there has lately been discovered in the vicinity, a valuable and extensive quarry of Stone, suitable for building, and preparations are now making for sawing it into jambs, mantel-pieces, window-caps, &c. Every facility for building, is afforded in abundance.

The Road from Detroit to Chicago, which is shortly to be opened, passes through one of the most delightful countries in the world, and when completed, will, no doubt, in connexion with Lake Erie, become a great thoroughfare from New-York and the Eastern States, to Indiana, Illinois, Missouri, and the country bordering on the Mississippi River.

The unexampled rapidity with which the county of Washtenaw has settled, is evidence of the value of this section of country; and the local position of Ypsilanti, with its abundance of water power, render it one of the most eligible situations for a large manufacturing town, in the western country, where the enterprize of the capitalist, the mechanic and manufacturer, will be sure to find a speedy reward.

LUCIUS LYON.

Detroit, May 24, 1827.

Printed by Chipman & Seymour, Detroit.

This opened the way for permanent settlement of the hinterlands.

Around 1822 or 1823 two former French fur traders, Gabriel Godfroy and Romaine de Chambre, gave up their trading post near what is now Huron and Pearl streets in Ypsilanti and sold their land patents. The buyers were Augustus Woodward, Andrew McKinstry and Henry Hunt, who almost immediately resold his share to John Stewart. Woodward had no interest in settling the land himself, and he shortly sold his tract thereafter to Lucius Lyon, another prominent Michigan land speculator who later became one of the state's first two senators. In 1823, almost at the same time, Major Benjamin Woodruff purchased 160 acres in Ypsilanti Township and founded a settlement called Woodruff's Grove. By the next year settlers occupied eight log cabins in his little hamlet.

All this activity signaled that Michigan was politically stable and ready for development. So was Washtenaw. By 1822 Governor Lewis Cass had already laid out the county with 40 townships and given it a name. People were gathering in Detroit looking either for speculative property or new homes in the wilderness, and many shared both motives.

John Allen, one of Ann Arbor's founders, was among them. He had both a compelling need to speculate and considerable experience in business. Allen was born of Scots-Irish ancestry into an old Virginia landowning family. His father James Allen had farmed and had owned a large milling establishment. But James came close to bankruptcy, and John Allen assumed many of his father's debts. By 1822 he owed some $40,000 despite two marriages to wealthy women. Allen left Virginia because of his financial difficulties and, like many others, saw speculation in western lands as a way of recouping his fortune. Allen also enjoyed meeting new challenges. Both motives combined to lure him into the wilderness.

Allen's partner, Elisha Rumsey, was of a similar bent. He had been accused of absconding to avoid his debts; he also may have deserted his original family for another woman. His financial affairs were settled on a trip back to Albany, New York, soon after he visited Michigan for the first time in 1824. But he promptly returned west to avoid the strong feeling against him in the East. He too looked to land speculation as a way to recoup his fortune; he had the added personal incentive to start a new life where his past marital difficulties were unknown.

Samuel Dexter, although still a relatively young man, had been on the move before. He had left his native Boston for Athens, New York, in 1816. But, after the death of his first wife in 1822, he traveled to Detroit and began the purchase of Michigan land that led to his settling in Washtenaw County in 1825.

Above: The early developers of Washtenaw reveled in pointing out the advantages of settling in the county. Easy access to water power, fertile land, quantities of timber, a healthy climate, nearness to Detroit, and the projected Chicago Road were several reasons why the "capitalist, the mechanic and manufacturer" should come to the Huron Valley, according to this advertisement. Courtesy, Clements Library, University of Michigan

Major Benjamin Woodruff, who founded the first community in the Ypsilanti area, came to Michigan from Ohio because he wished to invest his wife's inheritance in speculative lands. The estate was large enough so that he did not personally farm, at least at first, but spent his time assisting new settlers to make his investment multiply. John Dix was a restless man who spent less than ten years in Dixboro, the village he founded, before he pushed on to a new frontier in Texas.

Whatever the reasons—lure of wealth, the need to rebuild an economic base, or complicated interpersonal relationships—venturesome men, often with their wives and families, trickled into Washtenaw County and began to create homes, farms, and businesses. Most of them were in vigorous middle age. John Allen was the youngest at 28. Elisha Rumsey was ten years older. Samuel Dexter was 32, Woodruff was 39, and John Dix was 41. Most either had or once had

money and, at the very least, possessed a stake that permitted them to purchase the land they hoped would make their fortunes.

Although Benjamin Woodruff preceded Allen and Rumsey in putting down roots in Washtenaw, Ann Arbor became the county's intellectual and commercial center. Its lead came early, and was given an initial boost by its founding fathers.

John Allen from Virginia and Elisha Rumsey from Genesee County, New York, met in Detroit in January 1824. Allen had traveled through Canada and stopped in Detroit on his way to Ohio, where he expected to take up land. But in conversation with local merchants and political leaders, the Ohio plan was abandoned. In February the two men set out on the Indians' Great Sauk Trail for Woodruff's Grove, looking for a likely site for their town. On February 12 they returned to Detroit and registered their claims to a beautiful spot near the Huron River that promised fertile soil and

This log cabin built near Dexter in 1839 was still standing at the turn of the century. Erected several years after the first settlement in the area, it had several amenities that would not have been available earlier, such as sash windows, a shingle roof, and a real door. Courtesy, Dexter Historical Museum

convenient waterpower. Allen took 480 acres and Rumsey 160 acres for which they paid $600 and $200, respectively. One of their first acts was to petition Territorial Governor Lewis Cass to make their nonexistent community the county seat of the still-unorganized Washtenaw County. They left nothing to chance.

In less than a month they had obtained official designation of their town site as the county seat. By spring Rumsey and his wife had moved from a tent into a log house that doubled as the village inn. Four hundred lots had been platted and staked by June, a hundred of which had already been taken, and several frame houses were being built. Two sawmills and a gristmill were either contemplated or under construction. Ann Arbor was boomtown incarnate.

By the time John Allen's family joined him in October 1824 he had over 15 acres ploughed and fenced. He also had erected a log blockhouse on the northwest corner of what is now Main and Huron to shelter his family and anyone else heading west. In 1824 a visitor reported 35 people under its roof.

By the end of 1825 Washtenaw County boasted a population of 1,500 people. Growth, however, did not mean comfort. Despite the relative prosperity of the founders, the initial hardships cannot be overestimated, and the women—frequently pregnant, nursing infants, or carrying toddlers—felt the deprivations most keenly. Ann Rumsey gave birth to a baby girl at Woodruff's Grove on her way to Ann Arbor, a child that was stillborn or soon died. Ann Allen's daughter, Sarah, was less than two when Ann made the long and arduous trip on horseback to Michigan from Virginia.

Margaret Noble came with her husband to Dexter in 1825. She began her memoir, "My husband was seized by the mania." In 1824 he made a trip west to choose land. He promptly fetched his family and eventually settled in Dexter. Both Nobles suffered

from chills and fever during the summer months of their first years in the territory and were hard-pressed to erect a log house and plant crops between bouts of illness. Margaret Noble carried much of the burden. She raised the rafters and put on a roof, drew stones for the chimney, loaded and stacked hay, fed the cattle, and cut wood. During the first winter in Dexter she bundled up her two small children and brought them outside to warm up in the sun against the side of the cabin. The family was once over three weeks without flour for bread. She admitted the "want of society, church privileges, and in fact almost everything that makes life desirable, would often make me

Above: When Ypsilanti celebrated its centennial in 1923, the Kiwanis club erected an authentic pioneer log cabin from Willis in Gilbert Park. This reconstruction was probably a bit more comfortable than the first settlers' dwellings, which usually did not have windows or chimneys. Courtesy, Ypsilanti Historical Museum

Opposite page, below: No known portrait exists of Judge Augustus Woodward, who named Ypsilanti after a Greek hero and was one of its developers. However, Woodward may have resembled this drawing, made from a verbal description. Courtesy, Bentley Historical Library, University of Michigan

sad in spite of all efforts to the contrary."

Although imported supplies were meager, the land itself was bountiful. Venison was the staple of the settlers' diet, but ducks, prairie chickens, turkeys, and geese were available as well as fish. Wild berries were plentiful, and a good bee tree could yield a year's supply of honey. Maple sugar could be had for the labor of sugaring off. But even hunting and gathering could prove difficult. Game disappeared from the neighborhood for weeks. Berries only ripened in season, and equipment for sugaring was not always at hand. Preparing food over open outdoor fires was backbreaking work for the women, and their clothes often caught fire.

Despite these hardships there were lighthearted times. Independence Day was a secular holiday celebrated from the beginning. Benjamin Woodruff presumably invited everyone in the county to the Grove for the Fourth of July in 1824. Woodruff himself made a trip to Detroit for loaf sugar, cheese, raisins, rice, and a half-barrel of whiskey. A beef was killed and the meat roasted over an open fire. Dinner was served on rough boards, but the boards were covered with hand-woven linen brought from previous homes.

The menu represented real luxury: warm biscuits with butter and honey, cheese, rice pudding, new potatoes, peas and beets, chicken as well as beef, and loaf cake filled with raisins. A log was set up to resemble a cannon and rifles were fired to emulate salutes. Woodruff read the Declaration of Independence and all joined in singing *Hail Columbia*. A fiddler played for dancing in the evening. This gay interruption in the hardship and toil of the settlers' daily lives remained a vivid memory for the rest of their days.

CHOOSING A NAME

The origin of place names is often a puzzle, with legend frequently replacing fact. The Huron River was called *Cosscutenongsebee* (also transliterated *Giwita-tigweiasibi*) by the Potawatomi. The word meant "burnt district river," referring to the oak openings that graced its shores. White traders found that hard to pronounce and so named the river after the Huron people. The Raisin River was named by the French, *La Riviere du Raisin,* for the abundant wild grapes that lined its banks. The Saline River and the village that bears its name referred to the salt springs nearby. Manchester reflected the English origin of some of its early settlers. Base Lake acquired its name because the baseline of the early land survey ran through it, and Portage Lake refers to the portage made there by Indian travelers. Independence Lake received its name from a Fourth of July picnic held on its shores in the 1820s.

Legends abound about the origin of the name Washtenaw. Some say it was the name of an Indian who lived near the mouth of the river, that it was a Potawatomi corruption of Washington, the great white father, or that it meant large stream or river. Emerson Greenman, a former curator of the museum of anthropology at the University of Michigan, wrote that Washtenaw derived from the Algonquin and meant "far country," with Detroit as the point of departure. The early French applied the name to the Grand River, which they saw as far from Detroit, and its choice for the county that now bears the name was purely arbitrary.

Ypsilanti was first called Springfield, a name that would not have distinguished it from a dozen other communities. But Judge Augustus B. Woodward, one of the early land speculators in the area, insisted on Ypsilanti. Woodward, appointed by Thomas Jefferson as a territorial judge, was a classicist and a romantic. He closely followed the Greek war for independence, and was much taken with Demetrius Ypsilanti, the Greek republican hero. He felt that Demetrius Ypsilanti deserved celebration in the name of an American city. Thrilled by the American Revolution, Woodward journeyed to America and reportedly fought at the battle of Monmouth.

The touching story that Ann Arbor was named after the grape arbor that linked the property of the Rumseys and Allens and where their wives, the two Anns, rested on hot summer days is undoubtedly apocryphal. Ann Arbor was almost certainly named after the two Anns, for Mary Ann Rumsey was usually called by that part of her name. But "arbor" simply meant a woodsy place, and the early site was abundantly endowed.

Several communities in the county were given the names of their founders—Dixboro after John Dix, Foster Station after Samuel Foster, and Dexter after Samuel Dexter. Others like Bridgewater described the site. Webster was named for Daniel Webster and reflects Samuel Dexter's Whiggish propensities. A few towns such as Lima and Delhi exemplified the romantic early-19th century custom of naming new communities after exotic places but providing them with new pronunciations.

GOVERNANCE AND LEADERSHIP

Washtenaw County was organized apart from Wayne County in 1826, with Ann Arbor as the county seat. But the newly independent Washtenaw included substantial portions of what later became Livingston, Ingham, and Jackson counties. As settlement reached those western areas they in turn became separate political entities. Originally only three townships were created—Ypsilanti, Ann Arbor, and Dexter. Scio, Manchester, and Webster were originally part of Dexter. Northfield and Pittsfield were part of Ann Arbor. Ypsilanti included the area later split off into Augusta, Superior, and Salem.

Businesses, mills, houses, city lots, and farmland changed hands frequently in the first decade of settlement, often to the enrichment of the original owner. John Allen's first investment of $600 became a bonanza: six years after he purchased the acreage that lay north of what is now Huron Street in Ann Arbor, he was selling lots that had cost him 75 cents for several hundred dollars. By the 1830s he lived well in a house he had built at Main and Catherine and enjoyed carriages, servants, and the other accoutrements of the prosperous life. However, Rumsey's early death in 1827 prevented him from following as advantageous a course.

John Allen took his new fortune to New York City in 1836. He bought a house on Broadway for $16,000 and began to establish himself on Wall Street, but his financial empire crumbled in the panic of 1837. He returned to Ann Arbor and manfully faced his debts. His wife Ann left him in the 1840s, however, to return to her family in Virginia, where she lived with her son until her death in 1875. Allen then joined other adventurers off to California's gold rush in 1849. He died there in 1851 without finding the pot of gold he needed to recoup his fortune.

It was Samuel Dexter who put down the deepest roots. Dexter originally bought a thousand acres in what are now Dexter, Lima, Scio, and Webster townships. He built his first cabin in Webster Township in 1824. But he sold this building and the surrounding land to Charles B. Taylor, who in turn became one of Webster's founding fathers. Dexter originally owned all of the site of Dexter village, and he erected several buildings that he sold. But after 1841, when he built the great house that still stands on the rise west of town, he chose to stay put until his death in 1863; his third wife, Millisent, continued to live there for most of the century.

The early land developers also dabbled in commercial, manufacturing, and financial enterprises. Almost all took up innkeeping soon after their arrival. The general store was usually the next business venture

Top: This late nineteenth century photograph of the Dexter mansion depicts the original Greek Revival structure with its great columns, imposing entrance, and classic facade. On the left is a tower constructed by Mrs. Dexter after the judge's death in 1863. It may have offered a breathtaking view, but it did not add to the classical grandeur of the house, and it was removed after her death. Courtesy, Dexter Historical Museum

Above: Washtenaw County's first courthouse was built in 1834 on the square set aside by John Allen for that purpose. A classic Greek Revival building heated with fireplaces, it served as headquarters for the county government until 1878, when it was replaced by an elaborate structure with mansard roof and tower. The current courthouse, dating from the 1950s, occupies the same site. From Chapman, History of Washtenaw County

to appear. A sawmill was also a necessity if building was to go forward. Once the first crops were harvested there was need for a gristmill. In his first five years in Ann Arbor, John Allen—with the help of his partner Rumsey and his family—acted as innkeeper, storekeeper, mill owner, and newspaper publisher.

Even an ordinary carpenter could turn his skills into quick profit those first years. Asa Smith, an early Ann Arborite, made it a practice to build a house, move into it, build a second, and sell the first. He built and lived in a dozen of Ann Arbor's early houses in this way. John Shaw, an Ypsilantian, sold the crops in his fields (with the fields) a year after he established his claim.

Later the founding fathers played an active role in public service. The larger concerns of the community were always important to John Allen. He built a small schoolhouse in 1825 that was also used as a church. The original plat of Ann Arbor provided that Allen would donate land for a courthouse square, the Ann Arbor city block still used for that purpose, and Rumsey would give a plot on the other side of Huron Street for a jail. Many of the original developers also served as their community's first postmaster and judge.

The territorial court for Washtenaw County met for the first time in January 1827 with Samuel Dexter and Oliver Whitmore, an early settler of Pittsfield for whom the lake is named, as presiding judges. But the first courthouse, an attractive two-story Greek Revival building that was to serve the county well for half a century, was not erected until 1834. It was replaced in the 1870s by the imposing ornate structure (well-known through Milt Kemnitz's drawing) that was in turn replaced by the marble edifice of the 1950s.

Incorporation of villages came later. Ypsilanti was organized in 1832; Ann Arbor in 1833 when the county's population had already reached 4,000 people. Although Saline was platted in 1830, it was not incorporated until after the Civil War, as was Manchester. Woodruff's Grove remained unincorporated; it was eventually annexed by Ypsilanti.

Other than courts and the mail, government services were minimal. Not until 1836 did Ann Arbor organize a volunteer fire department and provide it with a hand engine and a hook-and-ladder wagon. Ypsilanti did not have formal provisions for fire fighting

until the 1850s. A village water supply, dependent on hand pump and cistern, was a private matter everywhere in the mid-19th century.

Even the streets were at best the recipients of benign neglect. Rail fences marked Ann Arbor's streets almost from the beginning, and after sawmills began operation, picket fences and a few boardwalks made their appearance. The streets themselves were, of course, mud or dust, depending on the season. Men tucked their trouser legs in their boots, but the long skirts of women must have been permanently embroidered with dirt.

If civic amenities usually received short shrift, on at least one occasion farsighted attention to detail improved the quality of life for generations. Judge Dexter's site plan provided that all streets intersecting Dexter's main thoroughfare (Ann Arbor Street) join it at an angle. The result was that the early Dexter houses were laid out, not directly north-south or east-west but across the compass, and consequently, as the founder planned, have sun in every room at some time of day.

MERCHANDISING AND MANUFACTURING

Washtenaw County was one of the best farming counties in the United States in the 19th century, but its abundant waterpower also provided manufacturing opportunities, all of which were tied to agriculture in the early years. Early industry followed the river. Grist- and sawmills, a tannery, and a distillery lined the Huron by the time settlement in the county was ten years old. Although mills were scattered everywhere, the commercial lumber industry was centered in Ypsilanti. At least three communities—Ann Arbor, Dexter, and Ypsilanti—had blacksmith shops. Distilleries came early in the larger towns, providing a convenient way to market grain. Ann Arbor had a tannery for processing the hides of farm animals as early as 1827, and Ypsilanti had a carding mill that fashioned wool into shanks of yarn by 1829.

Mercantile establishments also grew in number and degree of specialization. The improvised inns in people's homes of the mid-1820s were replaced in larger settlements by more ambitious buildings specializing in hospitality. Chauncey Goodrich built the Goodrich House, a respectable hostelry on a city

block he purchased for $1,000 just east of Court House square in Ann Arbor. Ypsilanti had its Perry House, built by Chester Perry and Salmon Champion in 1827. Specialized mercantile establishments such as grocery, shoe, and dry-goods stores joined the general store in the 1830s.

By 1833 the county had 12 mercantile establishments, 3 distilleries, a pail factory, a fanning mill, a gunsmith, a wagon maker, 5 flouring mills, 13 sawmills, and a carding mill. Many of these establishments changed hands frequently and were sometimes short-lived, but the essential economic services of an agricultural community were provided.

CREDIT OR BUST

Banking was slower than commercial and mercantile activity to establish itself in the county. But Washtenaw County, like the rest of southeastern Michigan, had its share of wildcat banks in the mid-1830s. The reelection of Andrew Jackson as president in 1832 ensured easy credit and an end to the financial power of the conservatively managed Bank of the United States. State banks multiplied and financed the phenomenal explosion in the sale of public lands that resulted from a flood of immigration into states like Michigan. Washtenaw County, where the population

was estimated at about 4,000 in 1832, had 21,000 inhabitants five years later. But this boom in credit, land sales, and population was not created without a little chicanery and a great deal of overoptimism.

The Michigan legislature had eased the high capital requirements for state banks—permitting their establishment with a small paid-in capital and the remainder secured by real estate. These banks' collateral was frequently paper lots platted in the woods that speculators had parlayed into imaginary cities. But even the liberal new banking rules were honored in the breach. It took only 18 months for the Huron River Bank of Ypsilanti to go broke. The Bank of Superior, organized by farmers in Superior Township, had securities so defective that it never actually opened. The failure of these schemes meant that no further banking activity was attempted in the county until the Civil War.

A MILITARY PRESENCE

Although the Indians were no longer residents of Washtenaw County when the first settlers arrived, the early settlers felt a psychological need for some kind of protection. Probably this feeling can be explained by the nearby presence of the British, who had long used Indian disaffection to stir up violence on the

Above: The Bank of Washtenaw was one of the short-lived establishments that flourished during the wildcat banking craze of the 1830s. No one knows if this three-dollar certificate was redeemed or not. If it had been, it probably would not have ended up in the scrapbook of Lucy Chapin, daughter of one of Ann Arbor's early businessmen. Courtesy, Bentley Historical Library, University of Michigan

American frontier. Settlers met in the Ypsilanti area in the spring of 1826 and organized a company—a makeshift affair of farmers and storekeepers under the captainship of Andrew McKinstry. The company had nothing to do except drill and parade, however, until the Black Hawk War created an excuse for a flurry of military action.

In the 1820s, the Sauk and Fox Indians had been forced beyond the Mississippi to make way for white settlers. But in 1832 their leader, Black Hawk, brought his people back across the river to reclaim their fields. White settlers were in a panic, reinforced when the Indians responded with violence to the use of federal force. Although the poor Sauk and Fox came nowhere near Washtenaw and were soon pushed back across the Mississippi, where most of them were slaughtered, Michigan was rife with rumors of invasion. Companies were mobilized to advance along the Chicago Road and save Michigan, including one that rendezvoused in Ann Arbor. But news of the Indians' defeat met them at Saline, and the troops were disbanded and sent home after six days under arms. The so-called Toledo War lasted somewhat longer and more intimately involved Washtenaw men.

In 1832 Michigan petitioned Congress for permission to write a state constitution. At that time, its southern boundary was designated as stipulated in the Northwest Ordinance of 1787: a line due east from the southern tip of Lake Michigan. The location of the southern rim of the lake, however, was unknown in 1787 and still uncertain when Ohio wrote its constitution in 1802. Ohio hedged and defined its northern border as either the ordinance line or the northern shore of Maumee Bay should the ordinance line fall below that point.

In 1805 Congress had organized Michigan Territory with the ordinance line as the southern boundary. Two United States surveys were made, one putting Toledo in Ohio, the other in Michigan. Until 1835 Michigan territorial officers governed the disputed area, its public lands were sold from Michigan land offices, and its inhabitants voted in Michigan territorial elections. Quite probably there were people in Washtenaw who owned land in the disputed strip that they had purchased thinking it was part of Michigan.

President Andrew Jackson meanwhile was determined to solve the dispute without force. Although the legal and geographical evidence favored Michigan, Jackson looked ahead to the election of 1836 when he wished to see his protege, Martin Van Buren, occupy the White House. Ohio was a state. Its citizens could vote in national elections, and Jackson was not about to alienate them. Michigan Governor Stevens T. Mason and Governor Robert Lucas of Ohio were equally determined. Mason could expect no help from Washington and felt he must call out the state militia to defend the so-called Toledo strip.

In April 1835 Captain Morell Goodrich, whose father owned the Goodrich House in Ann Arbor, was ordered to take his company to Ypsilanti. There he joined a cavalry troop under the command of Captain Lee Forsythe. The orders were to consolidate the companies, but who was to command? The local battle was settled by a throw of the dice, Ann Arbor won, and Ypsilanti had to be content with a second lieutenancy. But the victors were generous and provided, according to Goodrich's memoir, adequate liquid consolation at the Andrews House in Ypsilanti. Foraging the countryside for culinary and liquid rations along the way, the troops proceeded toward Toledo via Monroe. They camped on the outskirts of Toledo while two commissioners from Washington persuaded the belligerent governors to confer. The situation eased somewhat and Washtenaw's brave sons returned home. But the military phase of the Toledo War went on through September with the boundary still unsettled.

After another long year of wrangling, Michigan capitulated. Perpetual status as a territory was hardly appealing, and Michiganians were eager for full participation in the Union. A first Convention of Assent, as it was called, met at the courthouse in Ann Arbor in September 1836. But delegates voted to reject the compromise proposed by Congress to trade the Toledo strip for the western part of the Northern Peninsula. A second conference in December gave way, and Michigan entered the Union in 1837, two years after its constitution was written.

THE RAILROAD ENDS AN ERA

Washtenaw County's newspaper, appropriately named the *Western Emigrant,* reported on October 23, 1839:

Last Thursday was a proud and happy day for Ann Arbor. All was gaiety and delight. People came from all quarters to witness the arrival of the cars for the first time at our new and beautiful depot and to aid our citizens in the reception and entertainment of their civil and military guests.

The railroad had arrived! Over a thousand visitors from Detroit were on hand. The Brady Guards joined the Washtenaw Guards, the local militia, and pitched their tents in Court House square where a splendid banquet had been prepared. The end of an era was at hand. Washtenaw County was no longer a frontier community.

Plans for a railroad went back to 1831 when the Detroit and St. Joseph Railroad had been chartered, and settlements along its route were urged to subscribe capital. Construction began in 1836 and the cars reached Ypsilanti with appropriate festivities in February 1838. By 1839 Ann Arbor, the county seat, was linked to Detroit by rail. Four runs a day, a freight and passenger train each way, put the rest of the world at Washtenaw's fingertips.

The facilities were primitive. Thin iron straps covered the continuous oak rails and frequently came loose, curled up, and pierced the cars. Passenger injuries were common. But the new settler could now move in relative comfort across the Atlantic, up the Hudson River, through the Erie Canal, across the Great Lakes, all by water, and to Ann Arbor by rail. The county had truly come of age.

The railroad had made it from Detroit to Ypsilanti by June 1838, but the stage still transported passengers to points west. Courtesy, Bentley Historical Library, University of Michigan

Ypsilanti's Union School, the first in the county, was purchased from Charles Woodruff, son of Benjamin, who built it as a private academy. Originally there were dormitories in its upper stories, to accommodate the boarders who could obtain no secondary education in their own communities. Courtesy, Ypsilanti Historical Museum

II

A

PLACE OF

BOOK AND

PLOUGH

"Religion, morality, and knowledge being necessary to good government . . . schools and the means of education shall forever be encouraged."

Those words from the Northwest Ordinance of 1787, the first organic act to provide Michigan with political structure and tenets, were taken seriously in Michigan. From an early date Michigan had a constitutionally mandated state school system crowned by a publicly supported university, and the Northwest Ordinance's promise was abundantly fulfilled in Washtenaw County.

A PUBLIC COMMITMENT

Although concern for education was present from first settlement, provision for education had to be improvised in the early years. Tax-supported education was not even a dream; parents were expected to underwrite most of the costs, and no secondary education was truly public in the county until the 1840s.

Washtenaw's first schoolhouse was a little log building erected in 1824 in Pittsfield Township. Only 15 settlers occupied the neighborhood. But their families were large, and Harriet Parsons, the young daughter of Pittsfield pioneers Roswell and Agnes Parsons, taught the children for a season, just as she was to teach Ann Arbor youngsters two years later. In 1829 John Allen erected Ann Arbor's first school building, which also served as the church, and William Harwood provided similar facilities in Ypsilanti in 1831. Saline's town meeting appropriated public funds for a schoolhouse completed the same year.

School sessions were irregular, usually a winter and summer term, leaving spring and fall for planting and harvest. A single teacher, frequently a young woman working for a pittance, taught the rudiments to a mixed class of boys and girls of varying ages and was paid by the parents of her pupils.

Select schools, private secondary schools dedicated to studies that were called the higher branches, meaning some mathematics, elementary science, rhetoric, logic, and a smattering of classical languages, made their appearance by the 1830s. These schools typically met in homes or in second-story rooms over places of business.

The county's most famous private academy was the Misses Clarks' School for Girls, which educated Washtenaw young women from 1839 to 1875 in a half-dozen Ann Arbor locations. Four sisters, the oldest of whom, Mary, had been trained at Emma Willard's famous seminary in Troy, New York, were its proprietors, teachers, and matron. The Clarks' pupils either boarded or lived at home and studied a curriculum modeled on the Troy academy, learning botany and some French along with algebra, geometry, and literature.

At mid-century public union schools, teaching the upper division, were inaugurated in Ypsilanti, Ann Arbor, and Dexter. The Ypsilanti Union Seminary, purchased by the school district in 1848 from Benjamin Woodruff's son Charles, was the first of these. The three-story building and its 15 teachers attracted a sizable number of students from out-county, many of whom lived in the upper-story dormitory. During the years when Joseph Estabrook, a distinguished educator who later headed Michigan Normal, was principal, it prepared many country lads for college.

In 1856 Ann Arbor's Union School opened on the corner of Huron and State, a site used for the city's high school for nearly a hundred years. Although it never accepted boarders, 60 percent of its students came from out-of-town to prepare for the University of Michigan. By the 1880s it was one of the leading preparatory schools in the nation, but it was not a free (meaning tuition free) school in its early years. Although the building was erected with public funds, tuition covered most of the costs of staffing and maintenance.

Dexter was the only other Washtenaw community to attempt public secondary education before the Civil War. Its Union School opened in 1857. Manchester opened a union school in 1867 and Saline a year later.

A FRONTIER DREAM: LEADING THE WAY IN HIGHER EDUCATION

Washtenaw's heavy commitment to secondary education resulted from the presence within its borders of the state's first two institutions of higher learning. Michigan's first constitution in 1835 provided for a state university, and unlike many other states, denied public monies to sectarian schools. Thus all state resources for higher education went to strengthen public institutions. Two months after statehood was achieved, legislation was passed providing for a university with literary, law, and medical departments, as well as branches in several other counties to serve as preparatory and secondary schools.

Michigan's precocious commitment to higher education was made possible because the money to realize this ambitious dream was in hand. It was the practice of Congress to grant new states public land for the support of a university. In 1826, early in the process of settlement, Congress authorized that, in Michigan, selection of these lands should begin before the public land office opened new areas to sale. Some of the best land in southern Michigan was set aside for university purposes, and the subsequent sale of these lands realized an average of 12 dollars an acre, more than twice that of any other educational grant in the Old Northwest.

This generous endowment permitted considerable financial independence of the state legislature in the University of Michigan's first years, and it provided a solid base on which the growing institution later

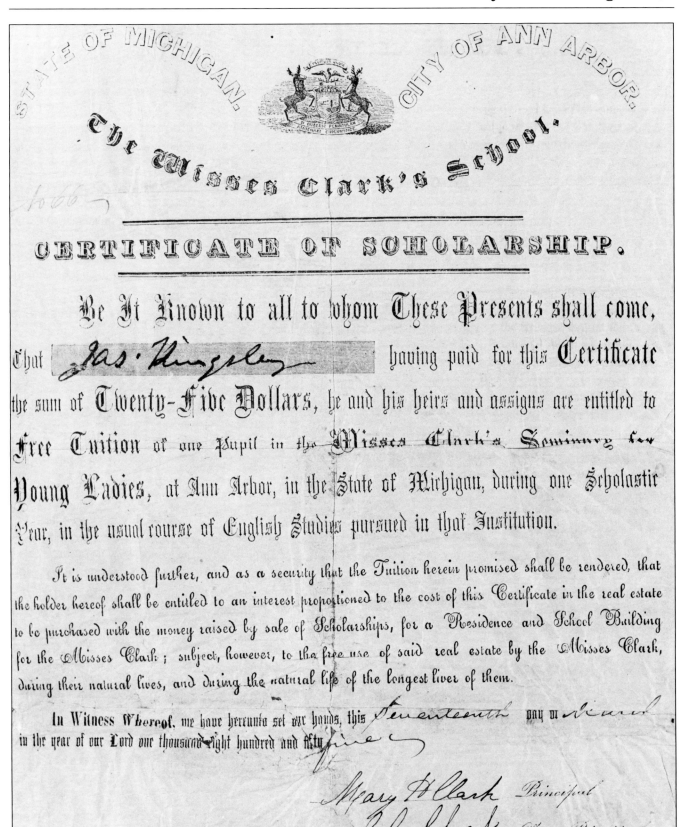

It was common practice in the mid-nineteenth century for a private school to sell scholarships to prospective patrons to raise capital for buildings. The Misses Clark employed this tactic to build a residence and school building. James Kingsley, early Ann Arbor capitalist who had promoted Ann Arbor as the site for a university, either bought this certificate for one of his children or as a favor to the Misses Clark. Courtesy, Lucy Chapin Scrapbooks, Bentley Historical Library, University of Michigan

expanded its fiscal autonomy. In the 1870s a part of the state property tax was set aside by law for the University's continuing support, thereby permitting its general funds to remain independent of the legislature until the 1930s.

Citizens of Ann Arbor, eager to profit from the projected institution of higher learning, won out over other communities competing for the school. A group of enterprising citizens calling themselves the Ann Arbor Land Company, and including among their members Charles Thayer and William S. Maynard, acquired all available land east of the village and offered a 40-acre site that still forms the central campus square. This land had previously been part of the farm of Elisha Rumsey's brother. James Kingsley and Orrin White meanwhile lobbied vigorously in the legislature for Ann Arbor as the final choice. At first the regents preferred a pretty, wooded, hilly site along north State Street near the river (one wonders at the beauty of such a campus), but the land company eventually prevailed.

The regents of the University at first hoped to add a touch of grandeur to the institution and hired a well-known New Haven architect to draw an elaborate campus plan that would have cost a half million dollars to construct. But the sale of University lands could not support such extravagance and forced the substitution of a more modest enterprise. It took four years to build six buildings—two dormitory-classroom buildings along the State Street side of the square and four houses for professors, two on North University and two on South University, all facing toward the cen-

Above left: Henry Tappan, first president of the University of Michigan, published a book in 1851 in which he declared, "In our country we have no Universities, whatever may be the names by which we choose to call our institutions of learning." Tappan came to Michigan to establish a true university, putting the older men's colleges of the eastern seaboard on their mettle. Courtesy, Ruth Bordin

Above right: James Burrill Angell became president of the University of Michigan in 1871 at the age of 42. A handsome, vigorous man, Angell left a lasting mark on the university. His family became something of a Michigan dynasty, and the 1984 death of his grandson, Robert Cooley Angell, a distinguished professor of sociology, marked the end of an era. Courtesy, Ruth Bordin

ter of the campus. In much altered form, one of those houses survives today as the residence of the president of the University of Michigan.

Not until the fall of 1841 were two professors and seven students assembled in Ann Arbor to begin instruction. There were more regents (18) than faculty and students combined that first year. Admission fees were ten dollars and tuition was not charged. Expenditures for University purposes averaged $8,252 a year for the first years; but, by the academic year 1851 to 1852, the faculty had increased to 6 and 62 students were in attendance.

At first the University had no president—a chancellorship rotated among the professors—but the new state constitution of 1850 required the regents to appoint a president. On the recommendation of historian George Bancroft, they chose Henry Philip Tappan, a New Yorker and graduate of Union College. Tappan was a distinguished philosopher whose work was recognized in Europe as well as in the United States. He had recently returned from a lengthy tour of European universities, much impressed by what he saw in Germany. He was eager to create "an American university deserving of the name," which would be a part of the public school system. He saw no hope of achieving this goal in the conservative East, where private academies and colleges were firmly entrenched. But he saw the state of Michigan as offering him his opportunity.

Tappan guided the little college at Ann Arbor toward true university status. Under his auspices graduate studies were begun, scientific courses were added to the Literary Department, and Michigan became the second university in the country to grant a bachelor of science degree. Although the Medical Department had opened in 1850, the Law Department (also provided for in the Act of 1837) was added during Tappan's incumbency. University enrollment tripled during the Tappan years, and space to provide for this rapid growth was obtained by eliminating dormitory quarters in the college buildings and converting them to classroom use.

Tappan's last years at the University were not happy. His imperious manner alienated many of the county's residents, some of the faculty, and most of the regents, and after a long battle over who should exercise administrative authority, the regents summarily dismissed him in June 1863. But he had made his mark on both the University and the community. Because of his tenure the University of Michigan would never again be a provincial institution, and its commitment to the international world of learning and scholarship was a reality.

James Burrill Angell, who served as the University of Michigan's president from 1871 to 1909, continued the work that was begun so auspiciously under Tappan. Angell was 42 when he came to Washtenaw County. Descended from stock that had migrated to Rhode Island with Roger Williams, he had been both student and professor at Brown University, as well as editor of the Providence *Journal* before accepting the presidency of the University of Vermont in 1866.

In his reminiscences, Angell described his first week in Ann Arbor as one of "fearful solicitude." He certainly faced his share of problems. The students were rowdy and undisciplined and did not endear themselves to the community's more sober citizenry. A long-lasting controversy over whether the University should develop a homeopathic medical school was at its height, and the admission of women (an innovation of the previous year) was still opposed by both faculty and male students.

Angell lent all the weight of his office to overcoming the opposition to coeducation and making it work, for he sincerely believed (albeit his vision was, by the late-20th century standards, limited) that the university-trained woman had much to contribute to the state's normal and secondary schools. Like Tappan before him, Angell was fully convinced of the importance of the University as an essential part of the state's educational system. He also believed that state and education would prosper or decline together. If Michigan moved forward, so would the University, and the University's gains would in turn be translated into gains for the state.

From the beginning University students were an economic asset to Ann Arbor. For 15 years the University provided housing in North and South halls. But these dormitories had no arrangements for feeding the men, and students contracted for their meals at several houses adjacent to the campus. Food service for students, eventually a major local industry, had

The rear portion of Michigan Normal's main building, shown at right, was built in 1852 and housed classrooms as well as the model school. As enrollment grew during the next two decades, the more elaborate front addition provided space for both instruction and demonstration. Michigan Normal could not fill Michigan's need for trained teachers in the nineteenth century, but it set standards that were pervasive; Michigan had exemplary teachers. Courtesy, Eastern Michigan University Archives

made its first appearance on the scene.

Private provision for student housing, another major Ann Arbor business, appeared in 1856 when the dormitories were adapted for classroom use, and the men had to live in town. When the first few brave women arrived on campus in 1870, the boarding-house-rooming-house pattern was well-established, and the women fit into the system as best they could, sharing the same residences as the men and eating at the same tables.

Students created other business opportunities. They required books and paper, laboratory supplies, and the candles that were the precursors to midnight oil. Local merchants were quick to supply their needs. The University itself was, of course, an important customer. Merely to stock the University's stoves with wood consumed the surplus of many a neighboring farmer's woodlot.

When a University hospital augmented the medical department in 1869, it both improved local medical care and provided employment to local citizens. In 1875 the city of Ann Arbor, recognizing the benefits of the hospital, contributed one-third of the $12,000 needed to construct a new building, a gift that was repeated and much augmented in 1891 when still another hospital was built.

And what was the result on the social scene of the presence of so many spirited young men in a relatively small village? By the mid-1860s over 1,200 male students were enrolled when the town's population was not much over 6,000. Local young ladies and the pupils of the boarding department of the Misses Clarks' School for Girls were well aware of their enriched opportunities. George Pray, a Superior Township farmer's son and later a physician and Michigan legislator, wrote in his diary in 1844 that at church "the girls possessed as many bewitching and enticing ways as usual," and the male students' "eyes often wandered in the direction of some fair object." Ann Arbor's young men must have found the student competition for young ladies a bit hard to bear.

Student energy and enthusiasm also found less desirable forms of expression. Students built bonfires in the streets, tore down street signs to decorate their rooms, stole fruit from local gardens and orchards,

and in the downtown saloons occasionally created serious disturbances that required police attention. When a student died of acute alcoholism during a fraternity initiation in 1857, an enraged and horrified community, supported by President Tappan and the University faculty, prevailed on the city council to proscribe the sale of liquor east of Division Street. The ban lasted for well over 100 years.

ANOTHER INNOVATION: TRAINING TEACHERS
In 1849 the Michigan legislature took another step with profound implications for the county. Lawmakers passed an act to establish another institution of higher learning, a school with the purpose of instructing "both sexes in the art of teaching." Teacher-training institutions had existed in Europe for over 100 years, but they had received attention in the United States for only a decade when the legislature took this action. A number of prominent educators had stimulated American interest by 1840, and the movement soon acquired powerful Michigan advocates, among them Governor Alpheus Felch of Ann Arbor and Michigan's first superintendent of public instruction, John D. Pierce. Michigan Normal School (now Eastern Michigan University) was the direct result of this movement.

After receiving bids from a number of communities, the State Board of Education selected Ypsilanti as the site of the new school. Ypsilanti's generous terms far outdistanced other contenders. The village offered a site and was prepared to contribute $13,500, which almost paid for the first building, and promised to pay the principal's salary for five years. There is no evidence that proximity to the University of Michigan was either a positive or negative consideration. But the two communities had been rivals from the beginning, and the generosity and attractiveness of Ypsilanti's offer was no doubt inspired in part by a desire to emulate the advantages that the University had provided for Ann Arbor.

A teachers' institute was held in 1852, the year the Normal building was completed, but no regular term was offered until March 1853. When the first students began classes, only four other teacher-training institutions existed in the United States and only three states supported normal schools. Michigan's was the only

one west of the Alleghenies.

Women were not only prominent among Normal's students, but served on the faculty from the beginning. The male principal, who headed the school, was seconded by a female preceptress, and many distinguished women educators taught at Normal during the years when its primary mission was to train teachers.

Normal's enrollment grew rapidly. Before the school was ten years old, its student body numbered over 300, two-thirds of them women. Adonijah Strong Welch, Normal's first administrative head, was a native Michiganian, trained in classics at the University of Michigan and the law in Detroit. He was a devoted advocate of the union-school movement and the pro-

fessional training of teachers. Welch shaped the direction Normal was to take the same way Tappan shaped the University. Joseph Estabrook, who became head of Normal the same year that James Burrill Angell came to Ann Arbor, continued Welch's emphasis on excellence in professional training.

Two major institutions of higher education, separated by less than a dozen miles, not only changed the character of Washtenaw County but also influenced the nature of the institutions themselves. Many of Normal's faculty were recruited from among the University's graduates. Some of Normal's students, having been well-trained in pedagogy, went on to the University to acquire advanced expertise in other disciplines, and a few joined the University's faculty. Well into the 20th century Normal and the University continued to benefit from competition, interaction, and cooperation. The founding fathers did not plan badly when they put one school so near the other.

Above left: Joseph Estabrook was the principal at Michigan Normal from 1871 to 1880. An Englishman described the students at Normal during Estabrook's tenure as having "bright earnest faces, the freshness of that Western school world." Estabrook improved Normal's professional training, and none of its faculty members "were remembered with kindlier feelings" than he. Courtesy, Eastern Michigan University Archives

Above right: Among the later waves of German immigrants was Samuel Heusel, an Ann Arbor baker, who had this family portrait made for a history of Washtenaw County. He was born in Wurtemberg, Germany, in 1860, migrated to the United States in 1880, and arrived in Washtenaw County in 1893. By the turn of the century his bakery was one of the county's major commercial concerns, shipping bread throughout southeastern Michigan. From Beakes, Past and Present of Washtenaw County, *1906*

THE GERMAN CONNECTION

One characteristic of Washtenaw's second phase was significant change in the county's ethnic mix. The first settlers, with notable exceptions like John Allen, came from upper New York State over the well-traveled route via the Erie Canal and Great Lakes to Detroit. But by the 1840s and 1850s a new migration was well under way.

In 1824 Jonathan Henry Mann, a skilled tanner by trade, left his home in the Swabian Rhineland for America. He moved around a bit until 1828, when he set out for Michigan. On his way he met two countrymen, Phillip Schilling and Daniel F. Allmendinger. Together they proceeded by boat from Albany to Detroit. They purchased land near Ann Arbor, and Mann and Allmendinger returned east for their families. Washtenaw's first German connection had been forged. By 1855, a quarter-century later, over 5,000 Swabians (a sixth of the county's population) had settled in Washtenaw. These German migrations continued in successive waves through the first half of the 20th century.

Loyal to their adopted land, active in its politics, and willing to send their sons to fight in United States' wars, Washtenaw's German minority put its imprint on the county. Thrifty, hard-working farmers and shrewd merchants, they soon established for themselves a secure niche in the county's trade and business.

In the 1840s political dissent was a major motivation for German immigration, and this desire for freedom also attracted Germans to the antislavery movement and the Republican party. German names are heavily represented on Washtenaw's Civil War casualty lists, and many letters in German script are found in local archives. The first generation of Germans kept their own language and stayed somewhat to themselves, finding continuity with their European past in the church. In 1833 the Reverend Frederick Schmid arrived in Ann Arbor, and the first church service was held in a log schoolhouse in Scio Township. A church was organized and before the month was out the struggling little society was planning its first building on land donated by Daniel Allmendinger. On the list of subscribers to that first building fund were Koch, Traver, Wild, Beck, Laubengayer, and Steffe, names that are still found in the county's directories.

Scio contained the bulk of the German population for at least another 15 years until the congregation and Pastor Schmid moved their church home to Ann Arbor. Then the southern tier of townships also began to attract German immigrants in sizable numbers. The German connection in Washtenaw has remained strong. In the mid-20th century stollen and lebkuchen were sold routinely in the county's bakeries at Christmastime. Advent calendars imported from Germany were a standard item in local gift shops. German names still adorn the storefronts of Washtenaw County's main streets and the stalls of its farmers' markets.

A GROWING ETHNIC MIX

The Germans were not the only new group of settlers. The Celts settled early around the northern lakes. In 1824 Benjamin Sutton arrived in Northfield Township. He built himself a double-hewn log house, one-and-a-half stories high, with a stick chimney and a fireplace.

The first Catholic log church was erected in Northfield Township in 1831, and by the 1840s names like Haran, Kearney, Kelly, O'Brien, O'Connor, Shanahan,

Above: This 1908 photo of Dresselhouse and Davidter's buggy, implement, and harness shop attests to both the prevalence of Germans in the Manchester area and the southwestern county's continuing strong ties to agriculture. Courtesy, Bentley Historical Library, University of Michigan

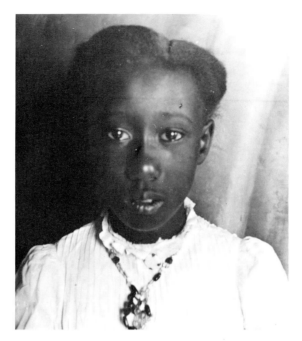

Top: Blacks in Washtenaw County frequently settled near Quaker families. Nora Johnson lived in a house near residents of Ypsilanti township who were members of the Ypsilanti area Friends Meeting. Courtesy, Fuller Collection, Bentley Historical Library, University of Michigan

Above: This photograph of the graduating class of Dexter's St. Joseph's Catholic school in 1921 shows the fusion of the county's various ethnic groups. Most of these students are Irish or German, and they all attended the same small school. The married names of the women, such as Mary Teresa Kelly Lusty (far right in the front row) attest to intermarriage. Courtesy, Dexter Historical Museum

and Ryan were common. By 1870 Scio Township was heavily Irish Catholic. The Irish also made their homes in Dexter Township, and a few found their way to Webster. Many of the Michigan Irish had first been employed on the Erie Canal, and with the canal completed they used the access it provided to move west. Many young women found jobs as servants and young men as farmhands, but landowners were among them. The great Irish potato famine of the 1840s increased their numbers, though not necessarily their prosperity as an ethnic entity, and as late as the 1880 census the rolls show large numbers of Irish hired laborers.

Not all the county's citizenry welcomed the newcomers. The Native American Association of Ann Arbor (and the name did not refer to American Indians) advocated a tax on foreigners and a 21-year residence requirement for naturalization. The Know-Nothing (or American) party unsuccessfully ran a few candidates in local elections of 1854 and 1855. But a third political force was gathering in the northern states, and by the mid-1850s "free soil" was becoming the paramount issue.

The census returns of 1850 show 231 blacks among Washtenaw County's population. Local legend has suggested that most of these settlers were escaped slaves who reached Washtenaw via the underground railroad. Escaped slaves, however, knew only too well the risks of staying in the United States. More likely most of the blacks who settled in the county before the Civil War were free blacks, who either were manumitted by their masters and left the South or had

left the Eastern Seaboard, where they faced increasing economic competition from European immigrants. When the Civil War broke out, the county had over 600 black residents.

During the antebellum period black Americans assiduously sought out homes in areas where antislavery sentiment flourished. Frequently they also looked for a community that included a Society of Friends (Quakers). Antislavery sentiment was strong in Washtenaw. The founding meeting of the Michigan Anti-Slavery Society was held in Ann Arbor's Presbyterian church in 1836. Although the state's first antislavery newspaper, the *Michigan Freeman*, began publication in Jackson, it moved to Ann Arbor in 1841 as the *Signal of Liberty*.

In Ypsilanti Township a Society of Friends had been organized in 1851 and many of the county's black residents settled nearby. At least two black families, the Robert Mortons and the Henry Johnsons, lived in Ypsilanti village by 1842, and an African Methodist Episcopal church was organized with 12 members in 1855. Three years later this congregation was able to purchase a lot on the corner of Adams and Buffalo, where they built a little frame church for $200. Ypsilanti continued to be the largest center of Washtenaw's black community through the 20th century.

Although the county's black population probably was not the result of underground-railroad activity, county citizens played a key role in that movement. Michigan's easy access to Canada made for heavy traffic through its southern counties.

Ypsilanti's chief stations were the homes of Leonard Chase and Mark Norris, white leaders of prominence and property. But the most dramatic rescues were the work of a black resident, George McCoy, a cigar maker with 11 children who lived on Forest Avenue. McCoy had connections in the Cincinnati black community, and he carried escaped slaves, who had crossed the Ohio River, in a covered wagon with a false floor over which he placed cigar boxes. Wyandotte was their destination. From there they reached

Above: The early Catholics in Washtenaw County were almost all Irish, and since most of them settled in rural areas like Northfield township, the first priests had to ride the circuit. By the mid-1830s headquarters were in Ann Arbor, and services for high holidays were celebrated there. The first brick church of St. Thomas the Apostle was built on Kingsley Street in 1842. The current impressive Romanesque building, seen here, was built beginning in 1896. Courtesy, Postcard Collection, Bentley Historical Library, University of Michigan

DINNER TO THE SOLDIERS.

To the Ladies of Washtenaw County:

The citizens of Ann Arbor propose to celebrate

THE FOURTH OF JULY

in a manner becoming the "days of yore." We appeal to you to aid us on that day in giving to the soldiers of Washtenaw a

PUBLIC DINNER

worthy of those who have sent fathers, brothers, and sons to the field of battle to maintain the unity of that Government the Independence of which the 4th of July commemorates. Mothers, will you do it? Daughters, will you attend to it? Then come with your provisions and aid us in spreading before our heroes a bountiful feast. Bring the fruits of a soil again blessed with the "smiles of peace." Bring the dainties of a household made once more happy by the presence of those who have fought to bring about this peace. Come one, come all, and let the people rejoice while the soldiers feast.

> D. CRAMER,
> Dr. A. NASH,
> J. CARPENTER,
> *Committee on Soldiers' Dinner.*

On the fourth of July in 1865, soldiers recently returned from Civil War battlefields were honored with a giant community potluck. Courtesy, Lucy Chapin Scrapbooks, Bentley Historical Library, University of Michigan

Canada by boat.

The depth of Washtenaw County's antislavery convictions is made clear by the level of its participation in the Civil War. Sixty residents of the tiny community of Saline served in the Union forces. Dexter provided the manpower for Company K of the Fourth Michigan Infantry that responded to Lincoln's call after Fort Sumter. A year later that little village provided the volunteers to form Company D of the Twentieth Michigan Infantry. Another company was composed of Chelsea men. Manchester's Union Guards served at Alexandria and Bull Run. Ypsilanti's Light Guards were mustered in as Company H of the First Michigan Infantry just after Sumter and participated in the first battle of Bull Run, the disastrous Peninsular campaign, Antietam, Fredericksburg, Mechanicsville, and Gettysburg. Both the University of Michigan and Michigan Normal School provided companies from their student bodies.

Casualties were substantial. The Ypsilanti Light Guards suffered 213 dead, 345 wounded, and 77 prisoners, a great many men from a village of 3,800 people. At a time when the standard size of an army company was 100 men, Ypsilanti recruits filled that company many times over.

THE PURSUIT OF POLITICS

Although European immigration and the slavery issue became the eventual rallying points for political loyalties, early political allegiances in Washtenaw County coalesced around Freemasonry. Most of Michigan's first settlers came from upper New York State, where in 1826, in Batavia, New York, a former member of the Society of Freemasons, William Morgan, disappeared after threatening to publish an exposure of the Masons. Rumor had the Masonic order murdering him. This possible atrocity sparked a national anti-Mason movement.

Eventually the anti-Masonic group, associating the order with privilege and fearful of its elitism, formed the Anti-Masonic party, the first "third party" in the United States, one that was rurally based and antiestablishment in its appeal. Samuel Dexter and John Allen were strong adherents of Anti-Masonry. Dexter was a fourth vice-president and a speaker at the new party's national convention in 1830. Dexter and Allen also purchased the county's first newspaper, the *Western Emigrant* in 1829, to serve as a vehicle for the distribution of the Anti-Masonic point of view. Ironically, Anti-Masonry represented the establishment in Washtenaw County.

However intense the county's feelings about Freemasonry in the 1830s and Know-Nothingism in the 1840s and early 1850s, by the mid-1850s one of its paramount political concerns was the presence of slavery within the Union. The state of Michigan, which with one exception had elected Democratic governors until 1854, remained firmly in the Republican column from that election until G. Mennen Williams forged a Democratic majority in the 1950s.

DEMOCRATIC MEETING.

ON Saturday, the 2d day of NOVEMBER next, there will be a

DEMOCRATIC MEETING,

at the Court House in Ann Arbor. The DEMO- CRATS of Washtenaw County are requested to attend.

It can not be expected that the Democratic candidate for Governor will be present to make *electioneering speeches for himself,* as was the whig candidate for that office at a recent meeting of the whigs at the same place. But it is promised *(and shall be done)* that the many falsehoods promulgated by the whigs; written and spoken by their imported speakers and *readers,* in which *they made even figures speak false to deceive* the people, shall be exposed *by citizens of our own county.*

E. Mundy,	W. R. Thompson,	James Kingsley,
G. Peters,	J. Tull,	J. Beedon,
R. S. Wilson,	J. B. Guitteau,	T. H. Rogers,
S. Sutherland,	C. Joslin,	A. Crossman,
G. Danforth,	D. W Bliss,	S Denton,
A M Gould,	M Smith,	C Thayer,
O Howe,	M Rider,	M Davis,
E Clark,	J Bardwell,	W A Buckbee,
N Noble,	A Goodwill,	D Petty,
F J B Crane	L Briggs,	J Anderson.
A Hecox,	E Root	W Anderson.

Right: Politicians could play a bit rough even before the Civil War. In this 1839 election poster the Democrats mince no words in accusing the "whigs" of telling lies. Courtesy, Poster Collection, Bentley Historical Library, University of Michigan

Washtenaw County at first shared the state's pattern, giving majorities to the Republicans in the biennial gubernatorial elections from 1854 until the Civil War, but suprisingly the county returned to the Democratic column in 1862.

Perhaps the sudden switch in 1862 can be explained by heavy casualties in local infantry companies. Washtenaw's young men had volunteered in substantial numbers after the fall of Sumter. But when they did not return or returned broken in body and perhaps spirit, Washtenaw's voters blamed the Republicans and in 1862 returned to their previous long allegiance to the Democratic party. The county voted overwhelmingly for George McClellan in 1864, and with few exceptions it remained in the Democratic column in both local and national elections well into the 20th century.

PROVISION FOR WORSHIP

Washtenaw County's first church service was held at Woodruff's Grove in 1824, but it was not until the 1830s that adherents of several Protestant denominations built their first frame sanctuaries and meetinghouses. Although there was an amazing need to preserve denominational identity, compromise was made with the realities of frontier life. In Ann Arbor Congregationalists and Presbyterians worshipped

together until 1847, as did German Evangelical Reform and Lutheran groups when they first arrived. Milan's first church building was a union church, a little, white-frame structure open to religious worship by all denominations.

Methodists, because of their circuit organization and itinerant ministry, were the first to organize on the frontier. Elias Patee preached regularly at Woodruff's Grove by 1825, as part of the Detroit circuit he served. Soon an Ann Arbor circuit was organized from which an Ypsilanti circuit was further split off as population increased.

Church services were held in homes and schools in the early years, but all congregations wanted their own buildings and were willing to make sacrifices to get them. Land was frequently donated by a prosperous parishioner. Ypsilanti's Methodist church, a white-frame, Greek Revival building on the corner of Washington and Ellis streets, was financed entirely by Thomas M. Town, a local merchant, who expected to be reimbursed by the sale of seats and pews. Eventually he received full restitution. Professor Edward Olney mortgaged his own home so that construction could go forward in 1880 on the new Huron Street building of Ann Arbor's Baptist congregation. Until Olney came to their rescue the Baptists had owned the vacant lot for ten years, unable to raise the money for building.

By the mid-19th century in the major towns and villages a wave of much more elaborate provisions for worship was under way. The Ypsilanti Methodist church that Thomas Town so generously financed in 1843 was a frame structure, but it seated 600 in 100 pews, and in the 1850s the auditorium was enlarged and a lecture hall built on the west end of the sanctuary. Ypsilanti's Protestant Episcopal congregation, St. Luke's, built a new structure, complete with bell and tower in 1856 and 1857, as did the Presbyterians. St. Andrew's in Ann Arbor was begun in 1868. In 1892 Ann Arbor's Catholics were finally able to afford the magnificent Romanesque building that still houses

Above: Except for a brief period just before and at the beginning of the Civil War, Washtenaw County was a Democratic stronghold throughout the nineteenth century. This photograph shows a Democratic caucus meeting in the township clerk's office above the Union Savings Bank in Manchester in the 1890s. These men wielded considerable power in local affairs. Courtesy, Manchester Public Library

the congregation of St. Thomas the Apostle. Ann Arbor's Bethel AME and Second Baptist congregations built new brick churches in the 1890s. Several of these beautiful Victorian churches, which marked the sturdy prosperity of the communities they served, are still in use today. New, less prosperous church groups often used the churches outgrown by older congregations until they, too, could afford more opulent quarters.

Nineteenth-century churches were the very core of community life. They were the meeting rooms, the public forums, the scene of public school and college graduation exercises, and friendly community suppers and socials. Sermons were reported in the local newspapers. And the clergy were among the most visible and respected citizens of the community. Church bells summoned young men to war as well as to Sunday services and tolled a doleful obituary when a member died.

THE COMFORTS OF LIFE

The first dwellings built by Washtenaw County settlers were little more than log huts. The early frame houses were only a bit more comfortable. But within 15 years of first settlement, especially during the decades of the 1840s and 1850s, pretentious residences were constructed to house the early pioneers, now

middle-aged, affluent, and eager to provide the comforts of life for themselves and their families. Many of these beautiful dwellings are still in use.

Work began in 1841 on the elegant house built by Judge Samuel Dexter that stands on the rise overlooking Mill Creek. Named Gordon Hall (Gordon was his mother's maiden name), the house was designed by architect Calvin Filmore, brother of the thirteenth president. Massive Greek Revival columns, two stories high and made of white-pine strips skillfully joined, adorn the front porch in a manner frequently associated with antebellum southern mansions. A pilastered doorway opened on a front hall that extended the entire width of the house. The banistered walnut staircase led in one unbroken flight to the second-floor bedrooms. Nine fireplaces heated its 20 rooms. The Dexter mansion was two years in the building. It was not completed until 1843. Not only was it built to last for centuries, it was also handsome in both conception and detail. The Dexter house is still used as a residence, albeit a multifamily dwelling, as it approaches its sesquicentennial.

The Dexter house was only one of many substantial houses erected in the middle decades of the 19th century. Division Street in Ann Arbor and Huron Street in Ypsilanti still display their Victorian splendor remarkably intact. Hundreds of comfortable farmhouses, on average less grand than the elegant urban residences, were built in the Italianate style, with parlors, lawns, fences, and cupolas. Cobblestone Farm is one of many surviving examples.

Local stone added warmth and depth to the county's grand mid-19th-century houses and churches. Guelph stonemasons from Ontario were brought to fashion Latin professor Henry Frieze's house on Washtenaw. The same colorful local stone was used in St. Andrew's church.

THE PURSUIT OF FELLOWSHIP

Clubs and social organizations appeared soon after set-

Above: Many large and gracious houses were built throughout the county in the period before and during the Civil War. Division Street in Ann Arbor proudly displayed the house Robert S. Wilson built in the late 1830s and 1840s, later known as the Wahr House. Ebenezer Wells built the next house north in the 1850s. St. Andrew's church, at the far left, was erected in the 1860s. Courtesy, Bentley Historical Library, University of Michigan

tlement. Temperance societies were among the county's first clubs, appearing in every settlement by 1829 and 1830. They were not without effect in reducing the consumption of spirits. In January 1830, for example, a barn was raised for Luther Boyden of Webster Township without whiskey but with a good supper, a novel but successful attempt at practicing communal temperance. Alcohol was plentiful on the Michigan frontier, and sober, industrious folk felt a compelling need to control consumption.

Temperance sentiment came in waves. Probably because of initial success, the problem waned and interest lagged; then drinking once again increased and a new spurt of organizing to control it began. The enthusiasm of 1830 had largely dissipated by mid-century. But after the Civil War the crusade against drink once more took off, and still other temperance revivals took place after 1894 and in the early 20th century.

Fraternal orders with purely social objectives also appeared in the county before the Civil War, but most of them were short-lived. Oddfellows and mutual protection societies were organized in several communities, but in light of the Anti-Masonic sentiments of the county's founding fathers, it is ironic that only the Masons continued without interruption.

Above: Ypsilanti's Ladies Literary Club, dedicated to self-improvement, was founded in 1878 as an adjunct of the Ladies Library Association, a service club. Seventeen women met in the Arcade building and formed the club, agreeing to have no officers, no fees, and no constitution. In 1923 they began to meet in this handsome Greek Revival house. For their centennial, the members dressed in costume and posed for this photo. Courtesy, Ypsilanti Historical Museum

The first women's organization was a short-lived secret society of young ladies founded in Ann Arbor in 1826 and dedicated to self-improvement. But most early women's service organizations were devoted to making the printed word more accessible. The Ladies Library Association of Ypsilanti was organized in 1865; the Ann Arbor association followed the next year, and Dexter's in 1879. These voluntary organizations eventually succeeded in promoting tax-supported municipal libraries, but they began by providing community access to reading material in storefront rooms, with donated books, and volunteer staff.

Although ecumenical in membership, many women's service organizations were church-related. The Ypsilanti Home Association, founded in 1857 and formally affiliated with the American Female Guardian Society in New York, aided poor families. The board of directors was composed of the wives of the pastors of the four major Ypsilanti Protestant churches, and its executive committee consisted of two members from each church. It continued to provide basic relief and social services for several decades.

The women's literary clubs that first appeared in the 1870s were gestated at the meetings of the earlier service organizations. The Ypsilanti Literary Club was

first proposed at a meeting of the Ladies Library Association. It studied Africa, geography, resources, art, and literature during its first year, an agenda not unlike those often undertaken by church missionary societies, although perhaps without as clear an evangelical thrust.

The earnest usefulness of women's service and self-improvement groups was not the only fellowship pattern. Music and theatricals received a large share of attention. Ann Arbor had a little thespian society in 1837. By the 1860s professional traveling companies were joining the amateurs, and the Whitney Opera House opened in 1871 with a performance of the *Spy of Shiloh,* a lurid drama that permitted the audience to relive the Civil War. Musical groups abounded, most of them strictly amateur. Productions of Gilbert and Sullivan's new operettas were popular in Ypsilanti. Before Ypsilanti's elaborate new opera house opened its doors downtown on Michigan Avenue in 1880, amateurs performed *H.M.S. Pinafore* at Hewitt Hall, one of a number of private auditoriums in the county.

Above: Manchester's Saturday Club, a ladies' literary society, met in the library of Mrs. Amariah Freeman's house on Ann Arbor Street. Its membership was small but bent on self-improvement. Members ranged from the young and unmarried to the elderly. Courtesy, Manchester Public Library

Top: The Manchester Dandies—Fred Blosser, Fred Freeman, August Nisle, Eugene Kirchgesner, and Will Nidmayer—donned derbies and chesterfields for this photograph. Note the German names in the group; by this time, Germans had been well assimilated by the Manchester community. Courtesy, Manchester Public Library

When **Pinafore** *was produced at the elegant Ypsilanti Opera House in the early 1890s, Ypsilanti society turned out in style. The opera house, in the center of downtown on Michigan Avenue, was constructed of red brick with black brick facings. Its imposing stone steps raised it above street level, and its ceiling was adorned with medallion portraits of Longfellow, Shakespeare, and Tennyson. Edwin Booth and Julia Marlowe both played there. Courtesy, Ypsilanti Historical Museum*

THE RAILROAD CONNECTION

Although some of the county's embryonic villages that were established in the 1820s and 1830s prospered until mid-century and then disappeared (Scio is an example), Chelsea was a late arrival, a product of the railroad.

In the 1830s Elisha and James Congdon had bought land and established farms in what became Chelsea. But not until the Michigan Central Railroad's route was established in 1848 did Elisha Congdon think of building a store on his farm. At that time the flimsy local railroad depot was two miles west, close to the county line. But Congdon's entrepreneurial enterprise paid off. In 1850 the Michigan Central erected a new station near his store, and Chelsea, first called Kedron, took off. Chelsea telescoped the usual patterns of settlement. Its Congregational church was organized in 1849. The village was platted in 1850, and its first select school was built in 1854.

Milan was the county's other latecomer. During its first half-century, Milan's history was like that of other small, unorganized communities. John Marvin began farming in York Township in 1830, and four years later a store and a pair of small grist- and sawmills took advantage of the Saline River's waterpower. But Milan's subsequent urban status was, like Chelsea's, the direct result of access to railroad transportation. The Ann Arbor Railroad was completed from Toledo to Ann Arbor in 1878, and the Wabash Railroad, linking Detroit with St. Louis, was fully in service by 1881. The two rights-of-way intersected at the little settlement, attracting both new business and an increased population. In 1885 the village of Milan was organized, and one of the larger urban communities in the county was under way.

By the turn of the century Milan and Chelsea had outstripped Saline, Dexter, and Manchester in population. Access to the railroad had replaced waterpower as the major economic asset fostering urbanization.

July Fourth 1874 marked the fiftieth anniversary of Benjamin Woodruff's little Independence Day celebration at the Grove. The time had arrived to celebrate the growth and prosperity that half a century had brought.

Thirty thousand people crowded Ypsilanti's wooden sidewalks, and every hitching rack was crowded with teams of horses. One special train of 19 cars brought people from Detroit. Another with 21 coaches arrived over the route from Hillsdale and still another from Ann Arbor. Cadets, national guardsmen, and veterans of the Civil War were on hand for the parade, which was long and splendid and concluded with a group of old settlers. The exercises in the park that followed the parade were conducted at a venerable table used at the Grove's celebration 50 years earlier. An arch at the station was covered with flowers and topped by a goddess of liberty. Fireworks brightened the evening sky.

No muskets masqueraded as cannon this time. Washtenaw County had reached a secure and affluent middle age. The amenities of life were at hand.

Right: This little Gothic Revival train depot, built in 1850, literally created the village of Chelsea, which had not existed two years before. The railroad both made and destroyed communities within the county. Distances between markets, accommodations, and supplies could now be lengthened, no longer depending on the distance a horse-drawn conveyance could comfortably travel in a day. Also, sites not convenient to river transportation could come into their own. Courtesy, Postcard Collection, Bentley Historical Library, University of Michigan

Potatoes were a major product of Maple Lane Farm near Ypsilanti in 1912, but the silo proves that dairying was at least equally important. Silage for dairy cattle was stashed there. Courtesy, Ypsilanti Historical Museum

III

A PLACE OF LEARNING, PRODUCE, AND MANUFACTORY

The decades from 1880 to the onset of World War I were in many ways a period when Washtenaw County's earlier promise was fulfilled and previous trends accelerated and solidified. But significant changes in direction also occurred. Many of the little local mills closed or were consolidated into larger enterprises. Farming was still the county's largest business, but agriculture looked increasingly to national and international markets. A growing urban population, fueled both by industry and by the expanding enrollments of its institutions of higher learning, forced the county's two major urban centers, Ann Arbor and Ypsilanti, to assume the responsibilities of cityhood.

A TRANSPORTATION REVOLUTION

Transportation routes were always important. The first tiny settlement at Milan was generated not only by a mill site on the Saline River, but also by the presence of a nearby tollgate on the plank road from Monroe to Saline, where travelers had to stop. James Kingsley, an Ann Arbor entrepreneur and attorney, petitioned Congress to build a canal across the lower part of Michigan in 1830. No doubt he hoped to match what the Erie Canal had done for upper New York State. When Congress did not cooperate, he switched his entrepreneurial talents to railroads and became a prime mover in the Michigan Central.

Stagecoaches still ran between Dexter and Pinckney in 1860 and continued to make two trips a day in 1875. The Dexter-Howell stage also operated in the 1870s. But railroads provided long-distance transportation in the late-19th and early-20th centuries. Transportation by rail was cheap, efficient, and amazingly available. Wheat and hogs could be put on trains. So could people. Sometimes, however, capital to implement grand dreams was less than easy to find. In Washtenaw between 1836 and 1869 at least ten railroad lines were contemplated, while only two major arteries were completed.

People marveled at the Michigan Central's speed and efficiency, but it was 30 years before a second rail line, the Detroit, Hillsdale, and Indiana, was built. Begun in 1870, it ran from Ypsilanti through Pittsfield, Saline, Bridgewater, and Manchester to Hillsdale. In June 1878 the Ann Arbor Railroad reached the city for which it was named on its way north from Toledo. The county now had usable and effective north-south connections.

The railroad had important side effects for the county. It virtually created Chelsea and had much to do with Milan's growth. By 1880 it had helped to make Saline a major agricultural shipping point in

GETTING OFF THE CAR

RIGHT WAY · WRONG WAY

Safe and Graceful · Dangerous and Awkward

ASSIST US IN PREVENTING ACCIDENTS

Above: The Interurban Trolley that ran between Ann Arbor and Ypsilanti was popular with the ladies. However, according to this circa 1890 poster, they needed to be taught the right and wrong ways to exit these modern contrivances. Courtesy, Hildebrandt Papers, Bentley Historical Library, University of Michigan

southeastern Michigan; and trains, heavily laden with livestock, grain, flour, wool, and apples, departed for markets via the Detroit, Hillsdale, and Indiana Railroad. Rail transport may well have contributed to the decline of Scio and Dexter in the 1880s. True, they were on the Michigan Central line, but, unlike Chelsea, they were so close to Ann Arbor that they couldn't tap another production area.

The interurban railway, lighter and cheaper to construct than regular railroads, made its debut late in the 19th century. It evolved from the steam-driven small rail lines used to haul logs from forest to sawmill and for over a generation provided quick, efficient intervillage transportation. The line between Ann Arbor and Ypsilanti was completed in 1890. Originally powered by steam, it was electrified in 1896 and became clean and relatively quiet as well. The cars ran every hour-and-a-half and carried an average of 600 passengers a day as well as a substantial quantity of freight.

As Junius Beal, local newspaperman, put it, the traffic was greatly helped "by the simple fact that while Ann Arbor had 3,000 boys [University of Michigan students] and not enough girls, Ypsilanti had 1,000 girls at the Normal and not enough boys. The street railroad helped to restore the equilibrium." Evening tickets on the Ypsi-Ann were sold at ten for a quarter (the usual fare was ten cents), and not only were the cars jammed during the school year, but in summer,

when most of the student swains had returned home, local people used the trolleys to cool off before going to sleep.

Local enterprise provided the first venture capital of $40,000, a sum soon recouped by the investors. Quite appropriately Junius Beal of Ann Arbor was president and Ypsilanti's Daniel Quirk was treasurer of the company. But the whole system was sold to the Detroit, Ypsilanti, and Ann Arbor Street Railway Company in 1898, and the line extended to Detroit and Jackson the next year.

The interurbans, like the railroads, had unintended side effects. For example, when the interurban was extended to Jackson it passed three miles south of Dexter but straight through Chelsea. This contributed at the turn of the century to Dexter's declining importance as one of the county's major urban centers.

As the decade of the 1890s wore on, interurbans were constructed to connect other villages and towns. The Ypsilanti-Saline line, whose carriage was called Old Maude, was completed in 1899 and provided service for the next quarter century. Interurban traffic, however, reached its peak in 1912. As automobiles increased in number, the street railway's usefulness as a short-run conveyor decreased, and in 1925 the local electric lines were abandoned and replaced, for better or for worse, by gasoline-powered buses that used public roads.

There were no roads other than Indian trails west of Detroit until 1827, when the Great Sauk Trail was converted into the Chicago Military Road, part of which ran from Detroit to Ypsilanti before veering south. In 1829 the territorial council authorized an offshoot of the Chicago road, heading west from Ypsilanti and eventually terminating at St. Joseph. This route, called Territorial Road, also followed an old Indian trail. Dexter Road had similar antecedents. No attempt was made to surface them.

The first effort at road improvement, the plank roads constructed as trunk lines in the 1850s, proved temporary. The crosswise planks that formed their sur-

John Wenger, a railroad crossing guard who lived on Huron Street in Dexter, posed gleefully in the touring car belonging to his son-in-law in 1919. Wenger probably could not actually drive when this picture was taken, but he certainly endorsed with enthusiasm the transportation revolution going on around him. Courtesy, Dexter Historical Museum

face soon rotted, and they were expensive to repair. A few macadam highways, consisting of layers of crushed stone, were attempted, but no real road improvement was realized or even contemplated until the 1880s, when the "good roads" movement got under way.

The real impetus for adequate roads was neither agitation by disgruntled farmers tired of having their horses mired in the mud nor the advent of the automobile. Instead, the bicycle fad sparked the demand for road improvement. By the 1890s bicycling was a veritable craze, and cyclers wanted adequate surfaces on which to pursue their sport.

In 1893 the state legislature authorized counties to replace townships as primary custodians of roads, but Washtenaw was slow to take advantage of this attempt to foster central authority. Not until 1905, when public roads were at last exempted from the 1850 constitutional provision denying state funds for canals, railroads, bridges, and roads, did the state participate directly in road building and maintenance. State subsidies for local road construction and a state highway commission were authorized at the same time, but again Washtenaw County failed to take advantage of this financial help until 1914.

Michigan's first trunk routes were authorized in 1913. The Old Sauk Trail, M-112, was the first state highway designated in Washtenaw County, and M-17 soon followed. M-17 was paved in 1919, but the Dexter-Ann Arbor road was not surfaced with concrete until 1926. Local streets received hard surfaces slowly, at best. Ann Arbor had no paved streets until 1896, and not until 1898 was the downtown portion of Main Street surfaced with brick. Ypsilanti's first paving was done in 1899, but Chelsea paved no streets until 1911. As late as 1930 most neighborhood streets were still gravel and received a daily sprinkling from the city's water wagon to subdue the summer dust.

URBAN GROWTH DEMANDS CITY SERVICES
Not only was the period from 1880 to World War I marked by revolutionary changes in public transportation, but other municipal services multiplied as well. At the beginning of this 40-year span, the only local public services were a minimum of street and walkway maintenance, a little police service, and com-

munity fire protection. The only public utility was gas lighting in the two urban centers.

Fire was an ever-present danger. In 1851 a disastrous fire in Ypsilanti destroyed the west-side business district, engulfing the north side of Michigan Avenue from Washington Street to the river. In 1870 Chelsea lost an entire block on the west side of Main Street and all the village records along with it. In Saline a full block of stores was consumed in 1881.

Although fire departments came early to Washtenaw County's communities, they were manned by volunteers. Their equipment was primitive, sometimes little more than a public well and a prayer. By the mid-19th century Ypsilanti had a hand pumper with a hose that could be dropped in a convenient cistern. Ann Arbor was equally well supplied, and the two companies were prone to friendly tournaments with their respective hoses.

Smaller communities acquired fire-fighting equipment much more slowly. In 1845 Dexter's frame business area burned and was replaced by brick stores that also succumbed to the flames in 1851. Other serious business-district fires occurred in 1866, 1869, and 1877. In 1877 Dexter called on her eastern neighbor for help, and Ann Arbor's pumping engine was loaded on a flat car and transported to Dexter by railroad to assist in extinguishing the blaze.

This experience inspired Dexter to acquire some equipment of its own. The village purchased a hook-and-ladder truck and a minimum of pumping equipment and constructed an engine house and a public cistern. The Dexter pattern was typical. The smaller towns began to acquire modern facilities, but volunteers continued to furnish most of the labor well past the mid-20th century. Ann Arbor authorized a full-time, paid fire department in 1889 and Ypsilanti in 1895. But Dexter, for example, did not hire its first professional fire fighter until 1970 and continued to supplement trained men with volunteers.

The first public water supplies were simply municipal wells and cisterns. Ann Arbor began digging wells in the 1840s. Their chief purpose was to provide a source of water for fire fighting. Everywhere, improvements in the public water supply invariably followed disastrous fires.

Householders made do with small cisterns or a bar-

rel to collect soft rainwater off the roof for bathing and laundry, and private wells, equipped with hand pumps, provided drinking water. Soon after settlement pollution forced abandonment of the county's lakes and streams as a major source of drinking water. Sewers were in even shorter supply; fortunately the backyard privy did not require drains to dispose of its wastes. Ann Arbor's sanitary sewer system was not begun until 1894 and storm sewers not until 1898, when modern plumbing was installed in houses and buildings because the earth itself could no longer deal satisfactorily with disposal problems.

The University of Michigan acquired a central water supply in 1874. Water from a large spring on Emanuel Mann's farm, near where the University of Michigan stadium is now, was piped to a 40,000-gallon tank on campus from which the University drew its water.

Although the need was acute, a dispute over whether a water company should be city owned or a private corporation kept the city of Ann Arbor from installing an adequate municipal water system until 1885. Ann Arbor's aldermen always resisted raising local taxes, and private enterprise won this contest. A franchise was awarded to a local company to establish a city water system. The site for the works was the present Barton pumping station, then on the farm of John Allen's son James. The private company, however, was unreliable and went bankrupt more than once. So, early in the 20th century sentiment began to shift toward public ownership. When the company's franchise terminated in 1913, the city bought the water plant and since then has owned and operated the city's water and sewer systems.

Ypsilanti opted for municipal ownership from the beginning. The city itself laid the first mains, constructed the first pumping station, and built the handsome stone storage tower, and by 1889 a fully functioning water system was a reality. Chelsea's plant was built in 1896 by Frank P. Glazier, a local entrepreneur, but he sold it to the village two years later. The county's other villages did not assume responsibility for

Ypsilanti's water tower was a product of the urbanization of the 1880s and the attendant increase in city services. Finished in 1889, the tower elevated a reservoir with a capacity of 250,000 gallons. From Art Work of Washtenaw County, *1893*

Above: One example of the increasing governmental services in the early twentieth century was free delivery of rural mail, instituted by the U.S. Postal Service in 1896. This jaunty driver, undaunted by the muddy road crossing the railroad track, delivered mail to the residents of Podunk, near Dexter. Although roads were still primitive, better roads and rural mail delivery helped to make the Washtenaw County farmer feel a part of the larger community. Courtesy, Dexter Historical Museum

Above: The symbiotic relationship between Washtenaw County and its educational institutions is clearly documented in this 1893 photograph of Ann Arbor's brand new State Street. State Street is a business district that developed in the 1880s to meet the needs of a growing academic community. Books, books, and more books, as well as a billiard hall and a green grocer, dominate the scene. From Art Work of Washtenaw County, *1893*

Facing page, top: Ypsilanti's bank block, built in 1893, was a three-story French chateau with neoclassic columns across its front. The YMCA was housed in the third story, and the offices of the Ypsilantian *were in the basement. From* Art Work of Washtenaw County, *1893*

a public water supply until the 20th century.

Decades before they concerned themselves with a residential water supply, several local communities granted franchises to gas-lighting companies. Both Ypsilanti and Ann Arbor acquired gas plants in 1858. Silas H. Douglas, the University of Michigan's professor of chemistry, was the organizer of the Ann Arbor Gas Light Company, from which the city contracted for 25 street lamps in 1859 to be lit from sunset to 1:00 a.m., except on moonlit nights when lunar power was considered sufficient. Ann Arbor made use of some gas streetlights until 1905, and the gas company continued to be locally owned in the 1920s. By then, however, its function as a lighter of lamps had been supplanted by electricity, and its main use was as fuel for cooking. Eventually the Ann Arbor plant became part of Michigan Consolidated Gas.

The 1880s and 1890s saw the development of electric power. The first electric companies were locally owned and operated and usually employed water-power from local dam sites. In 1884 Ann Arbor's privately owned VanDepoele Light and Power Company, named after the brilliant Belgian inventor, was ready to illuminate 36 stores and residences as well as to provide power for 33 streetlights. Ypsilanti's system was in place two years later. As with its water system, Ypsilanti chose public ownership. The city's plant was erected on Forest Avenue near the river. Lights on five high towers, one for each ward, provided illumination that resembled moonlight throughout the city. Another 50 lights were suspended at street intersections.

There was much merging and reorganizing of electric companies at the turn of the century. Chelsea's Frank Glazier also built that village's first electric plant, which he sold to the city in 1898 along with his waterworks. Dexter tried municipal ownership for a few years, but eventually sold its plant to Detroit Edison. By 1915 Detroit Edison was supplying most of the county's electricity. One exception was the University of Michigan, which supplied all its own power until 1925 when it installed a cross-connected system that permitted it to both furnish and receive electric power from the Edison network.

Around the turn of the century new communication networks added another dimension to commu-

nity life. Actually the telegraph had reached Ypsilanti in 1847, and Washtenaw County had been in direct and almost instantaneous communication with the rest of the world through Chicago and Detroit since the spring of 1848. But the telephone transmitted the human voice, not a series of dots and dashes that required special operators for translation.

The very first local telephone was just a plaything, a wire through the brick wall between Eberbach's Drug Store at 112 Main Street in Ann Arbor and Herman Hutzel's clothing store next door. The two men enjoyed the novelty of shouting to each other over the wires. Early telephone service consisted of unconnected private lines usually acquired for business purposes. For example Clark Cornwell, a prominent Ypsilanti industrialist, wanted easy communication between his downtown office and his paper mills on the Huron River at Geddes and Lowell, and he installed a telephone line to provide it.

In 1880 Ann Arbor devotees of the telephone managed to round up the necessary 25 subscribers and have a switchboard installed over Reinhart's shoe store at 42 South Main. Ypsilanti began with 60 sub-

at other occupations, the council became a purely legislative body and the mayor's responsibilities were considerably enhanced. For example the executive now had the power to appoint members of the rapidly increasing number of boards and commissions that supervised the new public service agencies and regulated public utilities.

In 1893 Ann Arbor constructed a new city hall, three stories of office space for municipal civil servants and meeting rooms for their unpaid overseers. Directly across Main Street the handsome fire station, occupied since 1883, housed the newly professionalized fire department. Ann Arbor was the only town in the county whose population had reached 10,000 in the 1890s, and fewer changes in governmental structure were necessary elsewhere.

Ypsilanti had written a new charter in 1877 that provided for a strong mayor, legislative council, and commissioners to supervise public services. The town did not substantially alter its charter until 1905 when it provided in detail for the regulation of street railways and public utilities. This charter also eliminated certain remnants of its rural past, for example, specifying what domestic farm animals could be kept and where. Urban population density proscribed some of the freedoms of earlier days.

A PLACE OF LEARNING

Although the first decade of James B. Angell's long tenure as president of the University of Michigan was marked by a return to the solid accomplishments of the Tappan era, the 1870s were not without uncertainties and divisive struggles. But by 1880 a large deficit had been eliminated, the University's relative financial independence of the legislature was assured, an internal scandal involving the chemistry department had been resolved, and an independent department of homeopathic medicine had been established. Where conflict once had festered, compromise and

scribers and a switching station housed predictably in the office of Cornwell's Ypsilanti Paper Company.

Mr. Bell's uncanny invention caught on. Long-distance communication was established between several Michigan cities in 1883, the year that smaller communities like Manchester also got service, and by 1915 there were nearly 4,000 phones in the county. The University and Normal were important customers, and the first private branch exchange was opened in 1904 to supply the University with more adequate service.

In the county's urban areas a growing population and the multiplying of public services required modifications in local government. Ann Arbor adopted a new city charter in 1889. Although both mayor and council continued to be unpaid and made their livings

Above: In 1880 Ann Arbor's State Street wore urban dress all the way to Hill Street, where sawmills and trees began to take over. Ann Arbor also had become a place of residences and multiple dwellings. The medical building on the central campus square faced a number of residences across East University Avenue. Most of Ann Arbor's population, however, resided in an area bounded by the Ann Arbor Railroad tracks on the west, Madison Avenue on the south, the Michigan Central right-of-way on the north, and a block or two of Forest Avenue on the east. Courtesy, Bentley Historical Library, University of Michigan

conciliation reigned.

The number of students tripled in the next 16 years, bringing prosperity with them. Never was the symbiotic relationship of the county and its educational institutions more apparent. Overall the presence of strong educational institutions was a stabilizing economic influence on the county. Although higher education was not completely immune to swings of the business cycle, downturns had relatively minor effects on payroll, enrollment, and local consumption, especially when compared to the wide swings experienced in areas dependent on heavy industry. After a brief enrollment decline in the early 1880s, Normal and the University grew exponentially and the county grew with them.

In Ann Arbor the student population explosion sent the University's budget from $150,000 in 1880 to over $2 million in 1916. The population of Ann Arbor grew too, increasing from 8,000 to nearly 15,000 during that period.

Michigan Normal expanded even more rapidly. Enrollment increased over seven-fold from approxi-

mately 400 in 1880 to over 2,800 in 1916. Appropriations at Normal went from a mere $27,000 in 1880 to nearly a quarter of a million dollars in 1916, and Ypsilanti's population increased from approximately 5,000 to 6,500, a smaller increase than in Ann Arbor. Ypsilanti was less tied to academia and more dependent on the business community than its sister city.

Dormitories did not appear at Michigan until just before the First World War, and Normal had no residence halls until 1938. Student housing was provided by private enterprise. As student enrollments soared householders could afford new dwellings by renting rooms to students. In Ann Arbor new subdivisions close to campus sprouted on the south side of Hill Street, Washtenaw beyond its intersection with Hill, and the far reaches of State Street beyond Packard. A new business district sprang up on State Street to accommodate this population's commercial needs.

Like the University of Michigan, Normal was originally on the edge of town, but by the 1890s residences were appearing nearby on Cross Street, Brower, Forest, and Summit, among them the

The Catherine Street hospitals, begun in 1891 and completed 18 years later, were a part of the expansion of the university's campus beyond the original 40 acres. At that time these buildings represented the last word in hospital construction. From **Art Work of Washtenaw County**, *1893*

Teachers at Normal were taught the importance of moral precepts, such as "Truth is the highest thing a man may keep," as seen on the blackboard. Every student pictured here looks earnest. Courtesy, Eastern Michigan University Archives

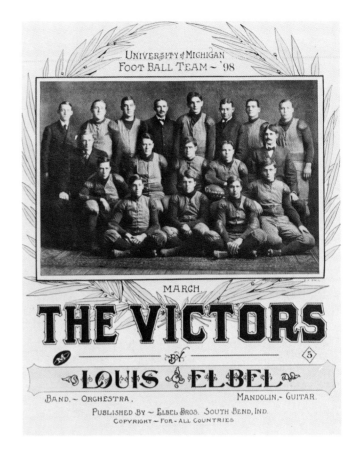

rooming houses that catered to students. Normal, which began with a small eight-acre site, purchased an additional four acres in the 1890s. But substantial additions were not made until 1910 when another 63 acres were acquired.

Both institutions launched major building programs at the turn of the century. The University added West Medical, West Engineering, a new library, a museum, Alumni Memorial Hall, a chemistry building, Waterman Gymnasium, and Hill Auditorium. The Michigan Union was well under way when the United States entered World War I.

Normal experienced its own expansion of physical plant. In 1887 north and south wings were added to Old Main, providing additional classrooms, a library,

and student meeting rooms. In the 1890s separate quarters for the Training School were completed and substantially added to a few years later. A science building, Starkweather Hall, a men's gymnasium, a botanical nursery, Pease Auditorium, which included space for the conservatory of music, and an administration building were major additions early in the century. This construction, plus the attendant private housing boom, made for a high level of prosperity in both cities that spread to outlying areas of the county as well.

In the 1880s another educational institution, dedicated to providing professional training especially for women, opened in Ypsilanti. Patrick Roger Cleary, a teacher of penmanship, the professional equipment of the 19th-century clerk, started classes in Ypsilanti

Above left: P.R. Cleary began his career in education by teaching penmanship in various Michigan towns. By 1883 he had moved to Ypsilanti and had expanded his enterprise to meet the growing business community's demand for clerical services. Young women were entering the business world in increasing numbers. In the class of 1893-1894, 20 of the 30 members of the shorthand class were female. Courtesy, Ypsilanti Historical Museum

Above right: Louis Elbel wrote "The Victors" in 1898 to celebrate the Michigan football team's victories that year. This is a reproduction of the cover of the sheet music. The tune has been heard in Ann Arbor's stadium ever since. Courtesy, Bentley Historical Library

in 1883. Cleary also trained telegraphers, a new skill for which the burgeoning railroads had created a brisk demand.

In the 1890s Cleary added shorthand and typewriting to his educational roster. Young women were increasingly eager to enter the labor force, and jobs using the new technology were multiplying. Cleary College, as he called it, moved in the late 1880s from his upstairs rooms in the Worden block to an impressive Romanesque building on Michigan Avenue, and enrollments soared.

An early informal relationship between Normal and Cleary was formalized in 1913. Normal students aiming to teach in high-school commercial departments went to Cleary for instruction in bookkeeping, stenography, and typewriting and continued to receive their academic courses and pedagogical training at Normal. This affiliation continued until 1938 when Normal began to offer full commercial training.

The University and Normal enriched the life of Washtenaw County culturally as well as economically and educationally. Because of the German connection music had always played a central role in both communities. But the presence of the two schools fostered that interest. Instruction in music, early seen as appropriate to teacher training, began in Normal's second year, and Albert Miller, the first purveyor of that instruction, was himself of German origin and educated at the University of Jena.

An early arbiter of Ann Arbor's musical life was Henry Simmons Frieze, a professor of classics. Frieze was a fine musician, both an accomplished organist and a talented choral leader, and in 1879 he gathered together several local church choirs to perform Handel's *Messiah*. In 1880 this group was formally organized as the Ann Arbor Choral Union. At about the same time the literary college of the University began to offer courses in music theory, under Calvin O. Cady, a graduate of Oberlin College in Ohio. Cady, along with other Ann Arbor musicians, founded a propri-

Above: Music lovers arrived at Pease Auditorium by both horse and automobile, circa 1920. The occasion photographed was probably tied to the Normal campus, but the auditorium also hosted concerts for the community. Courtesy, Eastern Michigan University Archives

etary school of music to supplement the University's minimal offerings. Frieze thereupon organized the University Musical Society to coordinate all these musical activities. But Frieze turned over managerial responsibilities to Cady, who became director of the proprietary school of music, the professor of music theory in the literary college, and the director of the Choral Union.

When Cady resigned in 1888, he was succeeded by Albert Stanley. Stanley was a distinguished organist and inspiring teacher. But his greatest contribution may have been his capacity to unite the community's musical resources with those of the University. He was joined in 1904 by Charles Sink, who carried on the tradition with flair and a canny knack for the profession of the impresario.

The role played by Professors Frieze, Cady, and Stanley in Ann Arbor was filled in Ypsilanti by Frederick H. Pease. Although his parents had strong Oberlin ties, Pease left that college as a very young man and settled in Ypsilanti. There he attended Normal and taught piano to local children. He joined Normal's faculty in the 1860s, but it was not until 1880 that Normal opened its conservatory of music under his direction. Normal's student body and townspeople joined together in the Ypsilanti Musical Union to perform Handel's cantatas, while Ann Arbor's Choral Union, a similar meld of academics and town, rendered the *Messiah* or the Bach *Passions*.

The University and Normal also brought the county far-flung fame. By World War I Michigan Normal School was recognized throughout the country as a source of highly capable teachers. Normal boasted a distinguished department of geography, the first in Michigan. It was the first institution west of the Alleghenies to offer physical-education training for teachers, the first in Michigan to teach industrial arts, and the first in the country to develop a program of special education for the handicapped.

The University of Michigan meanwhile rapidly acquired an international reputation. As its schools and colleges expanded both in number and in enrollment, many distinguished scholars and scientists found their way to Ann Arbor. Charles Kendall Adams introduced the seminar method of graduate instruction, and laboratories and clinical teaching in the scien-

ces and medicine were extended and improved by Michigan's scientific faculty. Requirements for admission to the professional schools were made increasingly rigorous. A formal budget was introduced in 1894, replacing the previous haphazard authorization of expenditures after they occurred. Foreign students appeared on the campus in increasing numbers, further indicating the worldwide nature of the University's appeal. Higher education in Washtenaw County had truly come of age.

A PLACE OF FACTORY, SHOP, AND OFFICE

Higher education began to have a subtle but unmistakable influence on the county's industrial base as well. The Eberbach drug firm was one of the first to show the heavy pull the county's educational centers exerted on the direction manufacturing would take.

Eberbach and Company dates back to 1843, when Christian Eberbach, a recent German immigrant, opened a drugstore on South Main Street in Ann Arbor. Eberbach had been trained as a pharmacist in Germany. But it was when Christian's son, Ottmar, joined the business in 1868 after obtaining technical training in Germany that the firm tied itself to the academic community. At first father and son began the manufacture of scientific apparatus and instruments. At the same time they ventured into chemical and laboratory supply. By the turn of the century they had developed a worldwide reputation in the scientific community, and their apparatus and instruments were shipped all over the globe. Without academic markets close at hand, it seems unlikely that Washtenaw would have become a center for the manufacture of scientific apparatus.

The growing musical life of the county no doubt helped to create a local market for parlor keyboard instruments. Ann Arbor's first organ works, owned by G.F. Gaertner, a native of Stettin, Germany, began operations in 1867. David F. Allmendinger, a distant cousin of the earlier David who settled in Scio Township, learned the trade working for Gaertner's firm. He also married Gaertner's daughter. In 1872 Allmendinger took over the organ factory, and under his leadership it became a major industry. Allmendinger began by building pipe and reed organs. Later the firm added the newly popular piano to its list. The Allmendinger

firm built many pipe organs for churches, three of which found homes in Ann Arbor, including one at Bethlehem Church. But the Allmendinger firm was best known for its parlor reed organs, many of them with elaborate wood carving. Some were shipped as far as Africa. Eventually Allmendinger's factory occupied half a city block on the corner of First and Washington in Ann Arbor, and his home with its gardens, pools, and woodsy dells spread along west Washington Street for four blocks.

Academia is much attached to the printed word, and printing and publishing, even papermaking, flourished and still flourish in this county. The advanced technology of Xerox and University Microfilms may have replaced the folk wisdom of Dr. Chase's recipe books, but Edwards Brothers, Ann Arbor's long-lived book printing firm, and Ypsilanti's Peninsular Paper have spanned the transition and are still important contributors to the economic life of the county.

The presence of the University was responsible for attracting Alvin Wood Chase, perhaps the best-known American physician of his day, to Washtenaw. Although he attended classes at the University's medical school in mid-life, his degree was from the Eclectic Medical Institute of Cincinnati, acquired after 16 weeks of intensive study. But by the time Dr. Chase was able to attach the professional suffix to his name,

he had been practicing medicine on the Michigan and Ohio frontier for nearly 30 years.

In 1864 Chase built a steam printing plant on the corner of North Main Street and Miller Avenue in Ann Arbor, and he began to publish an ambitious medical compendium. *Dr. Chase's Recipe Book* went through several editions, sold four million copies, and was the major 19th century best-seller after the Bible. It continued to sell well into the 20th century. Dr. Chase told you how to keep well, cure a boil, bake nutritious bread, doctor your horse, and dye your homespun yarn. The word eclectic in the title of his medical school was not for naught. He was, however, first attracted to Ann Arbor because of its medical school. Without that lure, the seat of his creative thrust in publishing may well have been Maumee or Jackson.

By the last quarter of the 19th century papermaking had become a major industry in Ypsilanti. Several small mills had existed in the county for some time. But paper manufacture was transformed in the 1860s and 1870s when a process was developed to make paper, especially newsprint, from cheap wood pulp rather than expensive rags.

Cornelius Cornwell, exploiting the new technology, embarked on a papermaking enterprise much larger than any the county had seen before. In 1874 he built on the Huron River in Ypsilanti the largest mill in Michigan, employing 500 workers. He also operated mills at Foster's Station, Hudson, Superior, and near what is now Barton dam. But Cornwell's extensive operation disappeared early in the 20th century.

The Peninsular Paper Company, incorporated in 1867 by a number of Ypsilanti businessmen, continues to exist, although it has been part of a large national corporation, the James River Company, since 1974. Peninsular has always made paper from rags. Originally Peninsular made newsprint and the Chicago *Tribune* was one of its customers. But by the end of the century wood pulp largely replaced rags as the raw material for newspaper stock. Peninsular, however, did not abandon rag paper. Instead it pioneered

Above: Warren Kimble's boat factory in Manchester, located on the Raisin River south of the Main Street bridge, is typical of the small industries that flourished in the county late in the nineteenth century. At the time local industry was often still based on the river. Courtesy, Manchester Public Library

specialty papers, developing color papers of high quality and cover and text papers for fine books. It has continued to make specialty papers throughout this century.

Until the mid-1970s one Ypsilanti family, the Quirks, dominated Peninsular's operations and was its major stockholder. The first Daniel Quirk was one of the original incorporators. His business experience was already extensive, including railroads and development, and he consistently exploited Ypsilanti's commercial opportunities. He was a prime mover in the First National Bank, the city gas plant, a woolen mill, and the interurban. But Peninsular Paper became a major interest. His son, Daniel Quirk, Jr., became president in 1914, and the most recent Daniel Quirk retired only after the firm's purchase by the James River Company.

Ypsilanti's industrial base was not limited to paper. Henry Colburn, Ypsilanti historian of the 1920s, described 15 "large manufactories" employing 600 persons in 1887, as well as numerous smaller enterprises. Threshing machines, coffee roasters, corn shellers, mill machinery, plows, baseball bats, bricks, pumps, and brooms were all made in this small city of 5,000 people. A dress-stay factory employed 170 women. There was also a bustle company and, of course, the usual woolen mills.

The Ypsilanti bottled-water industry, which developed in the 1880s, was a by-product of papermaking.

Cornwell bored a well in 1882 in search of pure water for processing paper, and at 750 feet he hit mineral water. A sanitarium was soon built on Huron Street to take advantage of the medicinal value of his discovery. A second deep well was bored on the sanitarium's site, and eventually a third in a different location. All tapped mineral-water deposits, and all three had different qualities. Most of the water from Cornwell's find was bottled and sent east, the sanitarium exploited its own well in treatments specializing in mineral water and electricity, and the product of the third was made into salts with substantial commercial value.

Trading stamps also originated in Ypsilanti. In the 1890s Shelley M. Hutchinson made a fortune from his ingenious green-stamp idea, only to lose it in other ventures such as the coffee roaster plant and an underwear factory.

The western side of the county joined the eastern townships in developing heavy industry. In 1891 Chelsea became the site of the Glazier Stove Works, founded by local entrepreneur Frank P. Glazier to manufacture a blue-flame kerosene cookstove, much in demand with the housewives of the day. The Glazier stove-manufacturing business was eventually worth over one-and-one-quarter million dollars. But Glazier also possessed a taste for power. He went on to organize a Chelsea bank. He had political control of Chelsea and, as we have seen, founded its public utilities. He became a state senator, and he wanted desperately to control the Washtenaw County Republican machine. He aspired to state office. Perhaps he wanted to be governor. His ambitions led him to attempt a political and economic empire that was beyond him. Although there is doubt about his actual guilt, Glazier, then Michigan's state treasurer, was convicted of fraud, imprisoned, and lost his public office and business interests. His stove works declared bankruptcy in 1907.

Chelsea was also the home of Washtenaw County's first automobile works. A.R. Welch was the proprietor of the Chelsea Manufacturing Company, a concern that made novelties such as knife sharpeners and tea

Above: This young woman is trying on a bodice extender in her farm home in Augusta township, circa 1902. We do not know the garment's origins, but it may have been made locally in one of Ypsilanti's underwear or corset factories. Courtesy, Ella Fuller Collection, Bentley Historical Library

strainers. Like many others in the 1890s, Welch caught automobile fever, and for ten years he schemed and planned to make a car. In 1903 his dreams were realized when the Welch Tourist, as he called his machine, made its debut at the Chicago automobile show. Welch's first cars were made in Chelsea, but in 1904 he moved to Pontiac, and in 1912, shortly after his death, his business was sold to General Motors.

Ann Arbor was slower than Chelsea and Ypsilanti to acquire heavy industry. As late as 1900 Ann Arbor's largest industry, aside from education, was milling. Not until the years 1910 to 1919 did American Broach, Hoover Ball, and Parker Manufacturing establish plants in the city, just in time to prosper from the industrial expansion fostered by World War I.

One local enterprise almost omnipresent was the newspaper. For several years the *Western Immigrant,* founded in 1829, was the county's only newspaper. Like most early 19th century newspapers, it did not see its purpose as the dissemination of local news, which everyone knew anyway; instead it served as an

organ for advertising the community and exerting political influence. In this case it was the blatant promotion of the Anti-Masonic views of John Allen and Judge Samuel Dexter. Ann Arbor had some 25 newspapers, if one counts name changes, in the 19th century, and mergers and changes of political allegiance were common.

The *Ann Arbor News,* founded by Frank Glazier of Chelsea to further his political ambitions, was part of the new wave that swept the country in the 1890s, daily papers having replaced the earlier weekly editions. When Glazier's empire collapsed, the *News* was merged with two older Ann Arbor papers, the *Argus* and the *Times.* Through that merger the *News* can trace its origins back to 1835 when the original *Argus,* again with many mergers and changes of ownership, was founded. The *News* continued to be locally owned until it was purchased by the Booth chain in 1919.

Ypsilanti acquired its first newspaper in 1844, a Whig sheet called the *Sentinel* founded by John B. Van Fossen, who was soon replaced as editor by Charles

Above: Many of the brick business blocks on Manchester's main street are still in existence. In this circa 1893 photograph, canvas awnings protect the merchandise in the store windows from the sun, and hitching posts line the unpaved street. An iron bridge facilitates traffic across the Raisin River. From Art Work of Washtenaw County, *1893*

Woodruff, son of the founder of Woodruff's Grove. The *Sentinel* was joined in 1864 by the Ypsilanti *Commercial,* a fiercely Republican paper. The Woodruffs continued as editors and publishers for two generations. In 1880 Charles' son, M.T. Woodruff, founded the *Ypsilantian,* dedicated to independence in politics and objectivity in reporting, a revolutionary break with the general tradition of the time.

Rural Washtenaw County also had its newspapers and, unlike those of Ann Arbor and Ypsilanti, they have remained weeklies. In the 20th century these papers have turned their attention mostly to local events. The editors of the early weeklies were essentially printers who frequently set the type themselves and did job printing on the side that provided much of their livelihood. The Milan *Leader* began publication in 1882. In 1871 Andrew Allison founded the Chelsea *Herald,* which was sold and resold several times. The Chelsea *Standard* began publication in 1882.

The Manchester *Enterprise,* founded in 1867 by George Spafford but purchased a year later by Mat

Blosser, had Blosser as its editor and publisher for 72 years, after which one of his daughters continued to be associated with the paper. This may be the longest span of editorial control by one family in the county.

A WIDENING SPHERE

At mid-century women had founded voluntary library associations, literary clubs, and charitable organizations that distributed relief to the poor. They continued to widen the horizons and aspirations of women as the century wore on.

First of all, late-19th-century women moved into the professions in sizable numbers, an influx that was not to be matched proportionally until the 1970s. Actually Ypsilanti's first female physician, Helen McAndrew, the wife of a local merchant, received her training and began her practice before the Civil War. By the end of the 1870s there were three women practicing medicine in Ypsilanti, and women had founded a Free Hospital Association to support charity beds in the infirmary staffed by two of these doctors, Ruth Gerry and Cynthia Smith. Women had served on the faculty of Michigan Normal since it opened its doors, and in 1900, of its 56 teachers, 34 were women. In 1895 Eliza Mosher returned to the University of Michigan campus, where she had earned a medical degree, to serve as professor of hygiene and dean of women to the 647 female students then enrolled. Otherwise women were conspicuous by their absence from the Michigan faculty. Women were, however, heavily represented on public-school and proprietary-professional-school staffs, although rarely in administrative roles.

Second, politics claimed an increasing share of women's attention. In 1881 women property owners received the right to vote in Michigan school elections. Many of these new women voters affiliated themselves with the Prohibition party, which also championed women's rights and permitted women to exercise full power in its councils. This alliance of women and Prohibitionists resulted in the election of Sarah Bishop in 1883 to the Ann Arbor school

Above: Ann Arbor's Beal Block, built in 1882 on the northeast corner of Main and Ann, housed the post office until 1909. It also sheltered a fraternal lodge on its third floor, bathrooms and a barber shop on the corner, and law offices on the second floor. From Art Work of Washtenaw County, *1893*

board. Another Prohibitionist and suffragist, Emma Bower, was elected in 1894, and in 1896, Anna Bach became the first female president of the Board of Education. Emma Bower followed her as president in 1899.

The Michigan Equal Suffrage Association held its 1894 convention in Ann Arbor, and a local Political Equality Club to foster women's rights soon followed. The local Woman's Christian Temperance Unions had been carrying on the fight for equal rights since the early 1880s, but at the turn of the century momentum increased and the campaign quickened. A state-wide referendum in November 1912 on women's suffrage passed narrowly in Ann Arbor (of course the voters were exclusively male) and failed narrowly in the county, 4,947 to 4,861. Not until November 1918 did Michigan women receive full suffrage, and the men of Washtenaw County supported that constitutional amendment 4,484 to 3,752.

By the onset of World War I Washtenaw County had begun to take on many of the features that characterize it today. Over 90 percent of its land was still agricultural, producing grain, hay, vegetables, fruit, dairy products, and sheep. But the factory had invaded both eastern and western townships while academia dominated its center. Highways and motor traffic had already begun to challenge the railroads as movers of freight and people. Cities were outgrowing their early boundaries and local government was increasing in complexity. These changes were occurring everywhere, but because of the presence of the University and Normal, Washtenaw's differentiation from the rest of Michigan's southern tier of counties was marked. The county was a place of learning, not just a place of farm, shop, and manufactory.

Top: Emma E. Bower was a prominent local club and church member and an 1883 graduate of the University of Michigan's homeopathic medical school. She was elected to the Ann Arbor school board in 1894 and later served as its president. From Beakes, Past and Present of Washtenaw County, *1906*

Above: Life was comfortable on Washtenaw County farms by the turn of the century. Franklin Fletcher is pictured resting in the parlor of his home on Bunton Road. Note the family portraits, the elaborate ceiling lamp (probably kerosene) reflected in the mirror, and the elegant Victorian sofa that perhaps dated from the 1860s. The bust of the Indian woman on the table may have been acquired at the Columbian Exposition of 1893. Courtesy, Fuller Collection, Bentley Historical Library, University of Michigan

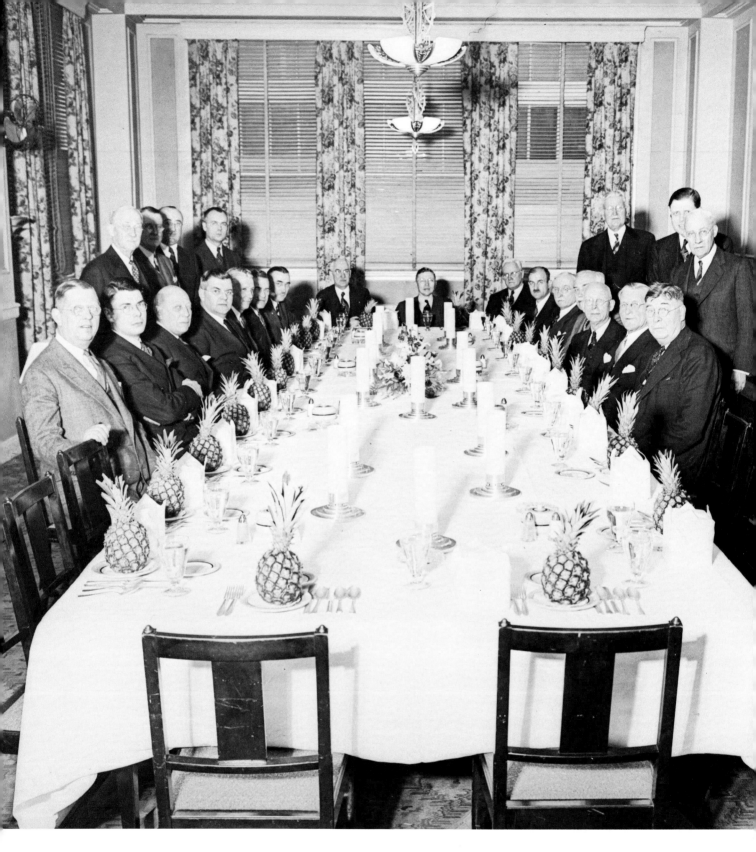

The Huron Hotel in Ypsilanti provided elegant banquet service in the period between the two world wars. The hotel was a genuine community project with many citizen investors, and it continues to fulfill a community function today as headquarters for the Heritage project. Courtesy, Ivory Collection, Bentley Historical Library, University of Michigan

IV

A
PLACE OF
STRENGTH AND
QUEST

After 1900 the uninterrupted confident optimism that characterized Washtenaw County's first American century was put to several severe and prolonged tests. Never again would Washtenaw's destiny seem quite so clear and untroubled, its citizens as certain that they had the promised land within their grasp. Two world wars and the Great Depression, plus the revolutionary changes that marked the postwar world, offered new and disturbing challenges.

AN ENGULFING CONFLICT

By 1914 the period of accelerating social and economic change that ushered in the 20th century had already penetrated Washtenaw County. An event that took place almost halfway around the world in July 1914 further accelerated that process. Within a month after the Austrian archduke was shot in Sarajevo, Yugoslavia, the major European powers found themselves at war with each other for the first time in a century.

At first the entanglements and the alterations brought by the war were subtle.

At the University of Michigan a young French instructor and his colleague in the German department hurried across the Atlantic to join their respective regiments. The farmers found a readier market for their produce and the new Hoover Ball and Bearing Company prospered. The income tax, which still touched only the upper-middle classes and business, began its inexorable rise as the United States mobilized to provide the nation with the military strength to assert its concerns in a warring world.

By early 1916, however, real change was in the air. An Ypsilanti National Guard unit, Company A of the United States Signal Corps, was called to service on the Mexican border. The men were to help contain a revolution that had no direct relationship to the war in Europe, but instead had its seeds in the endemic poverty of the Latin American masses. The border skir-

mishes that ensued, however, were only a dress rehearsal for men and officers soon to exercise their skills in the larger theater in France. Preparedness advocates and the declared supporters of the Allies became more vocal, German-Americans became more fearful of being accused of disloyalty, and the prosperity of business and agriculture became increasingly tied to the needs of the Allied armies on the western front. In April 1917 Congress, at President Woodrow Wilson's request, declared war on the Central Powers.

Ypsilanti's Signal Corps company returned from the Mexican border in March 1917, and only five months later, they found themselves back in service with orders to embark for France with the Thirty-Second Division. They fought at Chateau-Thierry and in the Argonne, lost ten of their number to wounds or disease, and went on to assist in the occupation of the Rhineland. They were not mustered out until May 25, 1919.

Ann Arbor's National Guard unit, Company I of the Thirty-First Michigan Infantry, was mobilized in July of 1917, went to France early in 1918 as a unit of the One-Hundred-Twenty-Sixth Infantry, and was sent to the Alsace front. Ann Arbor also supplied an ambulance company that marched down State Street on a rainy night in June 1917 and in August sailed on the H.M.S. *Baltic* to "hell," as one of them later wrote, the western front, where they lived with gassing, wounds, and influenza. This was one of the first United States army units to reach the French front.

World War I placed enormous strains on Washtenaw's German population. In several areas of the county, including Ann Arbor's West Side, German was still in use. Although German citizens and residents were almost universally loyal to their adopted country, ethnic tensions that had long been quiescent inevitably erupted. The *Washtenaw Post,* the area's German-language newspaper, was banned from the mails, and a few German businessmen lost trade for the duration. As the United States attempted to erase all traces of German influence, liberty cabbage, salis-

Above: This poignant photograph of Marie Wenger, a young girl of German descent, was made on the occasion of her confirmation just before World War I. She lived on a farm near Dexter, and her family probably spoke German at home. The Wengers were loyal Americans, but the times must have made them uneasy. Courtesy, Dexter Historical Museum

bury steak, and the hot dog replaced sauerkraut, the hamburger, and the frankfurter. But there were more abrasive, deeper wounds not so easily accommodated: the child persecuted by schoolmates, the shopkeeper boycotted by a favorite customer, and rumors of secret sabotage against an innocent victim. One member of the University's German department was dismissed, another granted indefinite leave and later refused reinstatement. It was not a time of tolerance.

Washtenaw County women played a leading role in the domestic war effort. Their earlier organizing efforts for temperance, charity, and political equality propelled them to the forefront in this crisis. Women took on many tasks that fit their traditional role. They knit socks, helmets, and sweaters for soldiers and refugees. Christmas packages were assembled and books collected for camp libraries. Women organized Ypsilanti's Allied Alley Fiesta, a splendid fair that occupied a full city block. Side shows, vaudeville performances, minstrel shows, and booths of every description enticed Ypsilantians and their neighbors to donate for war relief.

But women also filled jobs formerly held by men now in service, as well as enlisting in the armed forces themselves. Actually nursing was the only military assignment open to them. They also inspected munitions, learned to function as mechanics, and virtually replaced the male clerk in offices.

Nearly 13,000 University of Michigan faculty, staff, students, and alumni served in World War I, and 229 of them lost their lives. Such sacrifice was not accomplished without disruption and conflict.

Manpower was the first major war-related problem to confront the University. During the last half of 1916, as the cost of living rose and business and industry offered higher salaries, a quarter of the University of Michigan clerical workers resigned to go work elsewhere. Once war was declared the University's student enrollment declined precipitously. Its undergraduates and graduate students were still primarily male, and the men went off to fight. But this exodus reversed itself as the Student Army Training Corps

(SATC) was established on campus, and Washington urged students to stay in school until an appropriate niche could be found for them.

Faculty were also affected. Just a few months into the war 46 members of the University faculty were engaged in some kind of war service. Thirteen of these were making their contribution in Ann Arbor, but 33 had left the campus and were stationed in France, Washington, or in army camps around the country.

War also changed the curriculum. In 1917 almost a quarter of the University's student body was enrolled in classes in the Germanic languages and literature. When the war broke out those 1,300 students dropped to 150. A more fundamental shift is exemplified by a two-month course offered by the College of Engineering to train draftees at the technical, rather than the degree level, as gunsmiths, machinists, carpenters, blacksmiths, and mechanics. A number of women were enrolled in this program. Although the

Above: The army was conspicuous on Washtenaw's campuses by the fall of 1917. These two officers, standing on the boulevard in front of Hill Auditorium, trained the new ROTC units at the University of Michigan. Courtesy, Bentley Historical Library, University of Michigan

Reserve Officer Training Corps (ROTC) never became compulsory, 1,800 Michigan students were registered in the program at one time, the largest enrollment in any American university. By fall 1918, out of a total student body of 7,500, there were 3,750 men on the Ann Arbor campus under military discipline. They were housed, fed, clothed, and equipped by the federal government, a massive dose of federal support to education and an entirely new source of university support.

A proportionately smaller number of young males attending Normal meant that World War I's impact was far milder at that institution. In fact Normal was touched less profoundly than it had been during the Civil War, clear testimony to the increasing preponderance of women among professional teachers. Eleven Normal students died in World War I. The Student Army Training Corps organized at Normal contained only 76 men when the armistice was signed. Out of a total student body of 1,387, only 187 served in the armed forces.

Industrial development within Washtenaw County as a result of World War I produced more lasting economic effects than agriculture's comfortable wartime prosperity. By 1920 the Detroit area was well established as a major U.S. center of heavy industry. The First World War, with its need for transport, did much to accelerate this process. Parts and components, however, rather than the basic auto manufacturing process, formed the core of Washtenaw's industry.

In the spring of 1913 when the Federal Screw Works was founded at Chelsea as the Chelsea Screw Company, its 15 employees were housed in the Mack Building on North Main Street. In 1916 the company required a new building. By the end of World War I a large wing had to be added to this new structure, and the company's employees numbered over a hundred. Michigan Portland Cement, located in the same village, was incorporated in 1911. At the end of the war its plant was shipping over 400 carloads of cement per month. All over the county industry was booming, and with increasing frequency it was tied, in one way or another, to Detroit's growing monopoly of the automobile industry.

At long last, on November 11, 1918, Armistice Day marked the joyous end of the fighting. Although a false armistice and long days of peace rumors had preceded the actual event, this did not detract from the euphoria that met the silencing of the big guns in France. Church bells rang, community sings and parades were organized, bonfires were lit, and people indulged in a few last intemperate gestures, such as dragging the Kaiser's effigy through the streets. The war that for all time was to free the world of war had come to an end.

Before soldiers were released from the trenches on the western front, a new enemy at home and abroad had begun to claim its share of casualties. The so-called Spanish influenza made its appearance in the early fall of 1918. By mid-October all places of public assembly in Washtenaw County had been closed, and frightened citizens either stayed at home or went about their business protected by gauze masks. During the month of October 115 people died in Ann Arbor. Over 1,200 soldiers in training at the county's educational institutions fell ill. The Michigan Union became a hospital, Newberry Hall served as an infirmary, and a few private residences were pressed into care for the overflow. With no antibiotics to use against the plague, the Spanish flu could only run its course, and it was a rare household that did not face at least the threat of death.

PROSPERITY AND THE AUTOMOBILE

The prosperity of the 1920s, elusive and shallow in some parts of the United States, appears to have been real enough in Washtenaw County. Retail business and manufacturing both boomed. Population jumped substantially from 49,000 to over 65,000. The automobile began to monopolize transportation, facilitating suburban commuting, creating a demand for good roads, and introducing the family garage and parking problems.

At the same time rapidly increasing college enrollments mirrored real popular concern with broader educational opportunities and with professional credentials and competence. Prohibition was the touchstone of a return to Puritan religious values that prescribed strict discipline and government control of individual lifestyles. Meanwhile "nice," middle-class women for the first time smoked and drank in public places. Prosperity called forth a spurt in private and

Above: The Law Quadrangle, built in 1923-1924, was the gift of William W. Cook, a Michigan alumnus who made a fortune in Cuban sugar. The University of Michigan grew rapidly in the 1920s, but its most luxurious addition was undoubtedly this new home for the law school.

Top: In the 1920s the newly invented motor car and improved roads resulted in the construction of dozens of summer cottages on the lakes in the western part of the county. No longer did the middle class family have to vacation at a summer hotel close to a railroad line. Courtesy, Bentley Historical Library, University of Michigan

public building, and Washtenaw's largest city received its first quasi skyscrapers. Modern times had come to Washtenaw.

The direct and indirect repercussions of the automobile were myriad. Improved highways were built all over the county connecting major towns. The adventurous farmer who took his family to church in a Ford sedan and who thought about replacing his wagon with a small truck also began to be interested in good roads. And his young son could think of attending high school in town while continuing to live at home and help with the chores. The disruption on Ann Arbor's streets caused by the college boy's raucous tin lizzie in 1927 resulted in a ban on car ownership by University students until after World War II.

Small, summer cottages with ample front porches to catch summer breezes sprang up on the county's now much more accessible lakes—Whitmore, Base, and Portage. Suburban developments like Barton Hills could blossom on the outskirts of major urban centers. In fact, more accessible areas of the county, espe-

cially along the Huron River, became a residential haven for a number of Detroit's more affluent citizens.

Increasing college enrollments changed the shape of the county's major urban centers. By 1926 the University of Michigan had over 10,000 students, nearly double the prewar record. At Normal the change was more gradual, from less than 2,800 in 1915 to nearly 4,000 in 1925. Normal's appropriations also increased at a slower rate, from about $185,000 in 1916 to almost one million dollars in 1926. But during the decade of the 1920s the University's appropriations quadrupled, and the number of employees increased proportionately. The University was Ann Arbor's largest employer, and in fact more people worked for the University than in the city's manufacturing plants and retail trade combined. The economy of Ann Arbor and its outlying areas was tied to the University more firmly than it had ever been before.

An enormous building program doubled the size of the University's campus. The Law Quadrangle, Clements Library, Angell Hall, University High School,

Roosevelt School was the laboratory school for Michigan Normal at the height of its reputation as a first-class teacher training institution. In this photo, circa 1923, every student is properly dressed. Standards were high and rigidly enforced. Courtesy, Eastern Michigan University Archives

East Engineering, Randall Physics Laboratory, and a new Medical Building were erected during this decade. Away from the main campus, several blocks to the southwest, an imposing athletic compound, Yost Field House, the Intramural and Women's athletic buildings, and the new stadium, all financed by athletic-generated funds, were constructed. A new University Hospital overlooked the river valley.

Michigan Normal experienced a modest building program. Two training facilities were erected, Lincoln Laboratory School and Roosevelt High School. But, until after World War II, Normal was not as important to Ypsilanti's economy as the University was to that of Ann Arbor.

Other public construction also contributed to the county's prosperity. Perry and Bach schools in Ann Arbor received substantial additions, and Angell, Jones, and Mack schools were completed during the 1920s. Although it was not ready for use until 1931, Ypsilanti State Hospital was begun in 1929, and Beyer Hospital and nurses' home, both sponsored by a service organization with wartime origins, the Patriotic Service League, were completed. St. Joseph's Mercy Hospital, completed in 1914, built both a major addition in the 1920s and opened Mercywood, a 40-bed facility for emotionally disturbed patients, in Scio Township.

Private construction kept pace. Several new business blocks made their appearance. For the first time business rather than community buildings dominated city skylines. The Wolverine and First National buildings rivaled the courthouse tower in downtown Ann Arbor, and the Huron Hotel competed with the water tower and church spires in Ypsilanti.

THE GREAT DEPRESSION

From 1929 until the outbreak of the Second World War, the Great Depression afflicted the entire Western world. Banks failed, unemployment soared, and mortgages were in arrears. Protected in part by its link to education, Washtenaw County suffered less than the region of which it was a part. Nonetheless it could not bypass the tragic distemper that spread on every side. Although Washtenaw's diversified agriculture weathered the crisis better than single-crop ranches farther west, the farmer saw many of his markets disappear. The Depression years left students less confident of finding jobs at graduation. The construction boom of the 1920s terminated abruptly. The county's Detroit-dependent industry laid off workers by the score.

In Washtenaw County auto-parts suppliers—like American Broach, King Seeley, and Hoover Ball and Bearing—were almost immediately forced to reduce production and lay off workers. Although Ypsilanti found a large share of its labor force unemployed, Henry Ford, true to his iconoclastic ways, countered basic trends by expanding Ford Motor Company's interests in the eastern part of the county. In 1931 the old Cornwell Paper Mill site on the Huron River in Ypsilanti was purchased and converted into a parts plant employing several hundred men.

Although wages nosedived, it was the unemployed who really suffered. Personal savings, private charity, and local relief efforts were their only recourse until 1933. By 1931 the city of Ann Arbor was attempting

Above: In the 1920s Washtenaw County's second courthouse was still adequate for its needs. The county treasurer's office easily contained all of the tax records on shelves along the wall. The deputy county treasurer, Jennie Hatch (pictured in the foreground) had held that position for some time. Frank Tickner, seated behind the desk, was the elected treasurer, and Iva Limpert, left, was a clerk. A Mr. Ordway, standing in the rear, was a customer. Courtesy, Hatch Papers, Bentley Historical Library, University of Michigan

During the Great Depression, homeless men traveled around the country in railroad boxcars looking for work. This man is cooking his dinner over a fire built in an overturned washtub on the railroad siding. Courtesy, Ivory Collection, Bentley Historical Library, University of Michigan

to provide work relief. The unemployed improved parks, constructed sewers and sidewalks, and staffed the emergency facilities designed to aid them. But work relief was not enough. The city also provided direct welfare funds, food, and clothing.

That great stabilizer of Ann Arbor's economy, the University of Michigan, failed this time and instead proved responsive to the economic chaos in the larger community. University enrollment dropped from more than 15,500 in 1930 to just over 12,000 in 1933, a full 20 percent decrease. Appropriations decreased by a third during the same period. University salaries were cut from 8 to 20 percent on a sliding scale that favored those receiving the smallest wages.

Similar patterns unfolded in Ypsilanti. During the same period, 1930 to 1934, Normal's enrollment declined by 28 percent and its appropriations from the legislature were cut by a massive 49 percent, and this for a college that was much more dependent on the state legislature for funding than was the University. Salaries were precipitously cut, usually almost halved. Normal's president's salary dropped more drastically from $9,000 to $4,000.

Although the New Deal was not universally hailed in Washtenaw, Franklin Roosevelt's programs dispensed unusually large sums of money locally. A massive construction program was financed by the Public Works Administration (PWA). In Ann Arbor East and West quadrangles, Stockwell Hall, and Victor Vaughan dormitories were built with federal funds, as were the new Health Service Building and additions to the Dental School and the hospital. Fourteen percent of the University's students were employed by the National Youth Administration (NYA) at one time. These jobs were literally the ticket by which they were able to stay in school. University enrollments, spurred by these federal inducements, again began to rise.

Enrollment trends at Normal also were reversed by New Deal programs, and the number of students almost doubled between 1935 and 1940, although appropriations were never recouped. The legislature restored only 17 percent of the previous cuts, making for unreasonable teaching overloads and further strains on the instructional program. Normal also received a modest share of PWA funds, but did not

take advantage of available federal programs to the same extent as the University. Dormitories were built on campus for the first time: King and Goodison for women and Munson for men. Hoover Elementary Science Laboratory was completed in 1941. The major addition to Normal's athletic plant in the 1930s, however, was unrelated to federal programs but was a gift of Walter Owen Briggs.

Few communities in the nation, most especially Ann Arbor, were so well endowed by the New Deal. And Ann Arbor's penchant for subvention, especially for construction, helped the rest of the county. One might expect this largess to have some effect on the county's political affiliations. Washtenaw County, unlike the state, had voted Democratic, with few exceptions, from midway through the Civil War until the First World War, when it shifted its allegiance to the Republicans. It remained in the Republican column through the 1920s. In fact, it gave Herbert Hoover an overwhelming 78 percent of its vote in 1928. The Great Depression took a heavy toll from this Republican strength, and Hoover's share of the county's vote was reduced to 53 percent in 1932, although the Republican tally crept back to 63 percent by 1940. In short, the county voted Republican in a measure that reflected its prosperity rather than its receipt of aid from Washington. Ypsilanti and rural areas were more solidly Republican than Ann Arbor, which actually gave Franklin Roosevelt a majority of 52 percent in 1940. That figure, however, may indicate a peace vote, as had the county's shift to the Republicans in 1918. Once more the voters found themselves endorsing a president who had kept them out of war.

There were other ventures, more specific to local conditions, that were intended to solve or ameliorate the hardships of economic collapse. Although housing fees drastically dropped, students were still hard pressed to make ends meet. Spontaneous cooperative living arrangements eventually resulted in a thriving student cooperative movement that has persisted for over half a century. The Ann Arbor Farmers' Market in its present form had its origins in a sympathetic attempt to provide local farmers with a retail market for their produce and has enriched the county's quality of life ever since.

Other ambitious, Depression-related experiments

*These children are being hoisted onto a haywagon at Saline Valley Farms by Harold Gray,
president and founder of this community which was spawned by the Depression. Courtesy,
Harold Gray Papers, Bentley Historical Library, University of Michigan*

have not survived. Saline Valley Farms, a quasi-cooperative, idealistic venture initiated in 1931 by Harold Studley Gray, a wealthy Detroiter inoculated with a strong sense of noblesse oblige, is one example. At its height, this agricultural community of about 20 families farmed some 800 acres that encompassed orchards, dairy and beef herds, egg- and chicken-processing plants, a dairy, a canning factory, housing for members and employees, and even an artificial lake for recreation.

But World War II, as young men were drafted, severely tested the project's viability. After the war competition from corporate dairying became increasingly stiff, and the cooperative aspect of the enterprise was disbanded in 1953. In 1969 Saline Valley Farms was sold to the Teamsters Union as a recreation area.

Another creative response to the Depression originated in the fertile brain of Henry Ford. Ford had long nourished the idea of small, village industries that would provide work in rural areas for local people who would continue to operate their farms. Ford saw this decentralized industry as eliminating some of the brutal impersonality of large factories and huge cities and preserving a way of life that Ford remembered from his own early experience and forever idealized.

In six years he constructed 13 factories, almost always using an old gristmill site. In some of these plants Ford also experimented with using locally grown soybeans for the manufacture of plastics and paint. By the outbreak of World War II, 29 village industries were in operation. Saline, Milan, and Manchester were sites for three of Ford's experimental plants.

The little gristmills of the mid-19th century, some of which had been consolidated into impressive flour factories at the turn of the century, once again supported locally-based manufacturing, as they had in the beginning. Ford's experiment, however, was never profitable. Cheap energy and acute shortages of vehicle parts kept these small factories operating during World War II, but then they closed down. Not until the energy crisis of the late 1970s were their water-power resources reexamined as a possible source of oil-free energy.

WASHTENAW AGAIN GOES TO WAR
War came gradually to the United States in 1940 and 1941. Beginning in September 1940 the Selective Service inducted young men into growing armies, and after March 1941 the Lend-Lease Act supported a

Above: This large cannery, equipped in the 1930s, processed the produce and poultry raised on Saline Valley Farms. The canned goods were used on the farm and also sold outside. In this photo, women are canning chicken. During World War II the facilities were also used by ordinary citizens, for a fee, to process the produce from their victory gardens. Courtesy, Harold Gray Papers, Bentley Historical Library, University of Michigan

Above right: Local national guard units were sent off to training camp even before Pearl Harbor. The men in this photograph wave their farewells from the train as they prepare to leave Ann Arbor. Courtesy, Ivory Collection, Bentley Historical Library, University of Michigan

beleaguered Britain. Nonetheless, when Japanese bombs fell on Pearl Harbor, the shock was severe and the results cataclysmic. Michigan overnight had her role as the arsenal of democracy underscored and made absolute, and in less than two months automobile production for civilian use ceased altogether. Although Michigan certainly produced its share of fighting men, the state's role on the home front was crucial. Michigan supplied more munitions than any other state. Its industry became almost completely war industry.

The largest and most ambitious of the county's defense efforts took place on its eastern edge. The Willow Run Bomber Plant, erected in 1941, was built on the site of one of Henry Ford's Depression-related philanthropies. In 1939 Ford had established a camp for sons of World War I veterans at Willow Run. Sixty-five

disadvantaged youths lived in tents and farmed 320 acres. They were paid 25 cents an hour for their labor. In 1941 this land plus other acreage formed the tract on which the huge bomber plant was erected. Initially a work force of 50,000 was anticipated, but at the peak of employment 42,000 were actually on the job. Many of these employees commuted from Wayne County, but Ypsilanti was the city closest at hand, and large numbers of workers transplanted from Appalachia were housed there. At Willow Run Village on Ypsilanti's eastern edge, the Federal Housing Administration developed apartments, dormitories, and commercial services to serve 15,000 people. And a new expressway, the first in the state, carried commuters to and from Detroit. Only in the 1830s and 1840s had the county received a proportionate infusion of people, and then the gross numbers were, of course,

Above: Housewives contributed their old aluminum pots and pans for the manufacture of aluminum from scrap during World War II. This crib containing the county's discards graced the courthouse lawn in 1941. Courtesy, Ivory Collection, Bentley Historical Library, University of Michigan

much smaller.

Nearly a fifth of the 50,000 planes President Franklin Roosevelt promised an incredulous nation in 1942 were built in Willow Run's hastily erected hangars. By V-E Day nearly 9,000 B-24 Liberator bombers had come off the Willow Run assembly lines, one of the major wartime achievements of the automobile industry.

Like its factories, the county's campuses reflected the needs and concerns of the larger society. World War II early affected foreign students who found themselves without funds and physically unable to return home. Young men (and women also this time) enlisted or were drafted, especially at the end of the 1941 to 1942 academic year. The enrollment of Michigan Normal College dropped over 50 percent between 1941 and 1945, a reflection of the fact that men had been entering public education in large numbers. The University's enrollment, over 12,000 in 1940, had decreased to 7,000 civilian students by 1943, although another 4,000 recruits in uniform were also on campus. Over 200 members of the University faculty took leave in connection with war service, commuting to Washington or joining the armed forces.

Michigan State Normal College faced an additional hazard. Its very existence was threatened by a plan in 1943 to convert all the college buildings into housing facilities for the great bomber plant at Willow Run. Normal's President John Munson responded to the challenge, and students and alumni protested the wisdom of sacrificing so esteemed and venerable an institution. But as Normal's historian, Egbert Isbell, said, "by March the madness had subsided; the college was saved."

Little of the internal conflict and personal harassment that marked the campus responses during World War I was present this time. Enemy aliens and Japanese-Americans released from internment camps during the war were accepted on campus and in the community with intelligent sympathy and no trace of hysteria. The teaching of enemy languages was promoted rather than curtailed.

Once again campuses filled with uniforms. The University of Michigan played host to Army Specialized Training Programs (ASTP), Navy programs, the Judge Advocate General's School, and a Military Intelligence Language School. As it had during World War I, the

The huge Willow Run bomber plant was already under construction when the United States entered World War II. Thousands of planes made here saw service in the Pacific and European theaters of the war. Courtesy, Ivory Collection, Bentley Historical Library

University offered 27 courses at the nondegree technical level for defense workers, including training for ordnance inspectors. Michigan State Normal College provided ASTP Basic I training in mathematics, physics, history, English, and geography to men who would be sent elsewhere for advanced ASTP programs in engineering, medicine, or other professional curricula considered essential to the war effort.

The University's research facilities and scientists also contributed substantially to the winning of World War II. Even before Pearl Harbor, Engineering Research assisted with weapons development. By April 1942 the University had 31 federal research contracts, most of them classified. University faculty contributed to the success of military projects as disparate as the V-T Fuze that disabled robot bombs and knocked Japanese kamikaze planes out of the sky to an effective influenza vaccine. By accelerating the training period and lengthening the summer session Normal was able to help supply the need for public school teachers that increased rather than diminished as the war progressed.

Over 32,000 University of Michigan students and alumni served in World War II, over 500 of whom died in service. From its much smaller and heavily female roster, the Normal College sent over 1,000 young people to the armed services, 63 of whom lost their lives. Washtenaw County sent tens of thousands of its citizens into the armed services, of whom nearly 400 died, and nearly every adult and many children made some kind of contribution directly related to the war effort, from sorting and flattening tomato-soup cans for salvage or working a swing-shift assembly line, to contributing to the development of nuclear fission. The county displayed remarkable flexibility and resilient strength during this time of struggle.

BUTTER FOR GUNS

As victory in Europe was achieved and the recapture of the Philippine Islands made the Pacific seem less like a vast Japanese lake, a good deal of creative thinking about the postwar world went on in American society. Out of the rubble of war would come great technological advances, a consumers' paradisiacal cornucopia—clothing that would never need an iron, dehydrated food, plastic speed boats. After the Hiroshima blast, bountiful nuclear energy would make American society a utopia of cheap, abundant material goods. Or so the promises went. The accumulated demand from Depression deprivations and wartime rationing and shortages had starved people for consumer goods that wartime savings could now finance.

This time around demobilization was gradual. Selective Service was kept in place not only to police an orderly transition with our recent enemies, but also to keep in check the Communist nations we had

Above: Michigan Molded Plastics of Dexter had modest beginnings. Its offices were in the little white house pictured here, and its factory was located in the garage-like building next door. In a short time it was making plastic components related to war production. After World War II the plastics industry became enormously successful. Courtesy, Dexter Historical Museum

Top: Like other Washtenaw County industrial plants, King-Seeley converted to war industry and found itself increasingly dependent on women workers. Courtesy, Ivory Collection, Bentley Historical Library, University of Michigan

Above: During World War II women played a prominent role in the labor force of Michigan Molded Plastics, as they did in most war industry. These young women may have had husbands fighting in the Pacific or North Africa. Courtesy, Dexter Historical Museum

Ypsilanti celebrated Independence Day for the first time in 1823. Several generations later, on July 4, 1949, the zest for celebrating the holiday was still there, particularly among the young. Courtesy, Ypsilanti Historical Museum

recently counted as our allies. Late in 1945 the *Ann Arbor News* continued to carry its column, "With Our Men In Service," and it was to carry that column for a good many more years as later generations of young men were drafted and sent around the world to Korea, to Vietnam, and to the Middle East.

The county's war-related industry made the transition more easily and rapidly than anyone expected. Chelsea Products, for example, quickly converted to making power take-offs for the civilian trucks beginning to roll from the assembly lines. The Rockwell Standard plant made springs for trucks and cars. By December 1945, however, Willow Run Village was a ghost town of only 600 inhabitants, the bomber plant shut down, and its workers scattered. Willow Run's barracks-like housing was put to use as living space for the postwar bulge of students and faculty, and until 1953 the airport served as Detroit's major commercial airport, its giant hangar refurbished as a passenger terminal. Kaiser-Frazer made its ill-fated automobiles in the bomber plant's production area until 1953 when General Motors took over. Male unemployment was temporarily troublesome, but the backlog of demand for automobiles was such that economic decline in southeastern Michigan could not last long.

In the 1950s the county's traditional heavy industry, almost all linked to the auto industry, experienced major expansion. By 1959 the Chelsea Screw Works occupied an 85,000-square-foot plant, employed 250 people, and met a payroll of a million dollars a year. In Dexter, Michigan Molded Plastics, later acquired by the St. Regis Paper Company, had expanded to two plants. Three miles downriver King-Seeley was the largest industrial plant west of Ann Arbor. Milan's American Foundries Company was bought in 1948 by the Maumee Malleable Casting Company, and its production increased. Clark Perforating Company, an auto supplier, also located in that booming village in 1954. The old Chelsea Milling Company kept up with the times, while maintaining its agricultural roots, by converting to a Jiffy Mix factory.

But the trend toward research-based industry was already under way in Ann Arbor. By 1958 Parke-Davis, Bendix, Conductron, Federal Mogul, and Climax Molybdenum had Ann Arbor plants making use of the easy access to scientists and scientific know-how that

a university community could offer. And the Ann Arbor Chamber of Commerce promoted the trend, advertising the city with the slogan, "Research Center of the Midwest."

Industry in the county's small towns was reasonably stable until the late 1970s when the auto industry fell on hard times. But a substantial proportion of the out-county work force began to commute to major cities, where they were employed in service jobs at hospitals, universities, and even public schools. Their shopping habits tended to follow their work places. Small-town population did not decrease, as did the number of people employed in agriculture, but Washtenaw's villages became bedroom communities with fewer commercial resources of their own. When the auto industry became seriously troubled the county's smaller towns risked losing their industrial base as well.

But Washtenaw's small towns fought back. Manchester, the village most remote from the county's population centers, suffered the least and made the easiest transition. By the mid-1980s more jobs existed in its immediate area than the town had citizens, 2,500 to 1,686. Only ten percent of its work force commuted. A half dozen industries, Hoover Ball, Double A Products, and Manchester Plastics among them, were located near or inside its city limits. Much earlier its business area deliberately began to preserve its unique 19th-century flavor, and its peaceful rural charms continued to attract nostalgic visitors from more urban areas.

Milan faced a harder struggle. With three times Manchester's population it saw four of its major industrial employers shut down—the Freuhof plant, two foundries, and a plastics company. No one doubted the need for Milan to rebuild its economic base. Saline also suffered, and its businessmen organized the Uptown Saline Association to help them compete with the shopping malls. In the late 1970s Saline bought 160 acres of undeveloped land to be used as an industrial park. And like Manchester, Saline looked to the growing interest in the rural past and its artifacts and history as a new road to economic health. But Saline attempted to use its rural past in yet another way. It fostered new industrial development—including a soy milk factory, an ethanol plant, and an agricultural packaging firm—by calling attention to its agricultural resources and in the process created several hundred new jobs.

The industrial park, a device used by Ann Arbor to attract industry in the 1960s, became in the 1980s a major weapon of Washtenaw's smaller towns in their battle to stay alive and healthy. Chelsea, Manchester, and Saline were among those who chose to strengthen their economies this way. Manchester, Ypsilanti, Dexter, and Chelsea also experimented with preservation and restoration.

Ann Arbor had adopted in 1971 a municipal preservation ordinance proposed by its historical commission that was used in 1973 to set aside the first small preservation district at Ann and Division streets. Although historic preservation and restoration was only one factor, Ann Arbor was able to retain into the l980s a vital central business district that ranked second only to Detroit's in retail sales.

Agriculture, already rivaled by heavy industry as an economic mainstay of the county, fought its own battles to stay alive. The number of working farms in Washtenaw County fell more than half, from 3,500 to 1,400, in the 50 years from 1935 to 1985. By 1969 only slightly over one percent of the county's employed workers earned their livings on farms, and by 1985 that tiny percentage was reduced again by almost half.

But a healthy pick-yourself and retail, truck-farming business cushioned the decline, and, as had been true from the very beginning of settlement, farm products fueled auxiliary commerce, services, and manufacturing. The local saw- and gristmills were gone, but meat packing, milling, and the retailing of fertilizer, feed, and the provision of veterinary services took their place.

THE COLLEGE BOOM

The post-World War II period was marked all over the country by a rapid, almost precipitous increase in college enrollment. In Washtenaw such expansion had far-flung effects. The G.I. Bill of Rights, passed by Congress during World War II, promised further training to every returning member of the armed services, and the number of high-school graduates attending college more than doubled until over half went on to some form of higher education. In essence wartime university training programs were continued in a new form as direct subsidies to returning service people that were later replaced by student-loan programs. This was a massive, new dose of federal aid to higher education.

Michigan State Normal College significantly broadened its aims and the range of its offerings and became Eastern Michigan College in 1956 and Eastern Michigan University (EMU) in 1959. Eastern's enrollment increased astronomically. The teachers college that mustered 1,200 students at the end of the Second World War in 1945 had an enrollment of nearly

This view of the Eastern Michigan University campus shows the extent of post-World War II expansion and construction. The administration building and clock tower are in the foreground. Lincoln School, which dates from the 1930s, is at the left of center, with the newly constructed library directly behind it at the far left. Pray-Harold, a new classroom building, was still under construction at the time, as were student dormitories. Courtesy, Eastern Michigan University Collection, Bentley Historical Library, University of Michigan

Above: The campus of Concordia College occupies a scenic spot along the Huron River. The chapel where this scene took place dominates the campus, emphasizing the college's religious connection and commitment. Courtesy, Bureau of Alumni Relations, Concordia College

Top: Washtenaw Community College provides highly practical vocational training in a number of trades and professions. The auto shop shown here turns out competent mechanics. Courtesy, Washtenaw Community College Archives

18,000 by 1970, a fifteenfold increase. Increased demand for teachers, stemming from the baby boom, was part of that story. But teaching was only one of many disciplines offered at EMU by the late 1960s. The college's requirement that all its students must agree to teach on graduation had been eliminated in 1953. As late as 1966, however, Eastern was ranked ninth in the United States in the number of teachers trained.

A larger institution meant a greater economic impact on the city of which it was a part. But a true partnership between EMU and the Ypsilanti community did not develop until nearly 40 years after the war. By the 1980s one-quarter of the city of Ypsilanti's land was owned by EMU and was therefore tax free. Eastern was also expanding into the township. The city itself was surrounded by township land and could not grow by annexation. As expansion took place outside its limits the city proper suffered. But college and city combined to attempt to reverse this trend. One concrete implementation of the partnership was the EMU College of Business' plan for a new corporate training center on the south side of town, within the township, to attract increased economic activity to the area. More important was the decision to construct the new business school building on a downtown site on the edge of Ypsilanti's central business district. Administrators said they wanted to encourage interaction between the college and Main Street. With an enrollment of 20,000 and a budget of over 50 million dollars, there was no longer any doubt of Eastern's major role in Ypsilanti's economy. The investment of $13,500, made by the village in 1849 to acquire the normal school, had certainly repaid the city well.

Eastern was not the only Ypsilanti educational institution to experience phenomenal growth. By the mid-1970s Cleary Business School had become a nonprofit, degree-granting institution with over 600 students. Cleary had greatly expanded its scope and its physical plant, including a new building dedicated in 1960, which was financed partly from gifts and endowment.

In the late 1950s the desire for a local community college began to crystallize with much talk of easing the burdens of "teen jobless" and providing instruction for citizens who needed to be retrained or whose

education had been interrupted. A study commission was established, and in January 1965 county voters approved millage to support the two-year Washtenaw Community College.

Instruction began in the fall of 1966 on a temporary campus at Willow Run Village, using the buildings erected during World War II to serve bomber plant workers. But construction began on the handsome new campus in the Huron River valley midway between Ypsilanti and Ann Arbor, and graduates received their diplomas at a ceremony on the new campus grounds in June 1969. Temporary buildings housed most classrooms and offices in the early years, but by the 1980s essential facilities were in place, and in 1985 there were 8,000 students in attendance.

In 1962 Concordia College, a small, private liberal arts institution sponsored by the Lutheran Church (Missouri Synod), was established on the northern banks of the Huron River. Its site was the Earhart farm, one of the large, private estates that signaled the outreach of affluent suburbia in the 1920s. The original mansion was used as a student center, and a complex of contemporary classroom, office buildings, and adjoining dormitories was erected around a handsome central chapel that emphasized the college's primary commitment to religious values. Concordia began as a two-year institution. But by the mid-1980s, in addition to a four-year liberal arts course and training for church-related jobs, it prepared its nearly 500 students in nursing, education, and business.

The University of Michigan started from a much larger and broader base, and its postwar adjustment and expansion was inevitably less spectacular. Enrollment jumped to 12,000 in September 1945, and by fall 1948 had zoomed to over 21,000, about half of whom were veterans. To meet the housing shortage University-owned-and-managed student apartment complexes became a fixture of campus life. University Terrace Apartments, near the hospital and the Arboretum's Peony Gardens, were built first. But when postwar expansion resulted in a new professional school campus on the north side of the river, it included an extensive neighborhood of student apartments.

As enrollment climbed to over 46,000 by 1985, the central campus saw many changes. Its boundaries extended well beyond State Street on the west.

Dexter celebrated the centennial of its organization as a village in 1941. Flora Smith, Mrs. Jameson, and Genevieve Alley donned mid-nineteenth century costumes and posed in front of one of the oldest buildings on Main Street. Courtesy, Dexter Historical Museum

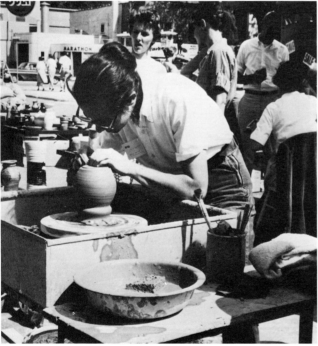

Administrative offices were moved twice in barely 20 years, ending up in new quarters west of the old campus square. Hill and Huron streets continued as the southern and northern boundaries of the campus, but the medical school and hospitals expanded northeast as far as the river. The riverfront location favored for the University by many early Ann Arborites had finally been achieved.

GROWTH AND DIVERSITY

In the 50 years after World War II Washtenaw County became increasingly urban. Its population zoomed from 81,000 in 1940 to 270,000 in 1980, and the population of Ann Arbor grew from 30,000 to 110,000. By the 1980s Ann Arbor contained nearly half of the county's population, and an urban belt joined Ann Arbor and Ypsilanti, crossed the eastern county line, and extended west almost to Dexter. Although there were still a few quiet woodsy dells and unharnessed rapids in the Huron River valley, they existed only because conscious effort had been exerted to keep them there.

The urban county faced quite different challenges than it had met in its rural past. The old sense of community was fragmented. Washtenaw's governing units were no longer villages, a small city or two, and rural townships with minimal responsibility for local schools and country roads. The urban township, eager for an industrial base to support its growing residential subdivisions, competed for both industry and residences with villages and cities. County services expanded markedly. No longer was county government primarily a record-keeping, tax-collecting, and justice-administering agency. Directly providing education for its citizens became, for example, one of the county's major concerns. Washtenaw Community College was a case in point, but other new educational

Above: Potters, painters, silversmiths, and other craftsmen from all over the country exhibit their work at the Ann Arbor Art Fair on State Street, first held in 1960. By 1970 dealers and crowds had taken over, and the fair was big business, but some of the folk festival quality remained. Children still watched the potters at work and experimented with clay themselves. Courtesy, Joyce Jones Papers, Bentley Historical Library, University of Michigan

Top: Washtenaw County's rich racial and cultural diversity is celebrated each September with an ethnic festival in Ann Arbor. Polish, Malaysian, Greek, and Vietnamese participants display their arts and crafts, offer their culinary delights to returning students and county residents, and engage in activities such as the folk dancing pictured.. Courtesy, Ann Arbor Conference and Visitors Bureau

services were provided by the Intermediate School District. Courts and rural law enforcement had always been a county function, but a wide range of juvenile facilities and a greatly expanded sheriff's department reflected new problems and many more people.

As the county urbanized it became diversified in other ways. German ancestry no longer represented difference; instead German origins were identified with the Anglo-Saxon establishment. In 1930, 87 percent of the county's population was native-born white, a percentage that had remained essentially constant since before World War I. By 1960, however, that figure had dropped to just over 80 percent. The ethnic mix was changing. The residents of Appalachia who had migrated to the county to work in defense plants during World War II blended easily into the county's earlier Anglo-Saxon meld. Blacks had also migrated into the county to work in war industry at jobs previously denied them. In 1980 they represented 11 percent of the county's population, and were still heavily concentrated in eastern areas in and near Ypsilanti, just as they had been in the 19th century.

Eastern Europeans, displaced from their Communist homelands, formed one new immigrant group. Orientals, who had scarcely figured into the county's ethnic mix in 1930, were heavily represented in Washtenaw's educational and scientific enterprises. The concealing headdresses and long skirts of Mideastern women no longer seemed alien in the county's shopping malls and supermarkets. Many of the newcomers were student families, some of whom would return to their homelands with their newly polished skills, but many stayed to become permanent residents and eventually U.S. citizens. Arab, Filipino, Korean, and Kuwaiti contributed their technical proficiency to college and university faculties and professional offices. And the local restaurants benefited from their culinary expertise and traditions.

The new ethnic mix also changed the religious complexion of the county. In 1945 church buildings were maintained only by the usual Protestant denominations, a few holiness groups, Roman Catholics, and a single Greek Orthodox congregation. The local Jews either worshiped in Detroit or met in homes for their religious observances. By the mid-1980s, however,

the county was home to 250 organized religious congregations with buildings, including three Jewish groups, a Buddhist temple, and an Islamic mosque.

CULTURE AND CONFLICT

The 1960s were a time of ferment, a season for bringing new ideas to fruition and challenging old values. As the colleges and population grew, the economy diversified, and so did the mix of theater, music, dance, and the visual arts. From the 1880s Ann Arbor had been on the national concert circuit, and good semi-amateur music had been performed in Ann Arbor and Ypsilanti almost from the beginning. But until the advent of the May Drama Festival—which flourished from 1935 to 1961 and brought such stars as Katherine Cornell, Helen Hayes, and Basil Rathbone to Ann Arbor—professional Broadway theatrical productions were relatively rare.

The postwar period saw a veritable flowering of professional theater. The parade of new theatrical ventures began with the Arts Theater in the 1950s, a vehicle for in-the-round productions of the classics, staged in an upstairs loft on Washington Street in Ann Arbor. It was succeeded by the Dramatic Arts Center, a similar enterprise with broader community backing, which was housed in Ann Arbor's former Masonic Temple (the site is now a parking lot and county bus station).

But the most visionary effort of all was the proposal for a Greek theater in Ypsilanti. The idea was first launched in 1963 at a dinner party given by Henry and Clara Owen who envisioned that Ypsilanti, capitalizing on its Greek name, would create a cultural center that would emulate the success Stratford, Ontario, enjoyed with Tyrone Guthrie's great Shakespearean venture. Alexis Solomos of the National Theater in Athens was engaged as director. A temporary open-air theater was improvised from the Eastern Michigan University's baseball diamond, and plans were made for a permanent structure. Bert Lahr and Dame Judith Anderson were secured for the first season. Six performances a week of Aeschylus' *Oresteia* and Aristophanes' *The Birds* in repertory were scheduled in the summer of 1966, and the productions received rave reviews in the national press. Ypsilanti's Greek theater was widely acclaimed an artistic success. But the fund-raising necessary to underwrite the project (despite generous local support) did not match its theatrical attainments, and the theater was unable to cope with overwhelming financial losses. The last performance took place in August 1966, and an audacious dream was permanently shattered.

In the fall of 1963 with the escalation of the war in Vietnam very much on young people's minds, the Free Speech movement originated on the Berkeley campus of the University of California. Three years later in the fall of 1966 the first teach-in to attempt to delineate and clarify the issues in the Vietnam struggle took place on the University of Michigan campus. At the midpoint of two turbulent decades, the academic year 1969 to 1970, the zenith of disruption and rebellion was reached on local campuses. The originally peaceful, thoughtful challenge to the status quo by questioning, anti-establishment students turned impatient, rebellious, and occasionally violent.

Never had the county witnessed the degree of disaffection it experienced in 1969 and 1970. Although students had created havoc and caused disruption in the past, this time the violence and discord had ideological overtones that had not been heard before. A campus branch of the Ann Arbor Bank received its share of broken windows in a "Liberation Party" in June of 1969. Eastern's just-completed classroom building, Pray-Harold, had its glass doors shattered, and spray-painted graffiti sprouted on every vacant wall on campus and off. State police contingents occupied Eastern Michigan University for a few nights in the spring of 1970, but the county's colleges and universities escaped rougher confrontations experienced elsewhere.

Students, however, were not the only protesters. On October 19, 1969, Charles Thomas, a heavy-set young black man with his hair in corn rows, scion of a Superior Township family, read his Black Manifesto

Black Action Mobilization, or BAM, struck the University of Michigan campus in the 1960s. In this photograph, black and white students parade in front of the LSA building, posters in hand. The militancy of the 1960s shocked some Washtenaw residents and triggered the guilt of others. Courtesy, John Sinclair Papers, Bentley Historical Library, University of Michigan

to the assembled congregation of Ann Arbor's St. Francis of Assisi Catholic Church. Thomas, citing the disadvantages and injustices forced on blacks during their American sojourn, demanded $10,000 in reparations from St. Francis. Sunday after Sunday that fall and winter, Thomas went to county churches, cataloguing black grievances and voicing his demands. Sometimes he was almost welcomed, but sometimes his interruption of services was clearly resented, and eventually an injunction and a criminal trespass charge were filed against him.

Thomas was part of a larger national movement, the Black Economic Development League (BEDL), that hoped to raise through reparations assessed on white institutions a minimum of 15 dollars for each black man in the United States. Thomas' efforts received substantial local support. Several churches contributed

to the fund. By 1972 he had collected $100,000 and was backed by an Interfaith Coalition of Churches. BEDL established an emergency fund for welfare families, made interest-free loans to black businessmen, sent children to camp, and loaned a total of $27,000 to poor homeowners for improvements on their residences. In 1972 one of its programs, with ties to Washtenaw Community College, trained 73 blacks in home construction, and the next year the Community Development Center was opened on Depot Street. Thomas himself eventually joined the First Presbyterian Church, where he had made one of his original forays. BEDL's activities continued into the 1980s. The means used to promote its causes became less dramatic, but there was no denying it changed the county in subtle ways.

The music was loud, the enthusiasm was obvious, and the dress was casual at the mass rock concerts held on the flats along the Huron River in the 1970s. Though the personna was different, the spirit was the same as that which marked the county's early Fourth of July celebrations. Courtesy, John Sinclair Papers, Bentley Historical Library, University of Michigan

A FINAL WORD

Nearly 165 years ago, Washtenaw County became a place for a new flood of westward-bound immigrants to live and farm and trade. The county's founders sought wealth as they cut down trees, staked out their fields, opened their mills and shops, and transformed the well-worn paths of the Native Americans into rutted wagon roads. But even Judge Samuel Dexter, probably the most affluent of the developers of the 1820s and 1830s, did not become a financial titan.

Most of the early settlers came looking for more than wealth. If asked, they might have dubbed their other vague yearnings as wanting the freedom of the frontier. For some the goal was escape from troubled personal relationships or past mistakes. Others were attracted by the hope of a patrimony they were almost certain would be denied their children on the Eastern Seaboard. Some, with dark skins and slavery in their backgrounds, sought physical liberty itself. And for those German and Irish farmers in Manchester or Bridgewater, freedom meant escape from a European destiny that included conscription, land deprivation, and an inflexible class system. Those who followed over the next century-and-a-half came for similar reasons.

Nonetheless they stopped here. At first newcomers halted their journeys at this spot because Washtenaw was accessible by river and trail, and because the local Indians had long since relinquished their rights and moved on. But they also stopped because it was a place of beauty, with its tall trees, open prairies, clean streams, and rushing rapids. Opportunity, aesthetics, and accident all played a role.

By the 1840s the opportunity Washtenaw provided included the availability of learning, an opportunity that widened exponentially over the years and played a larger role than any other in the county's development. But other forces also were at work. Although never a major commercial or industrial center, Washtenaw County has always been a prosperous work- and marketplace, almost a charmed circle semi-immune to the harsher realities of the surrounding economy. And enough of its natural beauty was preserved to keep it a lovely, if highly cultivated and contrived, garden.

In the 1980s Washtenaw County continued to attract newcomers. It was growing twice as fast as the state of Michigan and faster than any of the state's metropolitan areas. One projection had the population increasing by nearly 30 percent in the period from 1985 to 2005 and the number of jobs rising from 167,000 to 192,000, with government (which in this case largely meant education) continuing to provide the largest share of employment. Agriculture, manufacturing, and commerce also played significant roles in molding of Washtenaw's story, but from the 1840s on, the provision and the pursuit of education have been a constant in the county's economy and way of life.

In 1901 the Ypsilanti Whist Club enjoyed an excursion with equipage supplied by the Palace Livery. The club had its photograph taken to ensure that the splendor of its garments and the smartness of its transport would not be lost to posterity. Even the horses appear to understand the importance of the occasion. Courtesy, Ypsilanti Historical Museum

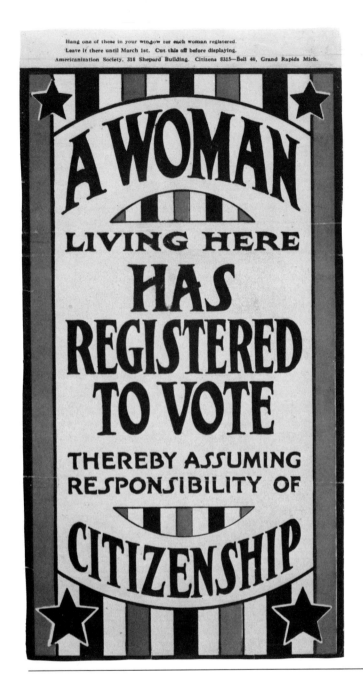

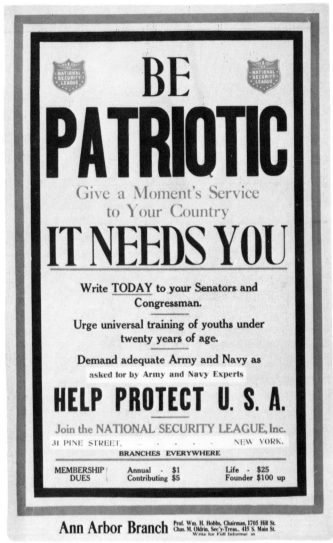

Above left: Women proudly and assertively assumed their new responsibilities when they at last were permitted to vote in Michigan in 1918. The nineteenth amendment to the U.S. constitution in 1920 solidified their newly won equality. Courtesy, Postcard Collection, Bentley Historical Library, University of Michigan

Above right: Professor William Hobbs was local chairman of the National Security League. The league urged "preparedness" and sympathetic support for the Allied nations, and anticipated American intervention on the Allied side during World War I. Courtesy, Poster Collection, Bentley Historical Library

This jazzy and colorful pictorial map of the University of Michigan was produced just as the Great Depression cast its sobering pall over student life as well as the rest of American society. Courtesy, Postcard Collection, Bentley Historical Library, University of Michigan

Returning war veterans enjoyed the companionship of their army buddies at this nineteenth century farmhouse converted to an American Legion Club. There was also a Veterans of Foreign Wars club on Liberty Street near the University of Michigan campus. The popularity of these clubs was enhanced by the presence of liquor, prohibited in Ann Arbor's public restaurants at the time. Courtesy, Postcard Collection, Bentley Historical Library, University of Michigan

Above: Daniel Quirk, Sr., built this imposing brick residence on North Huron Street in Ypsilanti before the Civil War. It was eventually given to the city, and its spacious lawns sloping toward the river form part of a city park. Courtesy, Ann Arbor Conference and Visitors Bureau

Top: The first fire station in Ypsilanti still stands and has been converted to an antique auto and truck museum. Photo by C.J. Elfont

Above: Stone School, at the intersection of Stone School and Packard roads, is an example of a rural school that survived into the twentieth century and was eventually incorporated into an urban school system. The original building became part of a much larger modern structure. Most of the early schools in the countryside were of frame construction and were much less imposing. Courtesy, Ann Arbor Conference and Visitors Bureau

Top: The Manchester Mill, built in 1832, still stands today despite being destroyed by two fires and two floods during the course of its history. Photo by C.J. Elfont

Above: Depot Town, a major concentration of Ypsilanti's effort to preserve its past, is seen here in a recent photograph. Photo by C.J. Elfont

Above: The rising standard of living in the post-World War II period fueled the rapid development of Washtenaw County's recreational facilities. Visitors throng to the county's lakes and rivers to participate in sports such as water skiing. Courtesy, Ann Arbor Conference and Visitors Bureau

Top: This path through the woods in Washtenaw County resembles ones used by early settlers. Those who visit the botanical garden or walk along Gallop Pond probably traverse other age-old paths. Photo by Dan Neill

Facing page: Barns such as the one pictured are reminders of Washtenaw County's predominantly rural past. Photo by Dick Pietrzyk

Above: These colorful apples are just a few examples of the abundant crop grown in Washtenaw County every year. Apple orchards have flourished in the county since they were planted by the first settlers. Photo by Dick Pietrzyk

Facing page: There are no downhill ski areas in Washtenaw County, but cross-country skiing is a popular winter sport. Photo by Dick Pietrzyk

Above: These draft horses pull a load of cheerful passengers at Domino's Farm, of Domino's Pizza fame, located just east of Ann Arbor. Photo by Dick Pietrzyk

Facing page: Many Washtenaw County residents own their own horses, and riding is a popular pastime in some parts of the county. Photo by Dick Pietrzyk

Above: Eugene Ormandy conducted the Philadelphia Orchestra in the May Festival concerts for over 30 years. This photograph was taken during one of his last appearances in the county. Courtesy, Ann Arbor Conference and Visitors Bureau

Top: The William L. Clements Library is one of several libraries available to the University of Michigan's 22,500 students. Photo by C.J. Elfont

By the 1980s Ann Arbor's State Street, seen here in a recent photo, had many more food outlets than bookstores but remained the campus commercial center. Photo by C.J. Elfont

Above: The University of Michigan's Burton Tower, built in 1936 to house the Baird Carillon, is a campus landmark. Photo by Jim West

Top: The Law Quadrangle, the gift of University of Michigan alumnus William W. Cook, was built in the 1920s. Photo by C.J. Elfont

This young fan of the Wolverines might grow up to attend the University of Michigan someday.
Photo by Jim West

Although agriculture is no longer the economic mainstay of Washtenaw County, fields of wheat and other grains are still a part of the landscape. Photo by Dick Pietrzyk

PARTNERS
IN
PROGRESS

It has been said that *business* is America's business. The American gospel of success has been reflected in exhortations from such disparate voices as those of Benjamin Franklin, *The McGuffey Reader,* P.T. Barnum, and Horatio Alger to David Riesman, Vance Packard, and Malcolm Forbes in more recent years.

"Business" was once the domestic production taking place in home and farm. It was rooted in the sales of crops and livestock, in the output of the farmer, miller, weaver, craftsman, and carpenter. The New World nurtured those pioneers who sought to acquire wealth and position. The American character honed itself on the element of risk and the potential for great wealth to be found here. The malcontent, the nonconformist, the gambler settled the East and then the frontier West that required, stimulated, and rewarded their ingenuity, resourcefulness, and individualism.

As Washtenaw County grew civilized, then citified, it reflected the experience of many communities as commercial processes shifted from home to factory and often from women to men. The experience of the American worker was transformed from artisan to administrator and tradesman to trucker.

At the brink of a new decade, the signs of industrial growth continue to be good. Even as the business arena widens to worldwide proportions, the challenge to individuals and industries is being accepted now as it was in the settlement days of Washtenaw County.

The following pages trace the spirit of commercial enterprise in Washtenaw County— through individuals and their endeavors—as it has struggled and prospered, dimmed, and sputtered to life again through periods of economic, political, and social change.

The organizations whose stories are detailed on the following pages have chosen to support this important literary and civic project. The civic involvement of Washtenaw's businesses, institutions of learning, and local government, in cooperation with its citizens, has made the county an excellent place to live and work.

WASHTENAW COUNTY HISTORICAL SOCIETY

Members of the Washtenaw County Historical Society's 1987-1988 board of directors are (back row, left to right) Carol Freeman, Arthur French, Pauline Walters, Peter Rocco, Lucy Kooperman, Louisa Pieper, Mary Jo Gord, Rosemarion Blake, Lawrence Ziegler, and Elizabeth Dusseau. In the center row (seated) are Alice Ziegler, impressions editor; Esther Warzynski, vice-president; Lucille Fisher, recording secretary; Patricia Austin, president; and Galen Wilson, immediate past president. In the front row (seated) are Karen O'Neal, Mary Jo Wholihan, Nancy Schuon, and Alan Jones. Additional directors not present: Robert Miller, Elaine Ference, William Wallach, Patrick Owen, Marilou Warner, Douglas Crary, John Dann, Coleman Jewett, David Pollock, Dalys Vogel, and Yvonne Blotner.

For 130 years the Washtenaw County Historical Society has been committed to collecting and preserving the rich history of a county once shaped by glaciers and inhabited by mastodons. Washtenaw County history includes the great explorer La Salle's expedition down the Huron River in 1680, a French trading post in what is now Ypsilanti, the lore of Indians and early settlers, log cabins, gristmills along the Huron, and one-room schools. The state's oldest local historical society was founded in 1857, when Washtenaw County was just 33 years old. Nineteen Ann Arbor citizens, chaired by John Geddes, adopted a constitution with the stated purpose "to collect and preserve the history of Washtenaw County, and to publish the same from time to time." After the Civil War the group was reactivated in 1873 as the Washtenaw County Pioneer Society, a name it kept until 1929.

In 1881 the society sponsored the publication of a 1,452-page volume, *History of Washtenaw County,* published by Chapman, which contains a wealth of information about the county up to that time. Now, more than 100 years later, it is sponsoring this volume on the county's history.

Today the society's more than 400 members hold meetings several times a year, publish a newsletter of reports and features, and sponsor annual tours of mill sites, centennial farms, local villages, museums, and battle sites.

During Michigan's sesquicentennial year in 1987, the society hosted a birthday ball, sponsored a play about the Toledo War that delayed Michigan statehood, and assisted with a commemoration of the Frostbitten Convention of 1836 that led to statehood the following year.

The organization fosters interest in local history by awarding certificates to churches, schools, and villages on their milestone anniversaries; maintaining two traveling historical exhibits; and restoring certain valuable artifacts. An Ann Arbor-built Allmendinger organ has been rebuilt, as has the city's first piano, which was hauled to Ann Arbor in 1827 by ox team for Lucy Ann Clark.

Over the years priceless articles have been donated to the society. Among them are the surveyor's chain used by John Allen in 1824 to lay out the city of Ann Arbor, Ann Allen's fan, Judge Dexter's rocking chair, early farm implements, carriages, wooden bicycles and skates, paintings, furniture, and clothing. The society also possesses the saddlebags used by Orange Risdon, who not only founded Saline but in 1825 surveyed the old Chicago Road (US 12) that followed the Indians' Great Sauk Trail through southern Michigan's swamps and hills.

In 1984 the Washtenaw County Historical Society donated $2,500 to help restore the log house on the grounds of Ann Arbor's Cobblestone Farm, built in 1844. The historic complex gives local schoolchildren and residents a taste of pioneer living.

The society's collection of books, manuscripts, and photographs is on deposit at the Michigan Historical Collections at the University of Michigan Bentley Library. Some artifacts are on public display at Cobblestone Farm, the Dexter Museum, and the Kempf House. A great many other items are in storage, awaiting the society's century-old dream of a permanent facility to house the entire historical collection.

The Washtenaw County Historical Society offers many different types of memberships and freely shares its accumulated information and artifacts with all—inviting Washtenaw County residents to explore their history and help preserve it for future generations.

Standing before an organ on display at the Kempf House Center for Local History in Ann Arbor are Nancy Schuon, chairman, book of county history, and Elizabeth Dusseau, chairman, collections committee. Seated is Esther Warzynski, vice-president. The organ was made by the Ann Arbor Organ Company.

GELMAN SCIENCES INC.

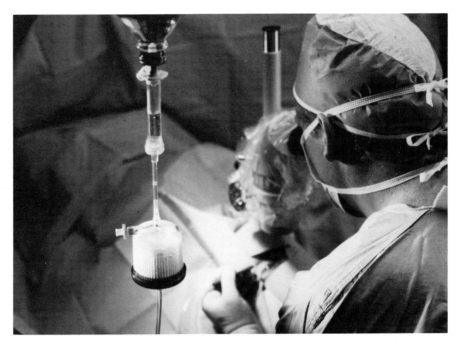

Is the story of good, old-fashioned ingenuity and courage relevant in today's sophisticated business climate? You bet!

Take Charles Gelman. At age 26, while working for the United States Health Service, he developed an air pollution sampling machine that collected precise air samples automatically. In 1959, just two years later, to meet the needs of his former government employer for additional sampling machines, he founded Gelman Instrument Company in his basement. Within another two years his interest had focused on the increasingly sophisticated performance characteristics required of filters used by new generations of his original sampler, and the business had moved out of his basement and into a rented storefront in nearby Chelsea, Michigan. He was soon manufacturing and selling filters for microfiltration—products that have established his name in the industry.

Microporous filters are made by creating bubbles in a polymer solution dried on long, stainless-steel belts to form thin, porous sheets. One of the most frequently used filters has bub-

Charles Gelman, chairman of the board and president, Gelman Sciences Inc.

bles that are approximately a half-millionth of an inch in diameter. Their ability to trap bacteria and minute particles makes them useful in purifying everything from pharmaceuticals to fluids used in the manufacture of silicon computer chips.

Gelman Sciences Inc. is a $55-million company cited for its superlative corporate profile by authors Ronald Paul and James Taylor in their book, *The Best-Performing Companies in America.* World headquarters and U.S. manufacturing facilities occupy a 54-acre complex in Ann Arbor, Michigan. Not bad for a young man who grew up in the depths of the Depression in neighborhoods of Manhattan and the Bronx that he describes as slums, spent his high school years in a Jewish orphanage, and went on to earn his master's degree in public health from the University of Michigan.

In 1986 Gelman was one of 10 recipients of the Michigan Trailblazer Award honoring outstanding professionals who have made significant contributions in science and technology.

Today Gelman Sciences is an international leader in microporous membrane technology research and the de-

An ophthalmic filter used in cataract surgery is one of the many products the firm developed for hospital use.

velopment of filtration products used for electronic and aerospace product manufacturing, genetic engineering and biotechnology, hospital diagnostic and care procedures, food and beverage processing, industrial laboratory testing and development, water and sewage testing, and air pollution control.

The firm's most recent innovation in membrane research has been the invention of the Sunbeam Process by which ultraviolet light is used to transform a liquid polymer solution into breathable, waterproof, sterile filter material that can be laminated or coated onto nonwoven fabrics similar to the familiar GORE-TEX® often used in sportswear. The Sunbeam production process developed by Gelman Sciences Inc. is capable of producing membrane at speeds of up to 1,000 feet per minute, 80 times faster than conventional methods. Potential uses for this material include surgical gowns, rainwear, and other consumer, medical, construction, and industrial products.

DOBSON-McOMBER AGENCY

The year 1893—when insurance policies were handwritten documents and horses pulled fire engines—saw the beginning of the Dobson-McOmber Agency.

The 1958 merger of the McOmber Agency and the Dobson Agency combined Ann Arbor's two oldest insurance firms. The McOmber Agency's first known location was in the Cornwell Building at 209 East Huron Street. The firm then relocated in 1935 to the Huron Valley Building and Savings Association headquarters at 116 North Fourth Avenue. In 1938 the agency moved again, this time to the State Savings Bank Building at 103 East Washington.

The Dobson Agency had been established in 1924 as a department of the Ann Arbor Trust Company. With the merger in 1958 both agencies relocated as Dobson-McOmber to 2361 East Stadium Boulevard. In 1981 the firm moved again, this time to the office building it occupies today at 1900 Manchester.

Doing business in more than 40 states and in a number of foreign countries, Dobson-McOmber Agency is the largest independent insurance agency in Ann Arbor, employing a staff of 36. The firm is unique locally in the variety and range of insurance coverages and services it offers, including the design and administration of property, liability, and employee benefits programs; life insurance; and financial services. As part of its intensive service program, comprehensive surveys and analyses of real and potential hazards are made as a basis for selecting the most cost-effective insurance and risk-transfer mechanisms for its clients. With about $10 million disbursed annually in claims payments, claims administration has also become a vital service.

Supporting the community has always been an important consideration for Dobson-McOmber, and to that end, charitable contributions are made annually to a variety of worthy local organizations. A formal contribution program was started in 1968, which marked the agency's 75th anniversary, whereby the firm contributes $100 for each year of its existence to various local causes that work for the good and improvement of Washtenaw County and its residents. Organizations that have received support include Park Washtenaw, local colleges, the Boy Scouts and Girl Scouts of America, the American Red Cross, the Ann Arbor Area Foundation, and many more.

The Dobson-McOmber Agency is the largest independent insurance agency in Ann Arbor, and is doing business in more than 40 states and a number of foreign countries.

APPLIED DYNAMICS INTERNATIONAL, INC.

During its 30-year history Applied Dynamics International, Inc. (ADI), has developed specialized computer systems for simulation applications worldwide. In its world headquarters in Ann Arbor, ADI integrates hardware and software systems that allow customers to effectively design and test new technology in the lab, thereby eliminating costly trial-and-error testing before proceeding to build expensive prototypes.

One of ADI's earliest applications assisted NASA's space program, which currently uses ADI equipment to simulate several functions of the space shuttle, including the engines, the remote manipulator arm, and the attitude control system.

In addition to modeling new products and processes for the aerospace market, ADI systems are used in several other areas including automotive, energy, transportation, petrochemical,

The SYSTEM 100 enables engineers and scientists, in a laboratory environment, to design, operate, test, and optimize intricate new products before proceeding to the expensive prototype stage.

and medical science. ADI customers include Boeing, Caterpillar, Ford, General Motors, McDonnell-Douglas, Rockwell International, and many others worldwide.

The company began with a few talented people solving a specific problem. In 1957 a University of Michigan engineering program in information theory and automatic control needed simulation computer equipment. Dr. Robert Howe, Dr. Edward Gilbert, Dr. Elmer Gilbert, and Jay King designed and built the LM 10—a tabletop, parallel processor analog computer. When AC Sparkplug expressed interest in the system, the founders, as Applied Dynamics, Inc., built the first commercial versions.

ADI next designed and built a small, affordable analog computer, the AD 1, that was used for a variety of tasks such as to simulate the fluid dynamics of the human eye, solve differential equations of chemical reactions, and simulate antiskid braking and control systems for aircraft.

Between 1957 and 1975 the growing company occupied several different locations in the area: a small building on North Main in Ann Arbor, two buildings on Platt Road, a Dexter facility on Huron River Drive, one on State Street in Ann Arbor, and another on North Maple Road in Saline. Beginning in 1975, the firm moved to its current manufacturing facility at 3800 Stone School Road in Ann Arbor.

In 1975 ADI's staff developed the AD 10, the first digital computer fast enough to do real-time continuous-system simulation. Since that year the Internatio-Müller Group, a major European corporation, has been ADI's parent company.

By 1985 Applied Dynamics had created its most powerful and advanced product to date, the SYSTEM 100. This dynamic-system simulation computer models continuous systems having more than 2,000 variables. Each of the system's four processors can work si-

The picture on the screen shows a plot of wheel velocity during the first 16 seconds of a simulated aircraft antiskid braking test. The SYSTEM 100 is capable of simulating the complete braking cycle.

multaneously on special tasks at a speed of approximately 20 million floating-point operations per second. The SYSTEM 100 has been used to develop satellite controls, helicopter systems, gas turbines, space shuttle avionics, auto power trains, and many other systems and products. ADI introduced major enhancements to the SYSTEM 100 in 1987. An integral part of the SYSTEM 100 is ADI's proprietary language ADSIM. This unique simulation language provides the user with an unequalled tool for programming and interfacing with his simulation.

Recently ADI moved its executive staff and various support offices to the 10th floor of 777 Eisenhower Plaza in Ann Arbor, keeping its hardware engineering and manufacturing divisions at the Stone School Road facility. Applied Dynamics International, Inc., employs some 130 people locally with additional staff at regional offices and at subsidiaries in England and France.

BRAUN-BRUMFIELD, INC.

Braun-Brumfield, Inc., started in business on August 28, 1950, at 308 South State Street in Ann Arbor with Carl Braun as founder and president. Carl and his fellow investors saw an opportunity to expand on an existing mimeographing operation and established a book-printing plant on Staebler Road, across the street from the present location. The firm's sales during its first year totaled $51,000.

Meanwhile, the Ann Arbor area was gaining in reputation with colleges and universities as a source for printing papers and journals plus other related textbook materials. Carl very soon initiated an added market: reprinting classic and antiquated books for publishers specializing in that field. Low-cost, short-run book printing made it possible for libraries across the country to stock these classics as reference materials.

Jim Briegel, the current vice-president of manufacturing, was the fifth employee, joining Braun-Brumfield in 1951. He has seen fantastic growth in both the company and the short-run book-printing industry, which has brought worldwide prominence to Ann Arbor. More book titles per year are produced in this area than anywhere else, including the 6,500 titles currently being produced annually by Braun-Brumfield.

In 1950 Carl Braun purchased Brumfield Mimeographing on South State Street. Four years later Braun-Brumfield purchased five acres at 100 North Staebler Road, building the initial structure that exists today in much expanded form.

Braun-Brumfield was purchased in 1967 by Shaw-Barton, who recognized the great potential for this established book manufacturer. Concerted sales efforts and expanded contacts in a major New York City market precipitated a period of rapid growth, from $1.3 million in 1968 to $2.9 million in 1973. At that time the company purchased Bindcrafters, a local case bindery,

which gave it complete printing and binding facilities for case-bound and perfect-bound books under one roof.

Dick Mellett was elected president, and shortly thereafter introduced the first outside sales representative for Braun-Brumfield. The sales force continued to grow, establishing contacts in major markets throughout the country, to its present size of nine representatives with three located in the major New York City market.

In 1981 the Shaw-Barton group was purchased by Heritage Communications, who again recognized the potential and Braun-Brumfield's position in the rapidly growing short-run book-printing industry. Sales at that time totaled $9.6 million annually.

The following year Bob Wilson assumed the presidency, bringing a solid financial background to the position. He worked with Heritage and Jim Briegel in initiating a concerted upgrade of equipment throughout the plant. A modest composition operation was expanded and modernized to allow for composition sales alone of one million

dollars in 1986. Investing well over one million dollars per year in capital equipment and expansion since 1981 has allowed for growth to an anticipated $25 million in 1987. An ambitious five-year plan is currently calling for the formation of a satellite plant in the southeast, in order to more efficiently answer major market needs. This expansion, along with continued upgrading and modernization of capital equipment at both facilities, should enable Braun-Brumfield to increase sales volume to $50 million by 1993.

Such impressive growth is evidence of a strong posture and sustained reputation as a quality book manufacturer maintained by Braun-Brumfield, Inc., in the continually expanding short-run book production industry.

The newly expanded offices and plant of Braun-Brumfield, Inc., in Ann Arbor. Braun-Brumfield has played a major part in the advancement of Ann Arbor's worldwide reputation in the book-printing industry.

CLEARY COLLEGE

The year 1883 was the year that Buffalo Bill opened his Wild West Show and the Brooklyn Bridge opened with considerable fanfare to New York traffic. It was also the year that a 26-year-old Irish immigrant, Patrick Roger Cleary, quietly founded a penmanship school in a room over a shoe store in downtown Ypsilanti, Michigan. Initial enrollment: two students.

In the succeeding 105 years his approach to education has been carried out with remarkable consistency: "Among the finest of our traditions is the right of expression by the individual to select a field of occupational endeavor and engage therein." Cleary College is an independent, four-year college of business dedicated to preparing students for careers in business, allied health, and other related professions.

Just as P.R. Cleary's penmanship classes in the 1880s met the needs of his students and those institutions that hired them, so, too, the curriculum has been adapted over the past century to offer the various technologies and personal skills men and women need to find satisfying employment in the 1980s.

The 32-member board of trustees has launched a $2-million capital campaign to guarantee steady progress toward the primary institutional goals: increased enrollment, appropriate class content to meet the needs of students and the marketplace, and effective placement of graduates in their chosen occupational fields.

A satellite 26-acre Livingston Campus, between Brighton and Howell, Michigan, now supplements the main campus on the outskirts of Ypsilanti. A third "campus" at the Milan Federal Correctional Institution, a medium-security prison, has in the past two years served the needs of 154 mostly full-time students in business computer systems and accounting degree programs leading to a four-year bachelor of arts, two-year associate degree, and one-year certification.

The requirements of a different audience for Cleary College programs—those individuals whose work schedules will only permit attendance at classes during evening hours—are also being met by continuing education classes.

A largely unheralded consistency of program and resolve have characterized the 105-year history of Cleary College. Its philosophy is exemplified by graduates who have demonstrated a commitment to occupational education in their professional roles in medicine, law, and business.

Cleary College's eighth president, Dr. Harry Howard, provides leadership for this advancing institution, meeting the challenge of technological impact on education for more than 1,200 students preparing for careers in the twenty-first century.

The original Cleary College building (1893), as shown on the 1888 diploma of May M. Clark (Mrs. May M. Gibson). Photo by Thomas Yanul, owner of the May Clark Gibson diploma

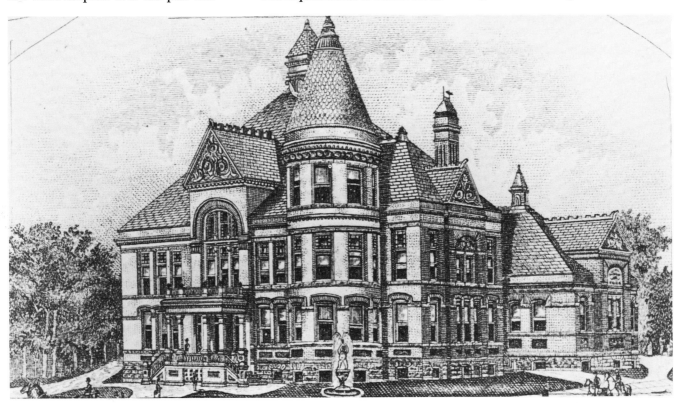

ENVIRONMENTAL RESEARCH INSTITUTE OF MICHIGAN

Although the Environmental Research Institute of Michigan (ERIM) has been physically located in Ann Arbor only since 1975, the institute and its staff have played a continuing and vital role in the intellectual life of the University of Michigan and the community for more than 40 years.

ERIM's story begins in 1946, when the university, at the request of the War Department, created the Michigan Aeronautical Research Center (MARC) to investigate the problem of defense against V-2 ballistic missiles. Based in university facilities at Willow Run Airport, MARC changed its name to Willow Run Laboratories (WRL) in 1955. In the 1940s and 1950s research at WRL was focused first on the problem of air defense, then one of the nation's foremost concerns, and later on problems associated with military reconnaissance and surveillance.

The first Symposium on Remote Sensing of Environment in 1962 marked the broadening of WRL's program by reporting ways in which some of the technologies used for mil-

itary reconnaissance and surveillance could also be used in civilian applications to detect, survey, and monitor various earth resources and the environment.

In 1972 the state legislature passed the Willow Run Amendment. This legislative action made possible a new structure for WRL's research programs. The result was ERIM—a private, not-for-profit research institute. Two years after its separation from the university, ERIM acquired its current headquarters building on Plymouth Road under a gift-sale agreement with the Bendix Corporation.

A look at just a few of ERIM's historical achievements amply demonstrates how the institute has contributed to Ann Arbor's reputation as one of the world's foremost research centers.

In 1957 ERIM physicists first demonstrated the properties of ruby as a maser material, a major contribution to maser and later laser technology. Maser amplifiers are used in long-range communication systems and for weak-signal amplification in radio astronomy; an ERIM-designed and -constructed ruby maser radiometer enabled the University of Michigan's

ERIM's pioneering work in coherent optical data processing led directly to the invention of practical holography. Here ERIM scientists Emmett Leith and Juris Upatnieks inspect an early hologram.

radio telescope to make the first unequivocal recordings of natural radio emissions from Saturn.

Using coherent optical processing techniques developed at the laboratories in the mid-1950s, ERIM demonstrated a synthetic aperture, high-resolution, focused airborne radar in 1957. In addition to military applications, this radar, which could map large ground areas in unprecedented

Part of ERIM's headquarters complex on Plymouth Road in northeast Ann Arbor.

fine detail, has proven to be invaluable in the observation of ocean waves and currents and in the study of large ice masses. ERIM designed one SAR, called STAR-1, especially to monitor ice movement in the Beaufort Sea, thus enhancing both the safety and profitability of offshore drilling operations in Arctic waters. Throughout the 1980s ERIM scientists have played a prominent role in the Marginal Ice Zone Experiments, a series of international studies that incorporate SAR data of ice and oceanographic processes in an area critical to global climate.

ERIM's coherent optical data-processing activities also led to what is perhaps its most well-publicized achievement. In 1962 institute researchers demonstrated a practical technique for optical wavefront recording and reconstruction, thus making possible the multitude of activities now occupying industry, other research organizations, and even artists the world over.

Building on its broad background

Former President Gerald R. Ford is one of many dignitaries, from both home and abroad, who have traveled to Ann Arbor to attend the International Symposia on Remote Sensing of Environment.

in surveillance and reconnaissance technologies, ERIM pioneered the adaptation of these technologies to applications involving earth resources. The institute played a leading technical role in the development of NASA's Landsat series of earth resources monitoring satellites. Today ERIM remains a world leader in the specification and evaluation of new scanning devices, the development of advanced techniques for data processing and geometric correction, and the transfer of these technologies to the rest of the world—especially the developing countries. Projects such as crop assessment for famine relief in the Sudan, monitoring of land erosion and accretion in Bangladesh, and the establishment of remote sensing centers worldwide—from Peru to Egypt and Nepal—demonstrates the tremendous impact this technology has had on the entire earth. Researchers come to Ann Arbor from the world over to attend ERIM conferences and training courses on remote sensing technology and its applications.

Ann Arbor's status as a nationally prominent center for high technology stems directly from ERIM's pioneering work in advanced computer systems for image processing. The Cytocomputer, a parallel, pipelined processor, can, when coupled with high-level sym-

bolic processing structures, power the image-understanding systems required for complex intelligent decision systems in a variety of environments—robotic factories, unmanned vehicles, reading machines, intelligent precision weapon systems, and unmanned space stations.

ERIM's powerful machine vision system is a demonstration of the kind of state-of-the-art computer vision technology that will support both the United States' economic development and its national security effort.

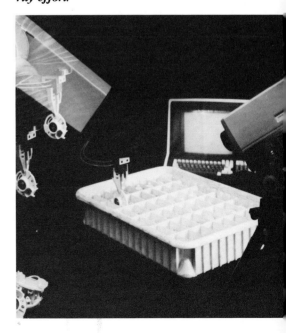

KERRYTOWN SHOPS

Kerrytown consists of 35 specialty shops and restaurants located in a quartet of early Ann Arbor buildings. It was one of the first shopping areas in the country developed by rehabilitating buildings destined for demolition in the central city. Now the original structural elements—open ceilings, brick walls, and wooden beams and floors—contribute to the warm atmosphere in this popular shopping area.

Kerrytown was the vision of Arthur Carpenter, an Ann Arbor attorney. In 1967 he formed Arbor-A, Inc., for the purpose of buying existing structures and adapting them to new uses. The name Kerrytown comes from County Kerry, Ireland, the birthplace of Marie O'Leary Sullivan, Carpenter's mother-in-law.

The land Kerrytown occupies, bounded by the Farmer's Market, Fourth and Fifth avenues, and Kingsley Street, was part of the original plat of the Village of Ann Arbor. Four buildings make up the Kerrytown complex: the Luick Building, erected in 1874 to house Emanuel and Gottlob Luick's lumber business (Gottlob Luick gave the land for the Farmer's Market to the city); the Godfrey Building, built in 1899 by Charles E. Godfrey for his moving and storage business; the Market Building, erected in the 1920s as a grain and farm center; and a storage shed at the west end of the Market Building.

Early in 1968 Arbor-A acquired the flatiron-shape Roach Printing Building at Fifth and Detroit, and converted it to offices. Kitchen Port was started in the basement of this building soon thereafter.

Subsequent acquisitions in 1969 were the Luick and Market buildings, then occupied by the Washtenaw Farm and Garden Center, obtained from the McCalla family. Initial renovation of the Market Building was finished in 1971. The doors were opened, and Kerrytown was off and running. O'Neal Construction performed the initial renovation, as it has all subsequent Kerrytown development. Renovation of the Luick Building was completed in 1973. Kitchen Port moved across the street into part of the newly finished second floor. The storage shed was next on the list for restoration. Work was completed in 1974, when Doug Smith and Morry Nathan brought their custom furniture-making business to Kerrytown.

In 1976 the 410-Four Partnership was created to buy the Godfrey Building for renovation and inclusion in Kerrytown. Restoration was completed the next year, and Workbench, a furniture retailer, moved in.

In 1981 O'Neal Construction purchased Arbor-A, Inc., and formed a partnership, Kerrytown Association Limited, to accomplish further development.

Entrance to the popular Kerrytown Shops in Ann Arbor.

Work was completed in 1982 on the addition of a second floor on the Market Building, enclosed connecting bridges to the Godfrey and Luick buildings, and a landscaped courtyard with benches and flower beds.

Kerrytown has become a tradition in Ann Arbor as the place to shop for fine quality foods and merchandise, and, especially on Saturday mornings, as a place to meet friends and neighbors.

A wide variety of food and merchandise is available in a unique setting at Kerrytown.

O'NEAL CONSTRUCTION, INC.

On October 17, 1961, O'Neal Construction began to dig its first hole. Six-year-old Ned Glysson, son of Eugene and Marie Glysson, performed the ground-breaking ceremonies at the spot where his family's home would later stand. Custom homes and residential remodeling made up the workload until 1966, when construction began on Northside Presbyterian Church and a complete renovation of the SAE house, which had been badly damaged by fire. The first labor agreements were signed, and O'Neal Construction was incorporated in 1966.

In late 1968 the Power Center for the Performing Arts at the University of Michigan was bid. This structure, designed by Roche Dinkeloo of Hamden, Connecticut, has been designated one of the 50 most significant structures in Michigan by the Michigan chapter of the American Institute of Architects. The Power Center contained numerous construction challenges—stage tower walls 100 feet high with no intermediate supports, a massive proscenium beam above the stage front, curved walls, and two spiral stairs that remain record holders for the number of turns in a concrete spiral stairway.

In 1968 a severe storm caused a major washout at Geddes Dam. Geddes Pond remained drained and overgrown until 1971, when Ann Arbor awarded a contract to O'Neal Construction to renovate Geddes, Superior, Barton, and Argo dams. These dams now form the backbone of Ann Arbor's Huron River park system and provide both flood control and water supply. Construction of the Mountain Park Dam in Mountain Park, Oklahoma, began in 1973 and was completed two years later. It was the first double-curved, thin-arch, concrete dam built in the United States.

Since 1975 the company has constructed numerous commercial and multifamily projects, completed several historic renovations, and recon-

Industrial Technology Institute, on Huron Parkway, was completed in 1987 by O'Neal Construction.

structed four dams. Among the buildings constructed during this period are the Industrial Technology Institute, Sloan Plaza, Michigan Theatre restoration, five buildings in Plymouth Park, Occupational Education Building at Washtenaw Community College, Sheraton University Inn, Central Fire Station, Parkway Meadows, Climax Molybdenum addition, Control Gaging, Stadium Centre, 222 South State, National Sanitation Foundation addition, Kerrytown renovation, First National Building renovation, Hands-On Museum, NBD-Briarwood, Almendinger Building renovation, John Bott Manufacturing, and Beta Theta Pi addition.

During the early 1980s, as the local construction economy slowed, O'Neal Construction looked for additional areas in which to build. Offices were opened in Orlando, Florida, and Austin, Texas. The Orlando office remained open for two years. The Austin office still contributes significantly.

In early 1987 O'Neal Construction, Inc., moved its office from 1342 North Main Street to the old Argus Building at 525 West William Street.

This 1866 structure has been carefully renovated into an office/light industrial complex that utilizes the most attractive features of the original building.

Sloan Plaza, on East Huron Street, under construction in 1986.

J.P. INDUSTRIES, INC.

"I like the way they have gone about taking sick companies and making them well . . . in the business world, he and his company are known as healers of undervalued companies in distinctly unglamorous industries."

Those bold statements are accolades from Gilbert Whitaker, dean of the University of Michigan School of Business Administration, in his role as judge in the 1987 Michigan Company of the Year competition. They reinforce the stated business strategy of J.P. Industries, Inc., to acquire underperforming companies that manufacture durable goods in developed industries, improve these operations to the level of their potential, integrate them into strategic business sectors, and manage them for growth.

The "he" referred to is founder, chairman, and president Dr. John Psarouthakis. His firm is now the leading secondary supplier of plumbingware in the United States and one of the leading independent suppliers of engine components to both original equipment manufacturers and aftermarket segments of the automotive market. The company has had record sales, net income, and earnings per share each year since it became operational in 1979. Over the past five years sales have increased 714 percent, from $47 million to $386 million. In both the plumbingware and transportation areas, 1987 marked a pivotal point in achievement of the corporate goals set in 1979: national distribution and recognition for a full range of products, with annualized sales in excess of $450 million.

A solid commitment to the encouragement and development of employees' professional growth has been considered crucial to the outstanding performance of the company. "Better Makes Us Best" is the corporate philosophy introduced in 1986 to provide a strong beacon for personal action and goal setting.

It could well be considered the

Dr. John Psarouthakis, founder, chairman, and president of J.P. Industries, Inc.

guiding principle of Dr. John Psarouthakis himself. An inveterate chess player, he admits that his business strategies may well find their basis in fundamental chess concepts. Psarouthakis immigrated to the United States in 1951 and subsequently became a citizen in 1963. His ability to identify and size up challenges and opportunities appears to be the greatest skill he brought to the pursuit of his professional career. He completed his education with a doctoral degree in mechanical engineering at the University of Maryland.

Implementation of his successful acquisition strategy began with a *Wall Street Journal* advertisement in 1978 that resulted in the acquisition of American Metalcraft Company to create a fully operational organization in January 1979. Since that time 12 firms have been acquired and two have been divested. On August 12, 1986, J.P. Industries began trading on the New York Stock Exchange. The company's approach to acquisition has been called "contrarian" by Wall Street analysts, acknowledging J.P. Industries' well-tuned strategy of ignoring tempting

high-technology companies in favor of underperforming, break-even manufacturing firms to be integrated into existing businesses operated by J.P. Industries.

Today J.P. Industries has 26 manufacturing operations in 10 states and three countries. Companywide employment exceeds 5,500, with more than 625 employees located in Michigan. Originally located in Ann Arbor to fully utilize the available Michigan and local educational and business resources such as the Industrial Technology Institute, the company has paid serious attention to its role as a corporate citizen by means of investments designed to improve manufacturing efficiency, relocation of staff and operating teams to Ann Arbor, charitable contributions to business-related organizations and institutions of higher education, as well as general community support for the arts, libraries, and athletic programs.

In response to questions about the company's ability to maintain its unusual growth in such unlikely industries as bathroom plumbing and automotive parts, Psarouthakis points out the firm's consistent success and well-honed policies: "We will need cars or transportation for the next 50,000 years. We will need bathrooms for the next million years or whatever. Companies that are prepared to adopt change and innovation, and understand technology, can move forward even though the product looks mundane." The company remains resolute in its belief that business in the United States is in the throes of change: "The ability of management to be agile, flexible, and receptive to change will be the key to business success through the twentieth century," says Psarouthakis.

In a recent commencement speech at Cleary College, Dr. Psarouthakis urged graduates to accept "the challenge of rapid change." He urged them to ". . . view change as an op-

Components for a wide range of transportation motor engines, including automobiles, trucks, locomotives, ships, heavy equipment, and off-road vehicles, are manufactured and sold worldwide by J.P. Industries.

portunity rather than an obstacle."

J.P. Industries has itself accepted the challenge of change as it has fostered change in the companies it bought and restructured to promote healthy growth. Change has been the catalyst for success and the foundation of strategic acquisition plans that currently aim for earnings to grow a minimum of 20 percent per year.

Applying the concept of Better Makes Us Best to the development of its people and the organization, J.P. Industries, Inc., will strive to continue the dramatic growth and ever-better performance of its short, nine-year history into the future.

The company is a leading maker and marketer of a full range of plumbing products such as bidets, tubs and whirlpool baths, lavatories, toilets, showers, faucets, drains, and strainers.

CATHERINE McAULEY HEALTH CENTER

Catherine McAuley Health Center today is a vital part of the community, offering comprehensive medical and mental health services to area residents and employing more than 4,000 people.

Catherine McAuley Health Center (CMHC) came into existence in 1979, when the Religious Sisters of Mercy, who had founded both St. Joseph Mercy Hospital and Mercywood Hospital, consolidated these operations. The Health Center was named in honor of Catherine McAuley, who, in 1831, started the Religious Sisters of Mercy in Dublin, Ireland, to serve the poor and the sick.

Since then CMHC, in response to community demand, has expanded to provide outpatient health care facilities, an outpatient surgery facility, a state-of-the-art Emergency Department, and a full range of chemical dependency treatment programs.

The first St. Joseph Mercy Hospital opened in this house at State and Kingsley on November 21, 1911.

A present-day aerial view of the Catherine McAuley Health Center.

But CMHC roots go back to 1911. It was in that year that a small group of Sisters of Mercy arrived from Dubuque, Iowa, to open Ann Arbor's first public hospital.

In that first facility the Sisters cared for the patients and did the cooking and laundry. Since there were no elevators, physicians helped to carry patients from the first-floor operating room up to their beds on the second floor.

This 17-bed facility, known as St. Joseph Sanitarium, was replaced in 1914 by a new 110-bed hospital on North Ingalls. The new hospital building was virtually taken over by the U.S. Army in 1918, when the county was hard hit by a flu epidemic.

The Sisters soon recognized that a medical hospital could not adequately treat those with mental or nervous disorders. As a result, the Sisters opened Mercywood Hospital on Jackson Road on Ann Arbor's west side in 1924. The first Mercywood was in an old farmhouse formerly owned by the Vandeveer family. Two years later it was replaced by a 40-bed mental health hospital that later expanded to 135 beds.

In the meantime, St. Joseph Mercy Hospital continued to grow. In 1977 a new St. Joseph Mercy Hospital was constructed on a 400-acre parcel at Clark Road and East Huron River Drive in Superior Township. Nine years later Mercywood Hospital moved into the new Mercywood Health Building on this same parcel.

CITY OF YPSILANTI

The Huron River, flowing through the gently rolling, treed land on which Ypsilanti stands today, played a key role in the area's early settlement. Five years after Michigan's lower peninsula was organized as a territory in 1805, three French explorers established Godfroy's Trading Post. This first non-Indian structure stood on the high west bank of the Huron River, close by the Sauk (Pottowattomi Indian) trail that ran from Bay City to Ohio.

In 1823 Major Benjamin Woodruff and companions from Sandusky, Ohio, founded a settlement known as Woodruff's Grove on the east bank of the Huron, one mile south of what is now Michigan Avenue. By 1825 the federal government had constructed a road for military purposes from Detroit to Chicago along the path of today's Michigan Avenue.

In 1832 Ypsilanti was incorporated as a village, named in honor of Greek General Demetrius Ypsilanti, a hero in his country's War of Independence. Generations have been mispronouncing and misspelling the name ever since. The period from 1837 to 1838 brought statehood to Michigan and the railroad to Ypsilanti. In 1848 the state legislature established Michigan State Normal College (now Eastern Michigan University) in Ypsilanti. Residents drained the heavily forested swampland to produce lumber, livestock, grain, and fruit.

Ypsilanti was incorporated as a city in 1858, after much wrangling between east and west. Many local businesses, churches, banks, newspapers, and civic organizations were established. As sentiment against slavery grew, Ypsilanti had at least two stations on the Underground Railroad that helped southern slaves escape to the north.

By the 1880s Ypsilanti had become a major manufacturing center with an impressive opera house. After two uneventful decades, interrupted by an 1893 tornado, Ypsilanti resumed growing in 1910, when many manufacturing firms, professionals, and workers moved to the area. In 1932 Ford Motor Company built its starter and generator plant along the Huron. The plant contributed to World War II military production and is a major employer today.

During World War II the Willow Run bomber plant drew an influx of workers and their families, many from Kentucky, Tennessee, and other southern states. At its peak the plant employed 42,000 people, creating a huge demand for more housing, stores, hospitals, and churches in Ypsilanti. The aircraft plant became the Kaiser-Fraser auto plant, later taken over by General Motors' Hydra-Matic and Fisher-Body divisions.

Today the City of Ypsilanti has some 25,000 residents, but its merchants, industry, and schools serve an area population of at least 70,000. Eastern Michigan University, Washtenaw Community College, and Cleary College have grown steadily in reputation and size; together they enroll roughly 29,000 students. Medical care in the area is excellent, with Ypsilanti's Beyer Memorial Hospital, nearby Catherine McAuley Health Center, and the University of Michigan hospitals.

Ypsilanti's 40-block Historic District, including more than 185 significant Victorian and Greek revival houses and buildings, is included in the National Register of Historic Sites. Depot Town's 125-year-old commercial and manufacturing district, Ypsilanti's Farmers' Market, the annual Heritage Festival, and other civic events are known throughout Michigan. Citizens of the City of Ypsilanti cherish their rich past while they look toward the future.

WASHTENAW ENGINEERING COMPANY

Washtenaw Engineering Company, formed in 1966, has provided civil engineering service to individuals, land developers, institutions, and municipalities throughout Washtenaw County. Site planning and land development, design of water distribution and sewage systems, construction engineering, and surveying are among Washtenaw Engineering's broad array of services. For more than two decades the firm has been on the ground floor of dozens of developments in the area, including road projects, subdivisions, condominiums, drains, and multiple housing projects.

In recent years the company's particular emphasis has been on the design and construction engineering of pavements for municipal and private roads, streets, and airports in Ann Arbor, Chelsea, and Manchester. Washtenaw Engineering has been involved in the reconstruction of Fuller and Glen streets, Ellsworth Road between South State and Platt, Huron Parkway from Geddes to Plymouth roads, and airport runways in Ann Arbor.

Significant commercial properties for which Washtenaw Engineering has provided services include the Briarwood Mall residual sites, the Bechtel Building, Atrium Office Center, Brock Residence Inn, Wolverine Inn, and the recent Cranbrook shopping and housing development in Ann Arbor.

Residential subdivisions to Washtenaw Engineering's credit include Ann Arbor's Earhart, Earhart West, and Travis Pointe, and several more in Scio, Superior, and Pittsfield townships. Condominium projects with the firm's stamp on them include The Woods, Walden Village, and Northbury.

Washtenaw Engineering is headed by two principals, Norman N. Fahrner and Walter F. Lewis. Lewis, who came from Toronto to earn a B.S.C.E. degree from the University of Michigan, is responsible for the areas of civil engineering design, construction engineering inspection, and project plan development. Fahrner, a registered land surveyor who also attended the University of Michigan, is in charge of construction surveying, mapping, and geometric layout.

Lewis worked for the Washtenaw County Road Commission, and Fahrner was employed by the state highway department and a local consulting engineering firm until 1966, when they seized an opportunity to go into business together as the engineering branch of Washtenaw Asphalt Company. The branch soon became a separate entity.

Lewis recalls the much smaller Ann Arbor he moved to in 1956. When Washtenaw Engineering began 10 years later, the area was beginning to move into a period of growth.

In 1981 the company bought its present headquarters at 3250 West Liberty. The architecturally charming brick structure was built in 1874 and served as the Wagner School building until 1954. Washtenaw Engineering bought the refurbished schoolhouse in 1981 and continued renovations and restorations. The organization plans to expand its offices to keep up with the continuing pace of development and consequent need for engineering services in Washtenaw County. Starting as a four-person operation in 1966, Washtenaw Engineering now employs some 35 people.

Fahrner and Lewis feel fortunate to be located in Ann Arbor, where the university provides stability, an engineering talent pool, and a demand for commercial and residential development. Despite the competitive market, there has been no lack of work for local engineering firms in the 1980s. Washtenaw Engineering Company's high-quality work on such projects as the new University of Michigan hospital, the Newport Woods subdivision, the Eisenhower Commerce Center, the Coreen Road drain, the Nixon Road reconstruction, and many more, has kept it among the area's leading engineering firms.

Washtenaw Engineering Company got its start in Ann Arbor more than 20 years ago and has been directly involved in much of the city's growth since that time. The firm moved into its present location at the historic Wagner School site in 1981.

ANN ARBOR TRANSPORTATION AUTHORITY

Service. That sums up what the Ann Arbor Transportation Authority is all about. Currently 93 percent of that service covers fixed routes through the city, and the remaining 7 percent is on a demand/response basis to provide service for the elderly and handicapped. Approximately 3.6 million riders per year take advantage of the fixed-route service that travels 3 million miles each year throughout the cities of Ann Arbor and Ypsilanti, plus surrounding townships.

Bus service in Ann Arbor was not

Creation of the Ann Arbor Transportation Authority in 1969 was the first step toward the organization needed to provide consistent and reliable service, but in spite of new funding sources and new plans for rider services, AATA was near bankruptcy in 1979.

Since that time the turnaround has been dramatic. New and refurbished equipment painted with AATA's eye-catching new maroon and blue color scheme took to the streets. Smaller vehicles more efficiently met

bor's annual Art Fair (the service carried 45,000 riders in four days during the 1987 fair) are extremely popular services that local riders have come to appreciate and expect.

Much of this new success is due to AATA's 157 employees, who are known for the pride they take in the system. Their safety record is enviable: only two preventable accidents per 100,000 miles. A recent rider survey indicated that 89 percent of the respondents believed that driver courtesy and professionalism was excellent or satisfactory. Incentive awards to employees amounted to $30,000 in 1987. Mechanics can now maintain the current fleet of buses from a portion of the new AATA facility built in 1984.

In 1985 AATA was awarded the American Public Transit Association Award for demonstrated achievement in efficiency and effectiveness.

With its introduction of a new pass program to allow stopover privileges on the same line, the Ann Arbor Transportation Authority still looks to new programs to meet rider needs.

From this new location the Ann Arbor Transportation Authority provides 3 million miles of fixed routes to Ann Arbor and Ypsilanti.

Longtime employee George Atchinson represents the customer service orientation provided by the AATA.

always extremely popular. Early intercity transit began with streetcars in 1886, with the official incorporation of the Ann Arbor Street Railway Company. But it was four years before the tracks were laid and the cars actually began to carry passengers. As buses followed streetcars and one transportation company followed another, private operators consistently failed to maintain financial stability.

the needs of less populated areas of the city and the sparser ridership during evening hours.

To address problems of senior citizens and the handicapped, AATA introduced the Good-as-Gold program, a shared-ride taxi service. Initial estimates predicted 4,500 trips per month. By the end of the second month 9,000 rides were being provided. Additional special services such as The Football Ride to all home University of Michigan football games from 13 major hotels and restaurants, and shuttle service to outlying parking areas for weary shoppers at Ann Ar-

ANN ARBOR NEWS

The *Ann Arbor News,* the largest daily paper in Washtenaw County, is a direct descendant of a four-page weekly, the *Michigan Argus,* founded in 1835. When 28-year-old Earle P. Gardiner started the *Argus,* Ann Arbor's population was little more than 1,000 people, and Michigan was still a territory. Four years later, after the University of Michigan and the railroad had come to town, Gardiner ambitiously attempted to put out a daily paper, but went back to publishing a weekly after three months.

The *Argus* underwent several name changes over the years. In 1846 Gardiner and a partner, L.W. Cole, reorganized the weekly as the *Argus-Democrat,* making its long-standing partisan position explicit. But it was not until 1889 that the *Argus* began daily publication, lagging eight years

The Ann Arbor News building at East Huron and South Division streets as it appeared in 1936 at its opening.

behind the appearance of Washtenaw County's first successful Republican daily, the *Washtenaw Evening Times.* Frank Glazier of Chelsea, state treasurer of Michigan, started a daily he called the *Ann Arbor News* in 1905, bought the *Argus* two years later, and published the merged paper as the *News-Argus.* When he was convicted of embezzling state funds in 1908, the Republican *Times* bought Glazier's daily at auction.

Two name changes later the paper was purchased by the relatively new Booth Publishing Company in 1919. The new publisher, Ralph H. Booth, referred to it as "a nice little paper." The paper has been the *Ann Arbor News* since 1937, the year after it moved into its present building at the corner of East Huron and South Division. The *News* remains one of eight Booth newspapers in Michigan, which were purchased as a group by Samuel H. Newhouse in 1976.

Statistics tell something about the

daily miracle of putting out a modern newspaper. By its sesquicentennial year in 1985, the *Ann Arbor News* had 177 employees, consumed 17 tons of newsprint each day, ran 1,840 daily classified advertisements, and published a 90-page Sunday edition. Some 650 carriers delivered more than 49,000 papers each day and nearly 60,000 on Sunday. But numbers do not describe the changes in size, appearance, production methods, and content of the *News* over the years.

Gardiner's *Argus* cost three dollars per year, sometimes paid to the publisher in firewood or fresh produce. It was printed with methods not unlike the movable type Gutenberg used to print copies of the Bible in the fifteenth century. In 1973 the *News* committed to a printing revolution. Its Linotype and hot metal equipment were replaced by high-speed computer-controlled phototypesetting. The newsroom's typewriters were replaced by computer terminals.

Editorial policy has also adapted to the times. In 1954 the *News* increased its publication of letters to the editor, because the editor believed that a community as knowledgeable and articulate as Washtenaw County would make a significant contribution to the paper. The *News'* letters column is often named as one of the best in the country. An innovative addition to the paper in 1958 was a daily language column to help readers learn conversational Russian. Beginning in 1962, the *News* ran a unique French language story strip for several years, and pioneered a child adoption column in 1966.

A restrictive, though temporary, change took place in 1962, when Booth Newspapers bought the *Ypsilanti Press*. The *News* was gradually withdrawn from competition with the *Press,* and Golfside Road became the eastern boundary line for circulation. This arrangement ended when Booth sold the *Press* in 1969. A Sunday edition was inevitable in a city expanding as rapidly as Ann Arbor in the 1960s. In 1968, despite the competition of the two Detroit papers' Sunday editions with their color comics and television magazines, the *News* began publishing seven days a week.

A major change in content and appearance began in 1982 under publisher Tim White. Reflecting the demands of its reading public, the *News* became more cosmopolitan. White's marketing background and pledge to see the paper among the nation's top 20 papers boosted staff morale. The Saturday paper was revamped, the Sunday paper beefed up. The new look included modern design, larger photographs, more charts and graphs, and contemporary headline type styles. The women's section was replaced by the "Connection" section, with local and national features of interest to both men and women. The *News* ran more national and international news, along with more professional and major college sports news, entertainment, health topics, and science. After the changes, circulation, the surest measure of a paper's popularity, climbed steadily.

In its long history only two events have ever shut down the *News*. The first was a strike against Booth newspapers by the International Typographical Union from November 24 to December 19 in 1958. After 21 missed editions, then-editor Arthur P. Gallagher remarked in an editorial that "a nonpublishing newspaper is colder and gloomier than a tomb." The second event was the devastating snowstorm of 1978 that kept the *News* from distributing for three days.

Herbert Spendlove, editor from 1976 to 1983, wrote that "it is an established tradition of the *News* to be a strong but candid friend of all elements of community life. This means vigorous reporting." That's the bottom line of the *News*: fair, balanced, accurate reporting. However, the early history of the *News'* predecessors suggests that there were lapses of good judgment. As a *News* reporter wrote in the sesquicentennial edition of the paper, "it was during the years leading up to the Civil War that the *Argus*. . . least distinguished itself." He added that the *News'* ancestors "seemed to have an uncanny ability to be on the wrong side of many of the great issues of the last 15 decades, but its editors did write wise and prophetic editorials at the outbreak of the Civil War and America's entry into World War II."

Today's *News* is committed to distinguishing itself by sensitive, conscientious, and credible local coverage, by appropriate selection of wire-service news, and by including topical features. The *Ann Arbor News* staff works tirelessly, not just to get the paper out on time, but to get it right. The "nice little paper" has come of age.

Crowds stream through the **Ann Arbor News** *newsroom during an open house in February 1985 observing the paper's 150th year. The newspaper that began as a four-page weekly has gone through many name changes and owners to become the successful daily publication that services the community of Ann Arbor.*

GENERAL AUTOMOTIVE CORPORATION

General Automotive Corporation (GAC), with headquarters in Ann Arbor, was formed in 1979 by Cruse W. Moss as a joint-venture partner with Bombardier, Ltd., to enter the international transit bus-manufacturing business in Shannon, Ireland, under contract to the Irish government. Privately held, GAC managed the Irish bus-manufacturing operation, transferring U.S. bus engineering, design, and manufacturing technology, and providing plant start-up, training, and ongoing operating leadership. During the period from 1979 to mid-1981 all GAC activities were focused on manufacturing buses in Ireland.

In mid-1981, after considerable success in Ireland, Moss decided to expand GAC's activities in the United States. Experienced automotive executives were recruited to develop automotive consulting, international marketing, and government vehicle development activities. As a result, a number of consulting projects were completed in North America, Mexico, and the United Kingdom, and GAC began the search for automotive-oriented acquisition opportunities to establish a U.S. manufacturing and marketing capability.

In 1983 GAC acquired The Flxible Corporation in Delaware, Ohio, from Grumman Corporation, and became the leading U.S. transit bus manufacturer. In a separate 1983 transaction GAC acquired Bombardier's interest in the Irish bus venture, and became the sole owner of GAC Ireland, Ltd. During this period GAC's international marketing activities began to grow, and GAC entered into a number of specialty government vehicle development programs through its Government Products Division.

In 1985 GAC acquired Hercules Bumpers, Inc., Pelham, Georgia, from private owners. The Hercules acquisition put GAC in the rapidly growing light-duty truck accessories business.

In mid-1985 GAC implemented plans to focus on U.S. manufacturing and marketing operations. The Government Products Division and international marketing operations were divested, and GAC Ireland, Ltd., became inactive when the contract to manufacture buses for the Irish government was not renewed, owing to a lack of government funding.

Today GAC provides operating direction, as well as financial and administrative support services, to GAC sub-

sidiaries. In addition, GAC is aggressively searching for and qualifying acquisition candidates to further expand established operations.

GAC's Ann Arbor location permits GAC key executives to be active participants in Washtenaw County educational, political, and cultural activities. GAC contributes both financial support and membership in advisory boards of many institutions of the University of Michigan, including the School of Business, the College of Engineering, Kelsey Museum of Archaeology, History of Art Tappan Hall, Museum of Art, Stearns Collection of Musical Instruments, Clements Library, Matthaei Botanical Gardens, and the Gerald Ford Library. Cleary College also receives financial support and trustee and advisory participation.

THE FLXIBLE CORPORATION

The Flxible Corporation, a wholly owned subsidiary of GAC acquired in 1983, is the largest manufacturer of transit buses in the United States. With more than 900,000 square feet of manufacturing space in Delaware and Loudonville, Ohio, and 1,100-plus employees, Flxible manufactures and markets the METRO™ model advanced-design bus in 30-, 35-, and 40-foot lengths. In addition to bus manufacturing, Flxible operates the most extensive transit service parts distribution system in the industry, with parts distribution centers in Loudonville, Ohio;

General Automotive Corporation's corporate headquarters, Ann Arbor, Michigan.

Cruse W. Moss (left), chairman of the board, and Mark J. Obert, president, of General Automotive Corporation.

Los Angeles, California; Newark, New Jersey; Dallas, Texas; Seattle, Washington; and Atlanta, Georgia.

Founded in 1913, Flxible has been a driving force in the transit bus market since 1924. Flxible buses are operating in almost every major city in the United States, as well as in many smaller but growing metropolitan areas.

The Flxible METRO advanced-design bus represents more than 70 years of transportation innovation and

One of the fleet of 252 Flxible Corporation METRO™ model advanced-design transit buses operated by the Washington Area Metropolitan Transit Authority, Washington, D.C.

development. The term "advanced design" is best represented by the METRO's proven combination of low maintenance costs and excellent operational reliability, as well as maximum passenger safety, convenience, and comfort.

Increased preference for the Flxible METRO model bus by transit systems nationwide results from the METRO's reputation as the standard for cost-effective life-cycle operation. Low operating and maintenance costs result from the METRO's optimum balance of proven components and advanced design technology.

GAC is continuing the proud tradition The Flxible Corporation has established over the years—transportation innovation, high-quality cost-effective products, and outstanding customer service and parts support.

HERCULES AUTOMOTIVE, INC.

Hercules Automotive, Inc., a GAC subsidiary acquired in 1985, is the largest independent manufacturer and marketer of light-duty truck step-bumpers and accessories in the United States. With in excess of 300,000 square feet of manufacturing space in Pelham, Georgia, and Mobile, Alabama, and more than 400 employees, Hercules markets its products to truck dealers in the United States, Canada, and Mexico.

Hercules Automotive provides GAC a strong presence in the rapidly growing light-duty truck segment of

A Hercules Automotive Inc. pickup truck step-bumper on a new Chevrolet.

the automotive market. Light-duty truck sales are increasing steadily in the United States, and Hercules accessories are important sources of sales and profit for new truck dealers.

Hercules manufacturing is focused primarily on the assembly of a complete line of painted and chrome rear step-bumpers for all domestic and imported light-duty trucks. In addition to bumpers, Hercules distributes a wide range of light-duty truck accessories to enhance the appearance and function of trucks. Hercules products are marketed through established truck accessory distributors serving new truck dealers, and in some cases direct to the new truck dealer. In addition, Hercules has established a strong position by supplying accessories to import truck, port of entry distributors.

Under General Automotive Corporation's ownership, Hercules Automotive has become the market leader in truck accessories.

Aerial photo of Hercules Automotive Inc., Pelham, Georgia. More than 500,000 step-bumpers are manufactured in this facility annually.

ASSOCIATED SPRING-BARNES GROUP, INC.

Springs are usually hidden from view, so it is easy to overlook how many household tools, appliances, and vehicles—and the machines to produce them—depend on these vital components. Associated Spring-Barnes Group, Inc., is a worldwide supplier whose Washtenaw County automotive spring division goes back nearly 60 years.

Associated Spring offers a broad range of precision springs and custom metal parts for the durable goods market, including cars, home appliances, farm machinery, heavy construction and electrical equipment, electronics, and communications. It is the largest of three business units owned by the Barnes Group, Inc., a *Fortune 500* company. The Washtenaw County division, which moved most of its 230 workers from Ann Arbor to a new plant in Saline in 1988, is one of 14 U.S. Associated Spring facilities, and there are five overseas units.

A growing demand for springs followed the incredibly rapid develop- ment of technology and industrial production since the nineteenth century. Before World War I, mechanical springs were usually made by family-run businesses in small plants—almost always to special order. At one time the Wallace Barnes Company in Connecticut was the nation's largest producer of flat springs, which were often used in clocks.

With the invention of the phonograph and agricultural machinery, the Wallace Barnes Company produced new types of springs for these manufacturers. The then-fledgling automobile industry began to demand more and varied springs for ignition systems, doors, valves, and clutches.

In 1919 the Wallace Barnes Company opened a sales office in Detroit to be near the automotive industry. The firm invited other family-owned spring-making businesses in the East to join forces, and the Barnes, Gibson, and Raymond companies were incorporated in 1922 as Associated Spring Corporation. In 1929 the group bought one of its longtime suppliers, the Cook Spring Company of Ann Arbor, producer of wire automobile springs. The plant became known as the Cook Spring division of B-G-R, Inc.

From its early years the Ann Arbor firm had an arrangement with the University of Michigan to research and develop new materials and springs. During World War II the local division was one of the principal suppliers of critical components supporting the war effort, particularly in making valve springs for aircraft engines. And during the energy crisis of the late 1970s Associated Spring helped General Motors develop torque converter clutch springs to improve fuel efficiency.

Associated Spring's Ann Arbor division remained in the Cook plant next to The University of Michigan football stadium and Crisler Arena for 58 years. Thriving in the university town, the division's sales climbed from a

Associated Spring-Barnes Group's new plant in Saline, Michigan.

monthly average of $80,000 in early 1929 to $275,000 in 1950 to $2 million in 1987—the year the company was the sole valve spring supplier for U.S.-built GM V-8 car engines and for Ford engines in the Tempo/Topaz and Taurus/Sable models.

But the 100-year-old Ann Arbor facility, which had once been the home of the Ann Arbor Ladder Company, could no longer house the expanding firm. In 1987 Barnes Group, Inc., announced plans to build a new $3.7-million, 100,000-square-foot manufacturing plant on a 12-acre site in Saline. Daniel Sebastian, manager of the Ann Arbor division of Associated Spring, explained the move: "We'd invented a new level of technology, but we just didn't have room to use it." In July 1987 ground-breaking ceremonies were held in Saline's municipally owned Donald E. Shelton Industrial Park for Associated Spring's high-

technology engine valve and torque converter operations. The Barnes Group has committed to invest $7 million in state-of-the-art equipment at the new Saline facility and at its Burlington, Ontario, plant.

Wallace Barnes, chairman and chief executive officer of Barnes Group, Inc., and great-grandson of the company's founder, praised the selection of the Saline site and the city officials for their cooperation. Barnes predicts that "our new automated production facilities will further improve valve spring quality to the level needed for today and tomorrow's high-performance engines, at the same time lowering costs." With these advantages, Associated Spring expects to substantially increase its share of the market for engine valve springs in the next few years.

Associated Spring's customers can order one-of-a-kind custom parts or

Associated Spring's automotive supply division, which has been in the Washtenaw area for nearly 60 years, is presently owned by the Barnes Group, Inc.

choose from an inventory of 50 million springs and spring washers, in thousands of designs and sizes. The company can locate, buy, modify, and develop the machinery needed to make special parts. It also offers customers access to design services, prototype development, sample testing, failure analysis, technical assistance, and production capability.

The firm continually explores new ideas—in computer controls, chemical polishing to improve durability, and innovative testing methods. Associated Spring's highly skilled work force in Washtenaw County will continue to play a part in keeping the U.S. auto industry moving forward.

UNIVERSITY LITHOPRINTERS, INC.

Ypsilanti's 1934 high school graduates may have worn knickers and sighed over Ginger Rogers and Fred Astaire, but interest in their high school yearbook was every bit as intense as that of graduates of the 1980s.

University Lithoprinters' founder, Alfred Lemon, understood that interest. His business on Cross Street specialized in printing these traditional memorial collections of friends, teachers, and activities. His business prospered, and he moved it in 1946 to Arbiter Hall on South Grove Street, but the majority of his business remained the production of yearbooks for local educational institutions.

Major growth for the firm took place under the leadership of Emil Schilawske and his son, Vern, who purchased the business from Alfred Lemon in 1952. This change in ownership brought about a corresponding change in the type of work sought and produced by University Lithoprinters. Schilawske and his son tackled the expanding business market in nearby Detroit, and soon their largest client—perhaps 90 percent of their business—was Ford Motor Company.

This is the way University Lithoprinters may have looked in 1934.

Today University Lithoprinters uses state-of-the-art, computer-controlled color presses, and has enlarged its capabilities to include a full range of services.

To support this burgeoning commercial business and enable the firm to provide four-color printing services, two, two-color presses were purchased and installed.

As the company became recognized in the area, and business continued strong, the printing plant and offices were moved in 1957 to their present location at 4569 Washtenaw Avenue in Ann Arbor. By 1968 expansion of the building was necessary to accommodate new bindery equipment. By 1975 the first four-color press had been added.

University Lithoprinters currently provides its clients a full range of printing services. Printing is performed on multiple-color presses, and most recently the firm has added warehousing and distribution to meet its clients' needs.

This company has always operated as a business strongly supported by its family orientation. That tradition was carried a step further on November 3, 1986, with the purchase of the firm by David and Suzanne Frink. They proudly acknowledge the assistance of their employees, some of whom have been with the company as long as 30 years.

The Frinks consider their greatest asset to be the family commitment of all their employees. That commitment has proven successful as the firm doubled in growth in the first nine months of the Frinks' leadership.

Carrying on the tradition of client growth through diversification that began in the 1950s, University Lithoprinters now provides high-quality color printing services to more than 200 clients in southeast Michigan, as well as Lansing, Jackson, and Flint.

NATIONAL SANITATION FOUNDATION

In these days of growing awareness and concern for health and environmental issues, it is hard to believe that it was not until 1952 that national voluntary consensus standards for sanitation were accepted and implemented.

The concept of national minimum health and sanitation requirements by agreement of all interested parties was the goal of the founders and early supporters of the National Sanitation Foundation. Chartered in Michigan in 1944, the foundation is an independent, not-for-profit, neutral agency serving government, industry, and consumers. At the invitation of the regents of The University of Michigan, it was housed first at the School of Public Health on the Ann Arbor campus. Research and education became the basis for NSF's programs. Early efforts by the NSF included a study of confusing and contradictory state and federal regulatory legislation and codes throughout the country.

Accepting the challenge to address a broad spectrum of critical public health issues, the first NSF clinics held in June 1948 discussed sanitation education, supervision and administra-

National Sanitation Foundation's international headquarters is located in Ann Arbor, with regional offices in California, Pennsylvania, Georgia, and Belgium.

tion, eating and drinking establishment ordinances and codes, dishwashing, detergents, sanitary requirements, installation of food-service equipment, a food handlers' training program, vending machines, and rodent and insect control, among other topics.

By 1952 the announcement was made of consensus sanitation standards and a Mark of recognition, to be placed on equipment meeting NSF standards. Administrative offices and some laboratories moved in the early 1950s to a newly purchased building on West Stadium Boulevard; by 1965 it had seen major additions.

Forty-four years after its founding NSF's services are available in 50 states and 26 countries. The agency's 110-member professional, technical, and support staff includes engineers, chemists, microbiologists, and degreed environmentalists.

Current NSF headquarters and principal laboratories are still based in Ann Arbor, in a facility purchased in 1972 at 3475 Plymouth Road and subsequently renovated to meet expanding needs. A wastewater equipment testing site is in nearby Chelsea, and regional offices are in California, Pennsylvania, Georgia, and Belgium.

Registered certification Marks are authorized for use in products shown to conform with NSF standards, or

Walter F. Snyder, founder of the National Sanitation Foundation, a nonprofit agency whose research and educational studies serve government, industry, and consumers.

with other consensus standards or official regulations. A major new program includes NSF standards for all drinking water additives products, including treatment chemicals and products in contact with water during its treatment, storage, or distribution. Further, NSF is currently inspecting international cruise ships that call at U.S. ports for overall vessel sanitation, in accordance with federal CDC guidelines.

EBERBACH CORPORATION

One of the oldest businesses in Ann Arbor, Eberbach Corporation has manufactured laboratory supplies and equipment for more than a century. The company's extensive line of scientific instruments and equipment is sold to major laboratory supply wholesalers in North America, Europe, and the Far East. Eberbach Corporation's long-standing reputation for quality and reliability has been maintained by a stable and highly skilled group of employees under the leadership of the Boehnke and Eberbach families.

Christian Eberbach came to this country from Germany in 1837, established himself as a pharmacist in Ann Arbor in 1843, and soon began to supply and import glassware and supplies for hospitals and educational institutions.

In 1880 Eberbach & Son Company established a shop to manufacture laboratory instruments. Ralph

The Eberbach building was located at Fourth Avenue and Liberty, and the manufacturing division of Eberbach Corporation occupied the third floor. It served the laboratory and equipment supply company until the newly founded corporation moved to its present location on South Maple Road.

Miller, an engineer from a prestigious Philadelphia supply firm who had wide contacts and expertise in the industry, became president of the manufacturing department in 1887. He was active in the company until his death in 1945. The manufacturing division occupied the third floor of the Eberbach Building, constructed at Fourth Avenue and Liberty in 1908.

Oscar Boehnke worked with Miller to develop equipment in the Eberbach & Son manufacturing department. Boehnke's son (and current president of Eberbach Corporation), Ralph Sr., was born in 1915 and worked in the manufacturing department before and after serving in World War II. A University of Michigan graduate in mechanical engineering, he was responsible for developing much of Eberbach's equipment in the decades after 1946.

The year 1951 was a turning point for the company. The manufacturing division became a separate Michigan corporation under president Ralph Boehnke, Sr., and Eberbach Corporation moved into its present facility at 505 South Maple Road. Third-generation Ralph Boehnke, Jr., now vice-president of the firm, joined the

The manufacturing division department in 1938.

business during the late 1960s. Robert Eberbach worked for Eberbach Corporation between 1967 and 1981, when the company bought out his shares. Four generations of the Eberbach family—Christian, his son Attmar, grandson Oscar, and great-grandson Robert—directed the Eberbach & Son laboratory supply firm until it was sold in 1966.

Eberbach Corporation's 30 employees design, produce, and ship a product line of more than 200 items. The company's many electromechanical products combine electrical components from outside suppliers with custom housings and parts produced in Eberbach's complete machine shop. Products range from special glass and steel containers for Waring blenders to machines that analyze metals used for electroplating.

Although the laboratory supply manufacturing industry is increasingly competitive and tied to the world economy, the industry is unique in one respect; even the large companies have relatively small production runs, and much manufacturing is still done by hand rather than mass produced. Now in its second century of manufacturing, Eberbach Corporation continues to provide the top-quality, reliable equipment that scientific and medical laboratories demand.

UMI (UNIVERSITY MICROFILMS INTERNATIONAL)

It is hard to imagine living without access to a photocopier. Like the photocopier, microphotography was developed within the time-honored pattern of entrepreneurs who address a need in the marketplace. Eugene B. Power, one of the pioneers of microphotography, sought a feasible way to produce small quantities of books and documents at a reasonable per unit cost. His initial concern was the publication of scholarly materials, which was particularly difficult because small demand made them unprofitable for most printers.

In a makeshift office that consisted of two small rooms in the rear of an Ann Arbor funeral parlor at 313 North First Street, Power had the vision and confidence in the process of microphotography and in himself to establish University Microfilms in 1938. The company first offered microfilm editions of rare books to scholars and libraries. One year later a dissertation publishing program allowed doctoral candidates to publish their original research and have it available to others on microfilm. Subsequent sophistication and refinement of microphotography and the on-demand publishing that was the result has permitted un-

Eugene B. Power, founder of University Microfilms International. Photo circa 1961

paralleled access to information, regardless of quantity. Copies of books, journals, and newspapers are produced upon receipt of the order, making the small order practical and fiscally possible.

A half-century later UMI's goal has not changed: to collect, preserve, and provide access to information via the most efficient and effective method, through agreements with thousands of publishers and authors. But the technologies used in 1988 to provide access to information are the technologies of the 1980s—paper, microforms, online transmission, and compact disc. Libraries and information centers worldwide have access to nearly every issue and every page of 16,000 period-

ical titles, 7,000 newspaper titles, 600,000 doctoral dissertations, 100,000 out-of-print books, and many of the world's outstanding printed materials, such as the Gutenberg Bible. The company also produces abstract and index tools that help users locate information easily.

UMI occupies more than 200,000 square feet of building space on Zeeb Road in Ann Arbor, with additional facilities at other Ann Arbor locations, as well as in Louisville, Kentucky, and Caguas, Puerto Rico. This $75-million company employs approximately 650 people in the Ann Arbor area.

In 1962 UMI was purchased by the Xerox Corporation. In December 1985 it was acquired by the Bell & Howell Company.

Among the new electronic options now offered are several premier abstract and index data bases on compact disc as well as on-line, providing fast access to the information contained in periodicals, newspapers, and dissertations. These electronic products support UMI's archival information base, which continues to expand to meet the needs of information users.

UMI, a Bell & Howell Company, is located on Zeeb Road in Ann Arbor.

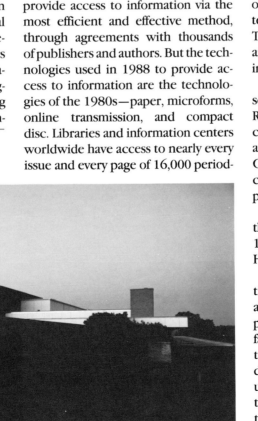

THE BARFIELD COMPANIES

In a 1987 ranking of black-owned firms by *Black Enterprise* magazine, The Barfield Companies of Ypsilanti were 27th, with annual revenues of $34.5 million. Already honored by the magazine as its black-owned company of 1985, the firm rose from 72nd to 27th place in just two years. The Barfield Companies top the list of the 470 black-owned businesses in Washtenaw County, according to the U.S. Department of Commerce. The three companies employed more than 1,000 people in 1987 and are Ypsilanti's second-largest private employer.

The janitorial service started as a part-time venture in 1951 by John and Betty Barfield was the foundation of three multimillion-dollar enterprises: Barfield Maintenance, Barfield Manufacturing, and Bartech, a supplier of contract engineering and drafting professionals.

John Barfield came to Ypsilanti in 1941 at age 15. His father, a share-cropper from Tuscaloosa, Alabama, had brought his family to Pennsylvania in 1936, where he worked first in a coal mine and then in a steel mill before coming to Ypsilanti to work in the Willow Run bomber plant. Barfield's own career began at age 16, when he dropped out of school to work in an Ypsilanti aluminum factory.

After serving in the U.S. Army, he returned to Ypsilanti, got married, and worked as a janitor for the University of Michigan and part time in his own residential cleaning business to help support his growing family. Just three years later, in 1954, the part-time business was so successful that John quit his job to devote full time to J&B Cleaning ("J" for John, "B" for his wife, Betty). A year later the firm had 12 employees and a new name, the Barfield Cleaning Company.

John had a simple strategy for success: Hire the best people and pay them more than anyone else. "We realized this would reduce turnover

and increase efficiency. I also wrote a training manual and established one of the first janitorial training centers in the country. Our name soon became synonymous with quality and dependability. We learned very early that there's no substitute for customer satisfaction," Barfield explains.

The strategy worked, and sales continued to grow. In 1969, just 15 years after starting the firm, Barfield sold the $750,000-per-year maintenance company to International Telephone and Telegraph Corporation, and at an early age. But he never lost his love for the business.

In 1976 John established Barfield Building Maintenance Company,

which offered commercial and industrial building maintenance services in southeastern Michigan. General Motors was one of the firm's clients. Barfield built up the company to sales of $3.5 million and 400 employees by the time he sold this second business to Unified Building Services, a minority-owned company in Washington, D.C.

Impressed with Barfield's managerial skills, GM offered him a chance to bid on design contracts—if he could recruit minority engineers and form a company within six months. The new firm, John Barfield and Associates, won the bid in 1977 to supply GM with contract engineers and designers, and had 30 employees within

John W. Barfield (left), chairman of the Barfield Companies, and Betty J. Barfield (right). John Barfield and his family have shared success and honor for their growing business ventures. They have been instrumental in providing employment for those in Washtenaw County for the past 36 years.

a year.

The company was renamed Bartech in 1985, the year Jon Barfield, John's eldest son and a graduate of Princeton and Harvard Law School, left his career with a prestigious Chicago law firm to become Bartech's president. To supply capital for expansion, Jon arranged for a 49-percent stock purchase by the Philadelphia-based architectural firm, Day and Zimmerman.

The sale marked one of the country's first investments of a majority-owned firm in a minority business. Today Bartech has more than 600 contract engineers and drafting professionals in Michigan, California, and New Jersey, plus a joint venture with a British firm. Sales reached $25 million by 1987.

Barfield's most recent enterprise, Barfield Manufacturing, produces precision sheet-metal fasteners and other specialty products for the Big Three automakers. In 1977 Barfield took up the challenge to be the sole supplier of four transmission pins for General Motors. Barfield Manufacturing started up with three old machines, three operators, and a cold, 100,000-square-foot factory warehouse. To meet GM's requirements, the plant had to run 24 hours a day, seven days a week—and it lost $260,000 its first year. Sales have since grown to $25 million, and in 1986 Masco Industries, a *Fortune* 500 holding company based in Taylor, Michigan, became a 49-percent shareholder, leaving control in Barfield hands.

"Our association with Masco puts us in a stronger position to serve our automotive customers and improve our technical capabilities. We are excited about the potential for continued growth and diversification," says Aaron Barfield, president of Barfield Manufacturing and vice-president of The Barfield Companies.

From corporate offices on Lowell Street near downtown Ypsilanti, the Barfields plan the future as a family project. Three of the six Barfield children have gone into the business. Sons Aaron and Jon are company presidents, and Lena Angela is corporate secretary for Bartech and vice-president of Barfield Manufacturing. "The fact that we have a second generation involved is one of the things in my life that gives me the greatest sense of pride," claims John Barfield, now chairman of the board.

Honored by Detroit's Booker T. Washington Business Association as its 1984 businessman of the year, and asked to give a speech at the Harvard Business School in 1985, John Barfield is committed to paving the way for other black business owners. He believes that "one way to meet the challenge is to offer incentives to large corporations to invest in established black businesses, or to engage in joint ventures."

Over the past 36 years four successful Barfield companies, and the spirit behind them, have indeed been a major asset to the Washtenaw community.

R&B MACHINE TOOL COMPANY

In 1942 the R&B Tool Company was opened in the former Wiedman Ford Garage at 118 East Michigan Avenue in Saline. This location has since been expanded, and additional plants in Redies Industrial Park on Woodland Drive have been built.

Modern metal-cutting and plastic blow-molding machines made today by R&B Machine Tool Company in Saline are helping the American manufacturing industry regain its strength, and R&B is developing machine tools for the future. "We don't buy the concept that U.S. manufacturing must be delegated to other nations. R&B is working hard to develop new process tools for the increasingly efficient U.S. Manufacturing plants that are emerging," says chairman of the board Robert Redies.

R&B itself has experienced steady growth since 1942, with no layoffs, despite some hard times in the machine tool industry. Its success can be attributed to following the traditions begun by founder Edward F. Redies: no debt, competitive prices on quality products, total commitment to service, constant innovation, and just plain hard work.

Today R&B's customers include most major U.S. manufacturing companies. R&B's metal-cutting machines are used by GM, Ford, and Chrysler, including machine tools for GM Oldsmobile Quad 4 engines and machines that change their own tools to eliminate production line delays. R&B's state-of-the-art machines for molding multi-layer plastic bottles are used by Owens-Illinois, and many R&B machine tools

are used to manufacture small engines and compressors.

The business traces its roots to a blacksmith shop on Ann Arbor's Main Street owned by Ed Redies' father, where Ed got his early technical training. After his first job in the machine shop at the University of Michigan Engineering School, a friendly recommendation to Joe Buhr, Sr., resulted in Ed's move to Buhr Machine Tool Company, where Ed became shop foreman.

In 1942, with a minimum amount of financing, Mr. Redies and Mr. Buhr started R&B Tool Company, a small retool and repair operation, in the former Wiedman Ford Garage at 118 East Michigan Avenue in Saline. During the first year R&B had five employees, and its first customers were Buhr Machine Tool, King Seeley Corp., and Tecumseh Products, which remains an R&B customer to this day. Three years later a small group at R&B started designing and building special heads and fixtures that are basic components of R&B machines today.

By 1947 the small organization ventured into manufacturing complete machine tools. Some of the first dial machines were indexed by hand. Often R&B would buy machines from used equipment dealers in the Detroit area and retool them for their customers. Several people moved from the Buhr Company to R&B, gradually giving the firm a design capability to develop new machine standards.

In the past three decades R&B broadened its product lines, including many huge, complex, and specialized machine tools. Between 1950 and 1965 R&B developed a complete line of heavy-duty index tables and way units, and the first R&B center column machine. From 1965 to 1975 Mr. Kuo Tu, now vice-president of manufacturing, developed a complete line of light-duty, high-speed tables known as the TK series. R&B brought out its first air lift precision boring table in the late 1970s, and a 96-inch center column

The third generation carries on the tradition begun in 1942 by founder Edward F. Redies. Redies was active in the business for more than 30 years.

machine in 1982. Three years later R&B developed a circular transfer machine and, one year later, a smart spindle and two new tool changers.

Meanwhile, three major additions to the original building on Michigan Avenue were no longer enough to contain the rapidly expanding business. Between 1976 and 1985 R&B built three additional plants in Redies Industrial Park on Woodland Drive off Maple Road in Saline, bringing plant space to more than 200,000 square feet.

In 1982 R&B developed its first blow-molding machine for plastic bottles. Plant number four now serves as the assembly plant and engineering center for the Plastics Division, headed by its originator and vice-president, Mr. M. Warren Martin. Beginning in 1985 R&B installed computer-aided design (CAD) systems for controls, and expanded the system for mechanical design work in 1987.

In 1970 Mr. Redies turned the management of the company over to his eldest son Robert, who became chairman of the board in 1974. In the

A 12-station circular transfer.

The Computer-Aided Design Facility.

1980s three of Robert's sons have started their life's career in the machine tool industry to carry on the family business.

The machine tool recession of the 1980s, resulting from major competitive problems in America's heavy industries, brought a wave of new challenges and problems to R&B. Quality and cost requirements narrowed profit margins and increased pressure for better quality machines. R&B responded with a "world class" strategy, including investment in a five-year modernization program, 100-percent in-house quality inspection processes,

and the fastest service response time in the business.

The third generation of this progressive company carries on the tradition of fast and effective customer service, competitive prices, tailor-made machinery for low-cost manufacturing, and innovative engineering through extensive use of computers and a functional CAD/CAM system.

Innovation and hard work continue to be the trademark of this privately held corporation that supplies "made in Saline" machines to so many U.S. manufacturers. R&B recognizes that companies that are not moving ahead today are falling behind. Armed with an AAA financial rating, modern facilities, and a stable, highly skilled work force exceeding 230 people, R&B Machine Tool Company is beating the competition and the odds in the difficult machine tool industry, its present management, Milton Stemen, president, and Robert Redies, chairman, is preparing for manufacturing in the twenty-first century.

Drill heads for manual drill presses were R&B's first product in 1945. The company makes more elaborate drill heads for semiautomated and automated equipment today.

CITY OF ANN ARBOR

Those young entrepreneurs who were the founders of the city called it Annarbour in honor of their wives and the commanding trees that covered attending hills and valleys. John Allen (more than six feet tall and "a very grand specimen of a man") from Virginia and New Yorker Elisha Rumsey were spurred by the same spirit that encouraged and challenged many of the entrepreneurs who created thriving businesses in Washtenaw County. They sought a new future out of economic necessity and, in this case, they saw frontier land as an opportunity for easy profit in land speculation.

Rumsey and Allen bought 640 acres at the government-established rate of $1.25 per acre and filed the plat for the new village of Annarbour on May 25, 1824. When Governor Lewis Cass later proclaimed the town of Ann Arbour as the county seat for Washtenaw County, Rumsey and Allen's

The Eisenhower Plaza Building is set in a parklike setting, surrounded by a pond, hills, and trees. It is the headquarters of the Bechtel Power Company and other Ann Arbor offices.

dreams came true: Half-acre lots soon sold for $100 or more.

A fortuitous location encouraged quick expansion of the city. It lay on the slopes of the scenic Huron River, surrounded by hills and valleys that sheltered good farmland. One year after its founding Allen reported that between 30 and 40 families were established in the town.

As might be expected, supporting amenities in the form of stores, tanneries, blacksmith shops, inns, churches, and banks kept pace with residential growth. As the commercial aspects of the town developed, so, too, did the educational. Following the erratic existence of private primary schools attended by only a small proportion of the city's youngsters, the Union School opened in 1856, unifying separate school systems in "Lower Town," north of the river, and "Upper Village," the area south of the river, originally intended as the site for the majority of city development. Union School was "one of the most expensive schools in Michigan, on one of the largest sites." Its assembly room held 700 citizens for local meetings and entertainment.

Magnificent as it was for its time and place, Union School was not the educational institution for which this

small midwestern town has come to be known. Opening in 1841 with seven students (all male—the university was not coeducational until 1910), "The Catholepistemiad or University of Michigania" was lured to Ann Arbor from Detroit with the promise of a 40-acre site of farmland east of State Street. Those early students lived, worked, and studied in one building, and shared the "common" with cows belonging to two faculty members. The university was funded by fees from students, income from a federal grant, and state aid—as it is now. Over time no institution has proven to be so crucial to the physical and intellectual growth of the city as The University of Michigan.

As new settlers from the east, as well as from Germany and Ireland, took up their new roles in the community, the resulting population increase in this unsophisticated frontier town caused predictable and unsettling problems. In 1871 the city council was urged to hire a police force to control the "general moral tone of the community as reflected by the great number of saloons, billiard and

Part of the University of Michigan Law School Quadrangle and Greek pillar next to Lorch Hall, the old Architecture Building.

gambling rooms, and the riot and disorder that prevailed on the city streets during the night and far into the morning." This was probably not unlike Ann Arbor on football Saturdays in the 1980s.

Shortly after the turn of the century, major new construction addressed the needs of the community. Hill Auditorium, the Law School, Michigan Union, Angell Hall, and the Michigan Stadium were built by the university, and the town's first skyscraper, the 10-story First National Bank building, appeared on its Main Street.

World War II brought even more rapid expansion, and business growth kept pace. Early enterprises such as the Mozart Watch Company, "once wound up, it is bound to run until it runs down," and the Mineral Springs House that accommodated up to 80 people indulging in the popular mineral baths, gave way gradually to manufacturing plants for milling, furniture making, brewing, and rug making, and, later still, to heavy industry such as Economy Baler, Hoover Steel Ball, and American Broach and Machine.

Commercial aspects of the city have exploded to a size and diversity that could never have been imagined in the 1800s. Known now as the research center of the Midwest, the city is surrounded by major industrial and research parks, and individuals and national and international organizations convene there to take advantage of the enormous cultural diversity: Fine restaurants, theater, and musical performances (the University Musical Society-sponsored May Festival has performed annually since 1894) add to the professional stimulation available through contact with business and academic organizations.

Hundreds of thousands of visitors each summer attend the annual street art fair and concurrent summer festival of music, film, theater, dance, and mime.

Ann Arbor residents still cherish the recreation offered by the Huron River and surrounding countryside. Literally hundreds of sports, hobbies, and educational pastimes can be enjoyed through classes made available by schools, city recreational programs, or other nonprofit groups.

The Ann Arbor Street Art Fair is held every July.

It is a thriving city with often intense participation by its residents in city planning and management. The City of Ann Arbor also prides itself on its ability to meet the needs and desires of its citizens with grace and style.

The town's first skyscraper, the 10-story First National Bank Building, on the corner of South Main and Washington streets.

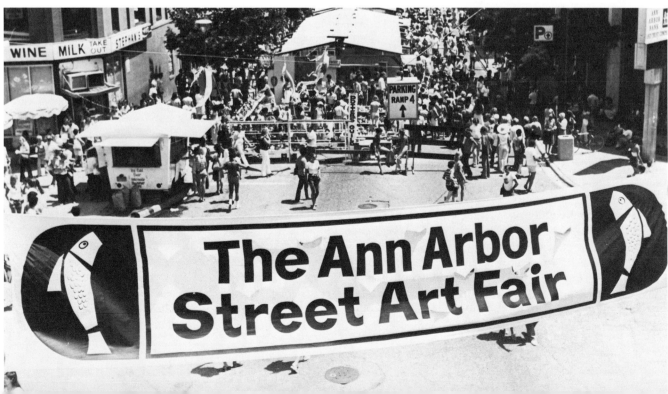

WASHTENAW REAL ESTATE

Although W.L. "Bill" Van Fossen, president of Washtenaw Real Estate, has worked for a number of large organizations, he has succeeded in the Washtenaw County real estate market by working fairly independently, keeping personal touch with his customers and getting many referrals from previous clients.

A native of Cincinnati, Ohio, Van Fossen graduated from Virginia Military Institute in 1956 and became an officer in the Army's armor corps. He came to Ann Arbor and within one year earned a Master's in Business Administration at the University of Michigan.

In 1959 Van Fossen took a job as an auditor with a large accounting firm, Arthur Anderson & Co., in Detroit and worked there until 1964. He bought a house at 333 John Street, Ann Arbor, for $12,500, and converted it into a two-family rental. That same year, as a client, he went to Kleiman Realty in Ypsilanti to look for other income properties. "While I was there going through the card file, a couple came in and we got talking about income properties. To my surprise, they asked me to take them around to look

at some. I explained the situation to the broker, Al Kleiman, and he said, 'Go ahead—give it a shot.' That was a turning point."

By the next year Van Fossen had his real estate license, was with Scope-Davis, and had joined the Ann Arbor Board of Realtors. In the 1960s and 1970s Van Fossen and other investors developed many small parcels of farmland in Washtenaw County and built several apartment buildings in Ann Arbor.

Van Fossen established his own company, Washtenaw Real Estate, in 1977. Today the business is fairly evenly divided between commercial/office and residential transactions, with many direct or indirect referrals. More than a few clients have come to Van Fossen to buy a house, returned to find quarters for his firm, and later for a site to expand the facility. Washtenaw Real Estate also manages several properties in the area, including the old artificial-ice house and granary properties in the 400 block of West Huron in which Washtenaw Real Estate has its own modest office.

Van Fossen handles fewer apartment buildings now. "With changes in

W.L. "Bill" Van Fossen, president of Washtenaw Real Estate.

the tax code in the late 1970s, people began buying apartment buildings as tax shelters. Prices shot up, and those investors didn't even care if they were rented. A building's value should stand on its own, not on someone's need to shelter income," Van Fossen states.

Since 1973 Van Fossen and his wife, Marcia, who teaches at The University of Michigan School of Nursing, have raised two children in a 180-year-old farmhouse in Salem Township. "Over the years I've discovered more about my own family's history, sometimes by chance. In the early 1800s one branch of our family went south down the Ohio River from Pennsylvania. Another branch turned westward to Michigan. William Van Fossen was the second husband of Ann Rumsey, one of Ann Arbor's first settlers. General John Van Fossen founded and managed the *Ypsilanti Sentinel* in 1844. I revere this heritage and these links to the past."

Perhaps that is one reason why Van Fossen has kept the business name, Washtenaw Real Estate, despite many offers to buy it.

FIRST OF AMERICA BANK-ANN ARBOR

A strong tradition as a business bank combined with a commitment to consumer services have made First of America Bank-Ann Arbor the largest commercial bank in Washtenaw County today. The institution benefits from being part of the 50-bank, $8.7-billion First of America Bank Corporation. However, the Ann Arbor bank retains control over loan decisions, construction financing, and local operations, and has its own board of directors. "First of America's philosophy," says Ann Arbor president Douglas D. Freeth, "is that we are community banks first."

First of America Bank-Ann Arbor celebrated its 50th anniversary in 1986. On February 17, 1936, the First National Bank of Ann Arbor (founded in 1863), the Ann Arbor Savings Bank (1869), and the Farmers' and Mechanics' Bank (1883), united their $13-million assets to become the Ann Arbor Savings and Commercial Bank. The original board of directors consisted of 17 prominent business leaders and University of Michigan officials. The bank's first president, Rudolph E. Reichert, was nationally known in banking circles for his part in creating the Federal Deposit Insurance Corporation (FDIC).

For more than 50 years the bank's headquarters have remained in the former Farmers' and Mechanics' Bank building at the corner of Main and Huron, although the structure has undergone renovations and expansions. The past decades have also seen the bank's name change three time—to Ann Arbor Bank (in 1942), Ann Arbor Bank & Trust (1974), and First of America Bank-Ann Arbor (1983).

From one branch in Nickels Arcade, the bank expanded to 11 branches by the end of the 1960s, including the 1954 Packard at Brockman branch that had the first drive-through bank window in Washtenaw County. Today there are 17 branches and 16 automated teller machines throughout the county.

In 1977 the bank's parent, American Bankcorp, Inc., merged with

Looking eastward along Huron in 1934, the Farmers' and Mechanics' Bank stood where the headquarters of First of America Bank-Ann Arbor is today.

First National Bank Corp. and today is known as First of America Bank Corp. By 1987 the Kalamazoo-based organization had grown to become the fourth-largest bank holding company in Michigan.

"First of America Bank-Ann Arbor takes pride in being a full-service bank. We are generalists, with resources for special situations," Freeth says. Keeping in close touch with the community and being able to evaluate the local market have made First of America a leader in what has become a highly competitive field. Residents often see "Financed by First of America Bank-Ann Arbor" signs in front of local construction sites, including the new $12.5-million One North Main complex in Ann Arbor. The bank has traditionally enjoyed a good relationship with The University of Michigan, and the annual influx of students is a major event.

Exceptionally stable leadership has no doubt contributed to the bank's growth. It had only four presidents in its first 50 years: R.E. Reichert, M.C. Taylor, Joseph B. Foster, and Bruce Benner, who is now the bank's chairman. In 1986 Freeth was named the fifth president, to set the course for First of America Bank-Ann Arbor's second half-century.

Striving continuously to keep up with changes in the field of banking, First of America Bank-Ann Arbor installed the first drive-through bank window in Washtenaw County.

MANUFACTURERS BANK

Manufacturers Bank of Saline was originally chartered by the State of Michigan as The Saline Savings Bank on May 23, 1908. Fifty-six original stockholders raised $25,000 in capital. Among those 56 stockholders was Gustaf Lindemann, grandfather of the bank's present cashier, Charles Lindemann.

By the end of the first year, December 31, 1908, the bank had deposits of $47,730.01, total assets of $72,790.99, and recorded a net profit of $60.08. The bank operated in the building at 109 West Michigan Avenue, Saline; still standing, it was purchased for $3,500. In the early years certain bank documents were printed in both English and German for the convenience of the community.

In 1915 the bank, under the direction of its new president, George Burkhart, a brother of Charles, purchased the property on the southwest corner of Michigan Avenue and South Ann Arbor Street, Saline, and erected a new bank building that, although remodeled, is still used as a financial institution. The bank's catch phrase was "The one-story bank on the corner."

The bank operated successfully through World War I and the many recessions until March 1933, when the governor of Michigan closed all of the state's banks for eight days during the Great Depression. The *Saline Observer* headlines reported, on March 16, 1933, "Local Banks Now Open 100 percent. Good News Flashed to the World Wednesday; Everybody Happy." As the world struggled with the Depression, so did the financial institutions. With the help of the Reconstruction Finance Corporation, the Saline Savings Bank survived 1933 and the Depression. Bank president George Burkhart passed away that year and was succeeded by Lee Tescher. Alwin R. Burkhardt succeeded Tescher in 1928 as cashier.

The bank continued to grow and

The new main office of Manufacturers Bank.

prosper through the World War II years. Due to the scarcity of basic materials, the bank started a Safekeeping Department as safe deposit boxes were not available. Bank board of directors' minutes during those years were written on the back of used and obsolete stationery in order to conserve resources.

In 1950 W.D. Crim and family bought controlling interest (51 percent) in the bank, and W.D. Crim succeeded Lee Tescher as president; in 1954 Wilson J. Scott succeeded A.R. Burkhardt as cashier. In 1964 the bank moved to a new 3,500-square-foot facility at 114 East Michigan Avenue with two drive-up windows and a walk-up window—the first of its kind in the community. The interior theme was "contemporary in style with functional furnishings in the officers' area and lounge-type furniture in the customers' waiting area" (straight-back padded chairs).

The next change in management came in 1968, when William Brittain of Saline purchased the Crim stock and became chairman of the board, appointing John R. Meadows of Ann Arbor, president, and Charles A. Lindemann, cashier. The bank's first branch was opened at the east end of Saline, featuring three TV drive-up stations in 1972.

Two years later the Saline Savings Bank joined Manufacturers National Corporation, a multibank holding company headquartered in Detroit. In January 1975 Thomas A. Collins became the bank's sixth president. The board of directors also elected Leon W. Eisemann as senior vice-president and Charles A. Lindemann, a 17-year employee, as cashier, vice-president, and secretary of the board—both men continue in these capacities. The bank had two offices in Saline, and deposits at the beginning of that year were $13.6 million. The merger resulted in an expansion of services to the community, a new name, and the capital to establish a branch system.

In 1978 and 1979 branches were opened in the Ann Arbor and Adrian areas, respectively. In 1980 an agreement was reached with The State Savings Bank of Clinton to merge into

The central corporate officers are (left to right) Charles A. Lindemann, vice-president/cashier; Michael J. Ross, vice-president; Thomas A. Collins, president and chief executive officer; and Leon W. Eisemann, senior vice-president.

what was now known as Manufacturers Bank of Saline. The bank had $62.3 million in deposits and six offices, three each in Washtenaw and Lenawee counties.

Interestingly, that bank on the Washtenaw/Lenawee County line started in the 1850s as the Exchange Bank of Clinton; later it was the Exchange Bank of Van Tuyle and Silvers, reflecting its ownership. In 1922 the Exchange Bank of Van Tuyle and Silvers merged with the Smith-Richmond Bank of Clinton under the name State Savings Bank of Clinton, with $50,000 in capital and $15,000 in surplus. At the time of the acquisition from the Van Tuyle family, State Savings Bank had $25.2 million in deposits, with offices in Clinton and the Irish Hills.

With the substantial and rapid growth of Washtenaw County, especially its principal city, Ann Arbor, Manufacturers Bank of Saline opened a second Ann Arbor office in 1984. The year 1987 again brought major change to the "one-story bank on the corner." The bank changed its charter from a state bank to a national bank, and in 1988 moved its headquarters to the heart of the financial district of Ann Arbor, occupying 12,000 square feet at One North Main. The institution's services again expanded to include on-site corporate trust services, international banking services, and private banking services, as well as the full-service banking function already in place. Currently assets exceed $110 million, and the bank has eight offices serving the communities of Ann Arbor, Saline, Clinton, Adrian, and the Irish Hills. The directors are Robert E. Betzig, president of Ann Arbor Machine Company; Jay P. Bunker, retired executive vice-president of Manufacturers National Corporation; Neil F. Haarer of Saline; Milton A. Hartman, president of Hartman Insurance Agency; Robert E. Merchant, real estate broker; Thomas A. Roach, attorney and regent of The University of Michigan; and Donald Staver, vice-president and senior corporate officer of Manufacturers National Corporation. Directors emeritus are Ernest Girbach of Saline and Raymond Service of Clinton.

As Manufacturers Bank of Saline celebrates its 80th anniversary, it is starting a new chapter as Manufacturers National Bank of Ann Arbor with the catch phrase of "That's my Bank." Interestingly, in 80 years there have been only six presidents and five cashiers, attesting to the organization's stability and conservatism.

The management staff in 1914 was (left to right) George Burkhart, president; E.D. Skinner, assistant cashier; G.A. Lehman, cashier; and George J. Feldkamp, director.

PARKE-DAVIS DIVISION
WARNER-LAMBERT COMPANY

Parke-Davis is located on a 40-acre site in Ann Arbor. Besides giving employment to the people of Ann Arbor, the Parke-Davis laboratories have been fortunate to obtain the professional services of many from the nearby University of Michigan.

Parke-Davis as it exists today is the result of several successful entrepreneurial mergers. One of the earliest of those was the formation, in 1866, of a small manufacturing business in Detroit to produce botanical medicines. The following year Duffield & Parke, Manufacturing Chemists (named for founders Hervey C. Parke, a Detroit businessman, and physician and pharmacist Dr. Samuel Duffield), added a young salesman named George S. Davis, and the rest, as they say, is history.

The newly created Parke, Davis & Company soon emerged as one of the leaders in the burgeoning pharmaceutical industry. Prior to 1879 medications varied widely from batch to batch, both in strength and efficacy. At that time Parke-Davis developed and established chemical standardization in medications. Uniformity was further improved in 1897, when the company introduced the additional concept of physiologically standardized preparations. Both of these innovations quickly became standards throughout the pharmaceutical industry.

By the late 1870s Parke-Davis established a collaboration with Detroit pharmacist E.A. Hubel, who had invented a machine to make empty capsules for medications, previously a slow, expensive manual procedure. The firm is now the largest worldwide supplier of hard gelatin capsules to the pharmaceutical industry.

At the turn of the century Parke-Davis introduced Adrenalin, only the second hormone to be isolated and marketed, and the firm had developed the first organized, systematic method of clinical testing of new drugs prior to marketing. On August 21, 1903, the U.S. Treasury Department awarded Biological License No. 1 to Parke-Davis for the manufacture, barter, and sale of vaccines, viruses, serums, and toxins. In 1907, to further its biological business, the company established a farm in Rochester, Michigan, with hundreds of horses, heifers, rabbits, and guinea pigs for the production of antibodies.

These early research efforts brought major medical achievements: in 1920 pioneer research and development of vitamins; in 1938 development of an experimental compound phenytoin (the company called it Dilantin), used as a treatment for epilepsy; in 1946 introduction of the first antihistamine, Benadryl, in the United States; and in 1949 the discovery and development of Chloromycetin, the first broad-spectrum antibiotic adaptable to large-scale chemical synthesis.

Firmly established by 1959 as one of the leading pharmaceutical companies in the world, Parke-Davis transferred a major portion of its research division from Detroit to a 40-acre site in Ann Arbor, Michigan, where a state-of-the-art research and laboratory facility was built to support pharmaceutical discovery and development in the fields of chemistry, biology, fermentation technology, toxicology, pharmacy, biostatistics, medicine, and computer and information sciences.

The location in Ann Arbor has proved to be so successful, underscored by the proximity to The University of Michigan faculty and resources, that five expansion projects have been undertaken in or on this facility since 1982.

Parke-Davis became a wholly owned subsidiary of Warner-Lambert Company in 1970, and seven years later it was established as a division of that company. Parke-Davis has doubled in size since 1982. It is committed to continuing leadership in meeting health care needs.

As a pioneer Parke-Davis pill mass manufacturing department (1880s) featured these bearded and mustachioed machine operators.

SALINE COMMUNITY HOSPITAL

From its first home in a historic stone building to its present modern facility high above Mill Pond, Saline Community Hospital has developed its acute care services to keep pace with the progress of medicine. Equally important, the hospital's many programs promote physical and mental health and wellness throughout the far-reaching community it serves.

The hospital's first building dates back to 1824, when Orange Risdon purchased the original Saline area land grant. Risdon gave a small parcel of his new land to a group of Baptists, who built a frame church on the corner of Ann Arbor and Henry streets that stood for 70 years. In 1904 it was replaced by a rugged masonry structure that served as a house of worship until 1919, when it was remodeled for use as a family dwelling and, later, a mortuary.

In 1935 John Schleh bought the building and leased it to Ralph McHenry and his wife, who transformed it into a 14-bed hospital to serve a community of some 1,000 residents. The building housed Saline Community Hospital until 1958. Many Salinians remember the dedicated service of Doctors Harold Miller and Gordon Prout—and the teamwork it took to carry patients up the torturously winding staircase from the operating room following surgery or delivery.

The town continued to grow, and a group of citizens arranged for the purchase of the present hospital site on Mills Road. Following a successful fund-raising drive, the new hospital was built, equipped, and staffed. It opened on May 1, 1959, with 26 beds and eight bassinets. The old downtown building served as the hospital's convalescent unit until 1967, and today it is the public library.

Between 1959 and 1974 the city mushroomed to more than 6,000 residents, and Saline Community Hos-

This charming building at Ann Arbor and Henry streets was used as the first Saline Community Hospital in 1935, and was in use until 1958.

pital's primary service area grew to approximately 67,000 people, including Milan, Manchester, Clinton, Willis, Dundee, and other surrounding communities. Saline area residents again supported a new facility.

In September 1974 a major expansion extended the hospital's capacity to 82 beds, including a six-bed critical care unit and many new and needed services. Today the hospital shares its 13-acre site with the Saline Evangelical Home and the Saline Professional Office Building. The latter houses many of the hospital's physicians and services, including the Head Injury and Hand Surgery & Rehabilitation centers.

Saline Community Hospital takes great pride in its more than 100 physicians, most of whom are also on the staffs of the Ann Arbor teaching hospitals, and in its more than 300 staff members. They provide

excellent care for 2,000 inpatient admissions and 35,000 outpatient visits each year. Medical staff expertise includes general and specialized surgery, emergency treatment, intensive care, and nuclear medicine, plus a variety of specialties.

In addition to continual updating of its acute care facilities, Saline Community Hospital's community focus has helped to maintain the institution at the forefront of health care. Programs and services include Greenbrook Recovery Center, which has treated more than 4,000 people for chemical dependency since it opened in 1977; Occupational Health Services; Home Health Care; the Millross Women's Health Center; and the Dimensions Fitness and Education Center. The hospital's many other health and educational programs reach thousands of community residents each year.

RAYCON CORPORATION

Raycon's symbol is an electrical spark and a hole. Briefly stated, Raycon develops and manufactures electrical discharge machines (EDMs) and laser systems that drill tiny holes in metal parts for the aerospace and automotive industries. But there is more to Raycon's story than sparks, laser beams, and microholes.

Entrepreneurs John Check and Gary Rupert, the president and vice-president, respectively, of Raycon Corporation, met when they were engineers working at The University of Michigan Space Physics Laboratory. They experimented with hole-drilling technology in their basements, looking for faster, better, and less expensive drilling processes. Rupert and Check succeeded, and in 1965 formed Raycon to develop and market the results.

Raycon revolutionized the industry with the first of many patented developments, an electrode refeed process—the most significant development in EDM since the spark itself. Electrode refeed increases productivity by automatically compensating for electrode wear, so the electrode is always positioned accurately throughout the drilling process. Electrode Management Technology (EMT) was born.

In 1967 Raycon was the first to combine numerical control with EDM, and in 1969 it built the first multiple-hole-drilling machine for mass production of jet engine turbine blades. That year the firm also introduced a new, completely automatic production EDM that could make up to 2,000 parts per hour. In 1970 Raycon was first to bring EDM to conventional machining centers, and the following year it created computer adaptive methods to control orifice size.

This succession of high-technology developments cemented Raycon's leadership position in a market niche—small hole production applications. More significant, how-

Vice-president and co-founder Gary Rupert surrounded by several state-of-the-art Raycon multihole drilling machines. This installation is used by a major aerospace jet engine manufacturer to produce cooling holes in engine components.

ever, is that the company's pioneering efforts were major contributors and paralleled milestone developments in the evolution of two major industries: automotive diesel fuel injection and aerospace cooling techniques.

The international reputation of Raycon products was well established by 1974, when the company delivered the first-ever million-dollar EDM installation in one plant. By that time Raycon had been settled comfortably for six years in a facility in the Enterprise Drive industrial park on the western edge of Ann Arbor. A major building expansion occurred in 1978. The following year the company established Raycon Machine Tool Corporation in Owosso, Michigan, to supply subcomponents.

In 1983 Raycon became a player in the global trend toward corporate mergers and was acquired by Detroit-based Ex-Cell-0 Corporation, a *Fortune* 300 company. Raycon benefited from the additional financial resources for research and development, and gained access to a market for the laser machining and non-contact gaging systems it began de-

veloping in the 1980s. Employees and sales increased substantially.

The emphasis remained, however, on the development of high-technology machines for the materials-processing requirements of the production floor. In 1984 and 1985 Raycon announced three major new products: a machine for drilling metering holes in auto fuel-injection systems, a computer-automated EDM for the aerospace industry, and a laser machine that cuts, welds, and heat-treats metal.

"Raycon has experienced many changes in the past few years," says Rupert, "from private to public enterprise, from $4 million to $20 million in revenues, from corporate restructuring to physical plant relocation. I'm not a fortune teller, but I believe Raycon is a survivor whose human resources will face the future with pride, ingenuity, diligence, and energy, and come up a winner."

President and co-founder John Check in front of a large Raycon laser system used to cut stainless-steel manifold parts for a major automotive manufacturer.

GT PRODUCTS, INC.

GT Products' plant on First and William streets manufactures diesel engine governors and automotive fuel vapor valves. The firm boasts 120 years of manufacturing on the same site.

In 1868 Henry Krause constructed a 30- by 120-foot, three-story brick tannery to make harnesses and leather goods. One of Ann Arbor's first industrial buildings, the tannery near Main Street and the railroad line saw one of the city's oldest residential neighborhoods, the Old West Side, grow up around it. The site has accommodated the changing needs of five owners, and business has continued unbroken.

After the tannery's owner died, the Detroit Gas Company occupied the building, between 1891 and 1925. That year the Seeley Corporation bought the structure to manufacture windshields, and immediately began additions.

In 1925 the renamed King-Seeley Corporation started manufacturing gas gauges for Model T Fords. Speedometers and tachometers were later added.

In 1938 King-Seeley purchased the Handy Governor Company, beginning the diesel governor line that has been produced at the plant since World War II. Construction of the first stage of a Scio Township plant started in 1948, and die casting and chrome plating were added to the firm's capabilities in 1952.

The 1950s and 1960s were a period of rapid expansion and diversification, under the leadership of the Gustine family. Neil Gustine started with King-Seeley in 1924 as a draftsman and

served as president of the company from 1947 to 1965. Richard Gustine joined the firm in 1934 as a material handler, and succeeded his brother as president, serving until 1971. A 1960 merger united the manufacturer of Thermos bottles, tents, and stoves with the automotive unit under the name King-Seeley Thermos Company. In the next decade both divisions expanded, with King-Seeley automotive supplying 95 percent of Chrysler Corporation's increasingly complex instrument clusters.

In 1968 Chrysler's Introl division bought King-Seeley's Ann Arbor and Scio Township automotive plants to keep its assembly lines running during a deadlocked strike. Later Household Finance Corporation acquired the non-automotive part of King-Seeley Thermos, moving the operation.

By 1980 rumors that the Ann Arbor plant was about to be sold sparked the interest of Amherst H. "Nub" Turner, then sales manager for Chrysler Introl. Turner, a lifelong Ann Arbor resident, had worked for GM's Detroit Diesel Allison before joining King-Seeley's sales force in 1966. Turner submitted an offer to buy the factory and the diesel governor line, with financing from Barclays and Ann Arbor Bank and Trust.

Chrysler and Turner worked out the details of the leveraged buy-out in

March 1982. "The hardest bargaining point was who would get the 50-yard-line University of Michigan football tickets!" Turner says. "We ended up splitting them 28 to 14."

Turner named the new company after himself and partner Robert Gustine, a friend since grade school whose family was an integral part of the plant's history. Gustine was with GT Products, Inc., during its first critical year.

Today the plant employs roughly 125 people, some of whom go back 30 to 40 years with King-Seeley and Chrysler. "GT managed to keep jobs in Ann Arbor when they were about to leave, and the company has been able to grow since then. We supply GM's Detroit Diesel Allison with engine-speed governors, and we've added a new product line of 'fuel vapor valves' that act as gas-tank safety devices in GM and Ford cars. In fact, we've become somewhat the expert in automotive valve technology," Turner notes. GT is also part owner of three southeastern Michigan firms: Adtech, Inc., GT Specialty Products, and CTEXT.

GT's president has been active in both the state and local chambers of commerce, and helped to found Ann Arbor's Innovation Center. Turner is proud that GT's plant, products, and people remain part of a long and continuing history.

After 120 years of manufacturing on the same site the GT Products plant is often referred to as "Ann Arbor's last smokestack industry." Though dormant since the late 1960s, when oil replaced the use of coal, the old smokestack still stands tall atop the original little tannery, one of Ann Arbor's first industrial buildings, constructed in 1868 and now all but obliterated by the many additions and expansions made to the facility between 1925 and 1945.

STARK FUNERAL SERVICE-MOORE MEMORIAL CHAPEL, INC.

Stark Funeral Service-Moore Memorial Chapel, Inc., in Ypsilanti carries on a 90-year tradition of compassion, community involvement, and closely knit ownership begun by its founder, Jay E. Moore. Born in 1865 when the country was still embroiled in the Civil War, the 33-year-old Moore established J.E. Moore & Company at what is now 22 North Washington Street. Stories are still being told about this well-liked, compassionate man and community leader who built up a leading funeral home in Ypsilanti and ran it until his death in 1952 at age 88.

In 1898, when Jay E. Moore began as a furniture store owner and maker of coffins, embalming was done in the home, and funerals were held either in homes or churches. Moore's business flourished, partly due to his reputation as "an undertaker." During these years Moore often rented a funeral coach and four horses from local livery stable owner William Schaffer. Schaffer's son, Lynn, and Moore soon became an established team in helping local families with funeral arrangements.

By 1930 the business had become too large to fit under one roof. During the Depression Moore bought the former St. Luke's Episcopal Church rectory at the southeast corner of South Washington and Ferris streets. A major addition was built to the home, and the business was renamed the J.E. Moore Home for Funerals. Moore and his wife had no children of their own; their niece, Madeline, married the young Lynn Schaffer, who later became manager of Moore's firm.

Lynn and Madeline Schaffer lived on the premises until Moore's death in 1952. They inherited the business and property, and continued the Moore tradition. However, after Lynn Schaffer suffered a heart attack in late 1955, he called in his three best funeral directors, Richard M. Wagner, William F. Jording, and Paul Block, and told them they would inherit the business

in equal shares upon his death. Lynn Schaffer died on February 24, 1956. Three weeks later his widow, Madeline, died suddenly in her sleep.

Six months after Schaffer's death, Block sold his interest in what was the Moore Funeral Home, Inc., to Wagner and Jording, who carried on the business for seven years. In November 1963 Jording ended his ownership. At that time Wagner agreed to share full partnership with a local resident and experienced funeral director, Leonard K. Stark.

Born during the Depression and raised as a southeastern Michigan farm boy, Leonard Stark attended Thorne School and Roosevelt High School in Ypsilanti. A high school test reflected Stark's strong interest in three careers related to service: doctor, clergyman, and funeral director. With encouragement from his uncle, a funeral director, to attend college, Stark worked his way through college and completed three years as a premedical chemistry major at Eastern Michigan University. He then transferred to Wayne State University, where he received his degree in mortuary science in 1955. On July 17, 1950, Stark served an apprenticeship at the Geer Funeral Home in Ypsilanti, and was employed by the Stevens & Rush Funeral Home on North Hamilton Street from 1957 to 1963, when he joined Wagner as a partner.

In the next 20 years Stark and Wagner worked together to improve the firm. The building was remodeled in 1964, and six years later a major addition more than doubled the facilities. The name was changed to reflect current ownership yet maintain the Moore tradition: Wagner-Stark Moore Memorial Chapel, Inc. Wagner retired as a partner in 1983. Starting in 1978, Stark shares ownership in funeral homes in Milan, Tecumseh, Clinton, Britton, Deerfield, and Petersburg, Michigan.

Stark's community involvement and his standing in the profession have

assisted the organization to become the foremost funeral service in eastern Washtenaw County. In 1963 the firm took care of 23 percent of funeral arrangements in the area; today it takes care of more than 85 percent.

During those years Stark's young sons literally grew up in the business. Both independently followed similar paths and entered the business. Rodney K. Stark, born in 1953, went to Ypsilanti High School, Eastern Michigan University, and Wayne State University, graduating in mortuary science in 1978. Rodney and his wife, Maria Kay, and their two daughters now live where the Schaffers, Wagners, and his parents lived before him.

Bradley W. Stark, the youngest of the four Stark children, was born in 1959, attended Ypsilanti High School and Washtenaw Community College, and graduated with a degree in mortuary science from Wayne State University in 1982. Both sons are now partners in the business.

In 1986 the firm's name was changed to Stark Funeral Service-Moore Memorial Chapel, Inc. Seven chapels accommodate groups of a few up to 400 people. Private consultation rooms, casket and vault selection rooms, and an experienced, caring staff help families to deal with funeral arrangements, 24 hours a day, seven days a week. Services for all religious faiths, traditional and nontraditional ceremonies, are conducted. Stark Funeral Service has also pioneered preneed planning, with one of the largest clienteles in Michigan.

Leonard Stark prefers to play down his extensive involvement, contributions, and honors from community groups, charities, and professional organizations in the past 25 years. Nevertheless, he served as chairman or president of 17 community organizations during that time, and participated in many more. As early as 1967 Stark Funeral Service was invited to join the 950 firms in 14 countries that belong

to the National Selected Morticians.

"We are proud to continue the 90-year tradition begun by Jay Moore," Stark says. "Every contact, every service, is carried out with consideration for the individual and the family. We are part of this community. We hope to remain a resource in times of need for another 90 years."

Continuing the 90-year tradition begun by its founder, Jay E. Moore, is (left to right): Bradley W. Stark, Rodney K. Stark, and Leonard Stark, of Stark Funeral Service-Moore Memorial Chapel, Inc.

CONTROL-O-MATION, INC.

From its modern facility on Huron River Drive in Dexter, Control-o-mation (COM) supplies customized computer-based control systems and components for a wide variety of industrial uses. Co-founded in 1972 by Richard Lundy, the company started with two employees, a 700-square-foot office on Ann Arbor's State Circle, and first-year sales of $45,000. By 1988 COM employed some 50 to 60 workers in its 25,000-square-foot plant and had annual sales of up to $7 million.

COM develops high-technology control systems, but people are its most important asset. "Our steady growth is a tribute to our employees, who provide high-quality systems that meet or exceed customers' expectations," Lundy says. COM's project managers, engineers, programmers, and assemblers form a highly skilled and stable team. A cooperative spirit, high productivity, and low turnover are fostered by the firm's profit-sharing plan and by the fact that COM is 100-percent employee-owned.

Control-o-mation headquarters in Dexter, Michigan.

Since 1972 COM has produced customized systems for an impressive array of clients. The company's first major control system was produced for GM Hydra-matic. Since then the firm has designed and produced an automation system to manufacture IBM printers, a materials-handling system for Ford car radios, testing systems for Ford and GM transmissions, and a robot and press system for Chrysler. COM has also manufactured all Prab robot control panels since 1979.

All electronic United Airlines passenger signs at Chicago's O'Hare and Denver's Stapleton airports originate at COM. And for customers as far away as Poland, the firm produced control panels to process meats and "real" Polish sausage.

In 1985 a separate corporation, COM 2, was established in Saline for high-volume manufacture of small electronic assemblies. COM 2's products are used in jukeboxes, vending machines, industrial terminals, and data multiplexers. COM is the majority stockholder in COM 2, which now employs 40 to 45 people.

COM has a strong tradition of community involvement. The firm is consistently among the highest per capita in gifts to the Washtenaw County United Way Fund, and contributed exercise course materials to Washtenaw County Park and Dexter schools. COM employees are active on the Dexter School Board, United Way, Michigan Technology Council, and many other civic and charitable organizations.

Lundy, now president and chief executive officer of COM, started out by working part time for Information Instruments, Inc., in Ann Arbor when he was a University of Michigan School of Engineering student, and worked there full time after getting his bachelor's degree in engineering. When that firm was bought by Allen-Bradley, Lundy founded COM to develop new applications.

"The applications we are developing at COM today are not being taught in any school. Our philosophy is to try to work a year or two ahead of the mainstream," says Lundy. "Control-o-mation will continue producing innovative, high-quality, and reliable process controls, test equipment, and automation for industries now and in the future."

Control-o-mation management (seated, left to right): Everett White, executive vice-president (since 1975); Dennis Salamin, vice-president/sales and marketing (1973); Donna Swersky, administrative services manager (1975); Robert Wallace, vice-president/engineering (1982); Henry Burgess, vice-president/manufacturing (1973); (standing) John Ritter, software services manager (1980); and Richard Lundy, co-founder, president, and chief executive officer (1972).

CHELSEA COMMUNITY HOSPITAL

Twenty years ago travelers to the Village of Chelsea passed by peaceful woods just south of town without a second thought, never imagining it would be the site of a sophisticated, acute care hospital and one of the area's largest employers. But in the late 1960s a group of forward-looking physicians and community leaders rec-

ognized the unmet medical needs of area residents and organized to meet those needs.

Until the hospital was founded in 1970, area residents faced at least a 15-mile drive to the nearest hospital. Plans for a comprehensive medical center took shape under the leadership of prominent area physicians, including Michael Papo, M.D., James H. Botsford, M.D., Jerry L. Waldyke, M.D., Bruce T. Stubbs, M.D., and James D. Shadoan, M.D.

Citizen involvement was built in from the beginning, through a team of community leaders that included Harold A. Jones, Ferdinand W. Merkel, and Paul E. Mann, who served as the hospital's first chairman of the board of trustees. "In 1970 few could envision the community resource

that Chelsea Community Hospital is today," says Mann.

Today the 63-acre campus of Chelsea Medical Center is the site of Chelsea Community Hospital, a 137-bed community-owned, nonprofit, acute care hospital; numerous physicians offices and clinics; and the University of Michigan Family Practice Center at

Chelsea Community Hospital is a community-owned, nonprofit acute care hospital that can boast of having the most up-to-date equipment and services. The institution offers intensive care services, emergency room, and a residential facility for treatment of alcohol and drug abuse.

Chelsea.

The hospital provides employment for 605 staff and has 130 physicians with privileges. With annual revenues of nearly $25 million, the hospital's annual payroll is approximately $9.5 million. Its acute care medical-surgical services and specialty medical programs are recognized for excellence and receive referrals throughout southeast Michigan and neighboring states.

The hospital has continued to grow and change to meet the varied

health care needs of the communities it serves. It opened one of the state's first ambulatory surgery centers in 1974, and it continues to be in the forefront of outpatient services. The hospital's specialty programs in psychiatry, rehabilitation, substance abuse, and pain management are recognized for their innovative treatment.

Over the years the look of the campus has changed, but the healing quality of the setting endures. The expansion that added ambulatory surgery also included an intensive care unit and an emergency room. In 1980 expansions in the therapy and radiology areas resulted in new construction, and the dining room was expanded and remodeled. Kresge House, the area's first hospital-based residential facility for treatment of alcohol and drug abuse, was opened in 1981 and was expanded from 12 to 24 beds four years later. In 1987 an earth-sheltered office building was completed, freeing existing space for expansion or relocation of patient care services.

Rarely does a Michigan community the size of Chelsea—3,800 residents—have a hospital of the quality and scope of Chelsea Community Hospital. It serves as a training center for medical, nursing, pharmacy, radiology, and other students from the University of Michigan, Eastern Michigan University, Western Michigan University, Washtenaw Community College, and others. Staffed by physicians in most major medical and surgical specialties, Chelsea Community Hospital is licensed by the State of Michigan and is fully accredited by the Joint Commission on Accreditation of Healthcare Organizations.

At Chelsea Community Hospital, change is a constant. As the hospital changes, it continues to improve the quality of its health care services to meet the needs of the communities it is privileged to serve—fully, compassionately, and effectively.

BEYER MEMORIAL HOSPITAL

Beyer Memorial Hospital celebrates its 70th anniversary in 1988. For seven decades the hospital's focus has remained solidly centered on personal, professional, and progressive care for community residents.

After 1910 Ypsilanti's population took an upward swing, aided by good rail connections and flourishing local enterprises. However, local physicians were often forced to perform surgery in their offices or patients' homes because the nearest hospitals were 10 horse-drawn-carriage miles away. Ypsilanti had only a small private hospital on Oak Street, operated by Miss Needlands, who later became the first supervisor at Beyer Hospital. City residents, led by Dr. George M. Hull, actively sought to create a larger local hospital.

In October 1915 Augustus Beyer, an Ypsilanti resident since 1850 and president of the Ypsilanti Savings Bank from 1901 to 1907, bequeathed $50,000 to the city to build a new hospital. He stipulated that Hull, Dr. Darling, and the county circuit court justice should serve on the board of directors, but placed the construction and future maintenance of the hospital in the city's hands.

Construction of the facility began in 1916, and in the fall of 1917 "the four walls, a sturdy roof, windows, new doors, unfinished plastering, and wet cement floors—nothing else" was complete. Furnishing and equipping the hospital was delegated to a committee of five women. Throughout the winter of 1917-1918 these women called upon their friends, local merchants, and residents to assemble the necessary beds, equipment, and supplies.

On June 15, 1918, opening ceremonies included a large crowd, a city band, and a hastily erected flagpole. Justice Martin Stadtmiller, who was to be the father of the first boy born at Beyer 37 days later (and of five more children and two grandchild-

ren later born at Beyer), presented a new flag to Mrs. Kirk, head of the volunteers. The most modern hospital in Washtenaw County officially opened. Two days later Dr. Hull admitted the first patient to the 28-bed hospital, and delivered the first baby on June 20.

Meanwhile, the Hull Contagious Hospital, located behind the main hospital, opened during the 1917-1920 flu epidemic. Named for Beyer Hospital's first physician, who often assisted patients that were unable to meet their hospital expenses, the Contagious Hospital was filled to capacity in later years to care for cases of diphtheria, typhoid, scarlet fever, and pneumonia.

In the years after 1918 the three staff nurses at Beyer Hospital worked 72 hours per week in 12-hour shifts, assisted by cadet nurses. Night-duty nurses also had to stoke the furnace. The year 1920 saw the purchase of a much-needed nurses' residence in a house across from the hospital. In 1923 the nursing supervisor's wage was $80 per month. In 1929 one patient's two-week stay for surgery cost $90.50.

During the 1930s many local residents and doctors, including Doctors J.J. Woods, H. Barss, F. Williamson, D. Martin, and B. Harris, drew community attention to the advantages of hospital care over home care. Increasing numbers of residents used the hospital during this decade, and in 1941 the Board of Commerce ap-

Before his death in 1915, Augustus Beyer provided funds for the first Beyer Hospital that cared for the ill in the Washtenaw area.

plied to the Federal Works Agency for funds to construct an 80-bed, three-story addition to the hospital.

World War II brought a sudden influx of workers and their families from southern states to the Willow Run bomber plant. The greater Ypsilanti population tripled to 45,000 by 1944. By then Beyer Hospital's planned expansion was much too small to take care of the community's urgent need.

After months of priority battles

The original Beyer Memorial Hospital, a stately, beautiful building, had accommodations for 28 beds when it was first dedicated in June 1918.

due to wartime conditions and re-stricted construction, the addition was finally dedicated on September 30, 1944, bringing Beyer's capacity up to 155 beds. Local organizations helped to furnish rooms and provide supplies. Dedication ceremonies ac-knowledged the efforts of hospital manager Minnie Smith, and the many community leaders and residents who worked so hard toward the new hospital.

In 1947 Beyer Hospital hired a superintendent, gained accreditation, and upgraded staff. However, the hos-pital still experienced financial difficul-ties. In the meantime a 1945 bill passed by the Michigan legislature allowed communities to incorporate to form a hospital authority in order to acquire, construct, operate, maintain, and man-age hospital facilities. In 1947 Beyer Hospital was purchased from Ypsilanti and became the first hospital of the new People's Community Hospital Au-thority (PCHA) that served western Wayne and eastern Washtenaw coun-ties. Beyer was the first hospital in Michigan to be operated by a joint authority.

At its 35th anniversary in 1953, Beyer Memorial Hospital already felt the need to expand its facilities due to increasing population shifts from the Detroit area and the opening of

Today Beyer Memorial Hospital pro-vides area residents with personal care, modern equipment, and a medi-cal staff drawn from Washtenaw Coun-ty's finest professionals. Courtesy, Michi-gan Hospital Association. Photography by Jill Seyler

the Ford and GM plants nearby. A Michigan Supreme Court ruling paved the way to expand PCHA. Plans were made and the present Beyer Memorial Hospital was built across the street from the former institution (now an extended care facility). A bond issue led to ground breaking for the 169-bed, 32-nursery-bed facility in 1967. The $10-million hospital opened its doors to community patients and residents on April 11, 1970.

The present 153,000-square-foot facility includes an intensive care unit as well as a step down unit between

intensive and general care. Beyer's mod-ern 24-hour emergency room is known for its qualified medical staff and equipment. Currently the institu-tion shares access to a $1.3-million CAT scanner, adding a valuable mod-ern diagnostic tool to is resources.

In recent years Beyer Hospital has introduced many innovations to bring individualized care to community res-idents. Beyer opened the first birthing room in Washtenaw County in 1986, giving parents the option of including family members in a homelike setting during delivery. PT Plus offers outpa-tients complete physical rehabilitation and cardiopulmonary services, and the Senior Advantage program provides extensive benefits, including a Medi-care adviser to help with financial concerns.

"Beyer Hospital strives to provide the most current technology and fa-cilities to give the community the best in medical care," says adminis-trator Jane G. McCormick, "but our emphasis has always been to serve as a community hospital where pa-tients receive the personalized care they deserve to maintain their dignity and individuality."

In an effort to keep up with the latest in modern medicine, Beyer Memorial Hos-pital introduced many innovations. It es-tablished the first birthing room, and shares access to a $1.3-million CAT scanner. Courtesy, The Ypsilanti Press. Pho-tography by Paul Hursehmann

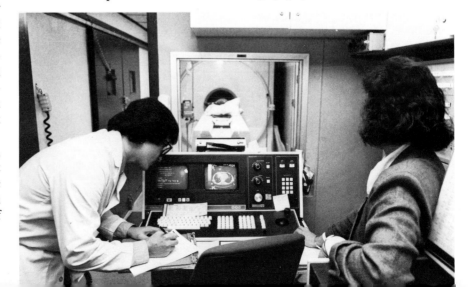

YPSILANTI PRESS

In 1954, after 50 years at the Huron and Pearl streets office, a mid-morning fire almost destroyed the Daily Press building.

"The first obligation of any newspaper is to stay in business," notes John Reynolds, publisher of Ypsilanti's *Press* since 1980. The history of the *Ypsilanti Press* proves that this is easier said than done. Since its founding in 1904, Ypsilanti's daily newspaper has come through several changes in name and ownership, economic hard times, and two major fires. Yet today's *Ypsilanti Press* is not only surviving but thriving.

Evolving from the Ypsilanti *Evening Press* to the *Ypsilantian Press* to the *Daily Press* to the *Ypsilanti Press,* the paper has remained a community-centered publication. Its first-edition editorial in 1904 promised "to concern itself with giving needed publicity to Ypsilanti projects and to advancing the educational and material welfare of the city." The *Evening Press* added this civic disclaimer: "It cannot say it has no friends to reward: for it considers every resident of Ypsilanti its friend."

The early issues of the *Evening Press* were put out by publisher Frank Codrington, business manager Hugh Van deWalker, and Fred Coe, who supplied the printing equipment and skill to print the paper at his 23 North Washington residence. On the second day of publication, 500 extra copies had to be run to fill the demand. But hard times were just around the corner. The community was too small to ensure immediate success of the daily, and losses during the first two years were greater than the entire capital stock investment. With bankruptcy a real possibility, stockholder Stuart Lathers, a professor of speech at the Michigan State Normal College (now Eastern Michigan University), took over the management.

In 1907 Detroit newsman G.H.D. Sutherland purchased the paper, selling it a year later to William Hatch. In October 1908 Hatch hired a young man named George Handy, who had been the paper's circulation manager when he was a student at Normal, to manage the paper for him. In 1917 Handy was able to buy the paper himself, and the *Press* remained in his capable hands for 45 years.

Some important events in the *Ypsilanti Press'* pages include its first big headline, two weeks into its publishing history: "Huron on Raging Tear." The study reported the heavy flood damage from high water and ice jams in the Huron River. (The Scovill Planing Mill's lumberyard and sawmill were flooded, and water reached the fires in the boilers at the Ypsilanti Underwear Company.) The first picture to appear in the *Evening Press,* done on a zinc plate, showed a plume of natural gas escaping from an oil well behind the Occidental Hotel.

Nearly 50 years later the *Daily Press* made its own front-page news, when its offices at Huron and Pearl streets were destroyed in a mid-morning fire on January 23, 1954. The paper managed to get out an edition later that same day, featuring a photo of the disastrous blaze under the headline, "Fire Destroys Press Building." But, with the help of other local newspapers and businesses, the paper never missed publishing a single issue while its offices were being rebuilt.

The 1954 fire also destroyed thousands of irreplaceable photographs and papers that were being sorted for the *Press'* 50th-anniversary issue. Community residents contributed whatever historic photographs and clippings they could find, and the issue came out in October of that year.

The *Ypsilanti Press'* instinct for survival has been strong, ever since its near failure two years after its start. When the community faces hard times, the paper's subscriptions and advertising also go down. But even during the Depression, publisher Handy answered every Dear Santa letter with the gifts of the child's choice.

It was after a second fire in 1965 that the Press *moved to its present facility at 20 East Michigan Avenue.*

owner, Journal News, in Ohio before coming to the *Ypsilanti Press* in 1978. To utilize the paper's trained staff and high-quality equipment, Reynolds has brought in outside work in recent years. The *Ypsilanti Press* currently prints the *Michigan Daily,* EMU's *Echo,* a cable television magazine, Domino's Pizza's *Pepperoni Press,* and others—an average of 125 press runs per month. It also prints and mails the weekly *Shoppers Showcase* to 18,000 non-subscribers' addresses in its distribution area.

With a circulation of approximately 16,000, the *Ypsilanti Press* employs 125 people in production and 280 in delivery. The paper puts out a "Heritage" section each year, sparking the strong civic interest in local history also fostered by the Ypsilanti Public Schools and the Ypsilanti Historical Society.

From the early days, when Ypsilanti was "the" city in Washtenaw County, to today, when the paper focuses on news in the eastern part of the county, mutual respect between area residents and the *Ypsilanti Press* has been evident. Hundreds of local businesses ran tributes on the occasion of the paper's golden anniversary, and the same 1954 edition thanked its readers for "the most gracious of public attitudes toward your home newspaper."

Having come through one devastating fire, the *Press* suffered a second one in August 1965. Soon afterward the paper moved to its 25,000-square-foot facility at 20 East Michigan Avenue, its present home.

Booth newspapers acquired the *Press* from George Handy in 1962. The *Press'* ownership passed to Panax Newspapers (1968) to Harte-Hanks Communications (1971) to its current parent group, Garden State Newpapers, in 1986. During the mid-1970s, under Harte-Hanks, the *Ypsilanti Press* switched from hot-type Linotype machines to its current computerized typesetting, laser printing, and offset press technology. Newswriting and ad makeup are done through a network of personal computers.

The paper contines to do well under publisher Reynolds, who was director of finance for Harte-Hanks'

During the 1970s this composing room was modernized. It was changed from the old hot-type Linotype machines to its present computerized typesetting, laser printing, and offset press technology.

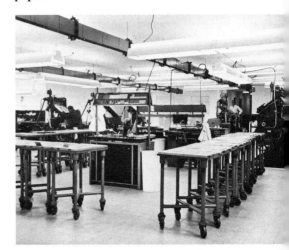

THE YPSILANTI SAVINGS BANK

The Ypsilanti Savings Bank celebrated its 100th anniversary in 1987. One of two nineteenth-century banks that still do business in Ypsilanti, Ypsilanti Savings Bank has operated continuously under its original charter for a century. During that time the bank has established a remarkable record of growth, stability, and community participation.

On May 1, 1887, eight prominent Ypsilanti citizens organized a bank corporation, subscribing to 500 shares of stock and accumulating capital assets of $50,000 by the next year. Three stockholders became the first officers: president Don C. Batchelder, vice-president Sullivan M. Cutcheon, and cashier Robert W. Hemphill. The bank's second president, Augustus Beyer, bequeathed the money to build Ypsilanti's first hospital.

One year after its founding the original Ypsilanti Savings Bank building was erected on the southeast corner of what is now Michigan Avenue and Huron, and it served as the bank's home for 89 years. The pump and watering trough in front of the bank made the corner a gathering place for talking or doing business while the horses quenched their thirst. For many years the building's upper floors housed the city's YMCA.

In the first three decades of this century the bank grew along with the city. During the Depression Ypsilanti Savings Bank closed only for four business days, complying with President Franklin D. Roosevelt's nationwide proclamation. The institution's customers received penny for penny on their deposits, which, in 1932, came to $100,000. New accounts continued to be opened by residents, and Christmas Club savings became popular.

The bank elected one of its most

The original Ypsilanti Savings Bank served the community from the corner of Michigan Avenue and Huron for 89 years. The location was a popular meeting place, and as the city grew so did the bank.

colorful presidents, John P. Kirk, in 1931. A graduate of The University of Michigan law school and a general during the Spanish American War, Kirk set up his law office in the first floor of the bank building in 1888, and was a longtime member of the bank's board of directors. In 1949 the building was renovated to allow the bank to expand to the upper floors.

Throughout its 100-year history Ypsilanti Savings Bank has had only nine presidents. After John Kirk, Mathew Sinkule, longtime resident and owner of a local meat market, served as president until 1966. State Representative James W. Warner was president until 1973 and later, as chairman of the board, played an important role in the bank's construction of a new main office on Michigan Avenue in

1976 at a cost of more than $3 million. Clarence J. Utley worked his way up through the ranks to become the bank's eighth president, serving until 1982.

Under the leadership of current president James B. Pate and chairman of the board Scott W. Woods, M.D., Ypsilanti Savings Bank began its second hundred years of service to the community by embarking on a new phase. On December 31, 1987, the papers were signed to formalize an association between the bank and Trustcorp of Michigan and its parent company, Trustcorp, Inc., of Toledo, Ohio. Already a full-service bank, Ypsilanti Savings Bank will gain access to more extensive capital resources and banking services for its customers.

By 1987 the bank had grown to 120 employees, 315,000 shares of stock, $140 million in assets, and four branch offices in addition to the main office at 301 East Michigan. The Ypsilanti Savings Bank's record of growth, stable leadership, and civic participation will continue into its second century of banking in the community.

An original painting created for The Ypsilanti Savings Bank's 100-year anniversary. It hangs in the bank's executive offices.

DOMINO'S PIZZA, INC.

The Prairie House, named after one of the architectural styles of Frank Lloyd Wright, at Domino's Farms. Included on the grounds are a children's petting zoo, a sports medicine/fitness center, a theater, and a museum.

Flags from eight nations representing countries where its stores are located snap in a brisk breeze before the half-mile-long, low brick building that is Domino's Farms, a $120-million office complex and world headquarters for Domino's Pizza, Inc.

In 1960 its predecessor consisted of one exterior sign, two small tables, and a pizza oven in a dingy shop on the Eastern Michigan University campus in Ypsilanti, Michigan. One of the two owners was Thomas S. Monaghan, whose transformation from pauper to pizza prince is one of the success stories of the decade, known well to county residents and, particularly since his purchase of the Detroit Tigers in 1983, to sports fans across the country.

His was a roller-coaster business experience in the classic tradition. The purchase of a small pizza store with his brother James was intended to be a temporary means of support while he studied architecture at The University of Michigan. He had no experience in the restaurant business, in pizza making, or in handling store finances.

But within one year he had developed the keys to success that were to support his business through 25 years of ups and downs: top-quality ingredients; fast, free delivery; constant employee training; and good advertising.

Raised in an orphanage and foster homes, Monaghan displayed the tenacity and mental toughness he is known for throughout extraordinary years of adversity that included bankruptcy, fire, and a lawsuit with Domino Sugar Company over use of the Domino name.

But by 1973 store franchises sold as briskly as the popular pizza. The 97 stores with sales of $20 million in 1974 escalated to 287 stores with sales of $60 million five years later.

It was obvious by 1983 that Domino's Pizza, Inc., had become an entrepreneurial phenomenon. The relentless expansion continues today, always emanating from its home base in Washtenaw County, offering a strong economic base to the area (800 employees work out of the world headquarters building in Ann Arbor), and around the world (more than 130,000 employees serve Domino's Pizza facilities in eight countries). It is possible that in future years Domino's Pizza will be the area's largest employer.

Nearly 3,000 people, including the governor and state and federal legislators, celebrated the opening of the world headquarters building and the company's 25th anniversary on December 8 and 9, 1985. Domino's Pizza finished that year with 2,839 stores and $1.1 billion in total sales.

Monaghan believes it is now more important than ever to offer the people in the surrounding communities an opportunity to share in the wealth they have helped to create. Washtenaw County franchises exemplify the corporate policy of involvement in and support for local social, religious, and educational activities.

A National Center for the Study of Frank Lloyd Wright is being established in conjunction with the Frank Lloyd Wright Museum in the world headquarters building, and includes the Domino's Pizza Collection of Wright's decorative designs, the largest of its kind in the world.

Domino's co-founder Thomas S. Monaghan is one of the success stories of the decade. He is shown amidst some of his 400 pieces of Frank Lloyd Wright-designed furniture, displayed in the Frank Lloyd Wright Archives located in the Domino's Farms headquarters building.

The first Domino's Pizza store, in Ypsilanti, to display the Domino's name.

MICHIGAN CONSOLIDATED GAS COMPANY

Today all but a small corner of Washtenaw County gets its natural gas for home heating and industrial use from the Michigan Consolidated Gas Company. MichCon's forerunners in the county go back 130 years or more, when coal gas was first used for lights.

Up until 1858 county streets were dark. Students at the University of Michigan made their way home from late study sessions by sputtering oil lamps. Ann Arbor residents lit their homes with oil or kerosene lamps and candles, sometimes placing one in the window to help light the street. Special occasions, such as Michigan's statehood 21 years before, were celebrated around outdoor bonfires.

But on the evening of September 1, 1858, Ann Arbor's stores stayed open after dark. Brilliant new gaslights gave the shopping area a carnival atmosphere, and people came into town from as far away as Dexter to see the sights. Several merchants had their names written across the front of their stores in gas jets. A new era had begun for the little town of 4,800.

That year Ann Arbor's first public utility, the Ann Arbor Gas Light Company, was incorporated by 82 prominent citizens, who bought 460 shares of stock at $50 each. The firm was organized by Dr. Silas H. Douglas, a chemistry professor at The University of Michigan. Douglas also helped organize the medical school, served as mayor of Ann Arbor, and managed the utility company for 33 years—the first 10 without pay. His son, Henry, succeeded him as manager for another 33-year term.

The first coal-generated gas-manufacturing plant, now long gone, was built at the corner of Beakes and Depot streets. At first, gas was used as a better source of indoor lighting by wealthy families. At the end of the first year, the company could boast five miles of gas mains—enough, with short extensions, "to reach nearly every portion of the city which is likely to

be built upon." The stockholders were told of "the cheerfulness and readiness with which the 180 customers have paid their bills, the company having lost less than $3 of the $2,400 worth of gas sold."

It was also in 1859 that the Ann Arbor Gas Light Company proposed lighting city streets with 25 gas lamps. The lamps would be lit at sunset and turned off at 1 a.m.—except when there was a full moon. The contract with the city ran until 1887, when the first electric utility obtained a contract for new street lighting. Existing gas lamps remained in use until 1905.

The gas company's loss of business to electric streetlights soon was made up for by the growing popularity of gas ranges and stoves. As more householders had their homes piped, gas increasingly was used for cooking and heating rather than light. The Ann Arbor Gas Light Company reorganized in 1888 as the Ann Arbor Gas Company.

By 1890 the growing demand for gas required a larger plant, which was constructed north of the New York Central Railroad tracks (the site of MichCon's Broadway Station service center today). The original plant was demolished and replaced by a barn for

the horses that pulled delivery wagons for coke, a by-product of gas manufacturing.

The plant began with an output of 100,000 cubic feet of gas per day, although it could store twice that much. A second, 500,000-cubic-foot storage holding tank was added in 1909. By 1925 sales had grown to the point where a 1.5-million-cubic-foot expandable tank was built. This holder was sufficient until 1939, when natural gas and compressors came on the scene.

In 1913 the firm reorganized, changing its name to the Washtenaw Gas Company to reflect its extended service to the villages of Dexter and Chelsea by means of a unique, new high-pressure line. An explosion at the plant in the coldest part of winter in 1917 injured only two employees, and service was restored before any pilot lights went out. Damage to the plant was quickly repaired.

In 1927 stockholders received a good price for selling their shares in

The municipally owned Ypsilanti Gas Company produced gas and coke, a gas by-product, in the horse-and-buggy era. MichCon leased and then bought the company in the late 1940s and converted the propane gas system into natural gas.

Today MichCon's Ann Arbor Broadway Station service facility is located on the site where gas was manufactured from 1900 until the late 1930s, when natural gas was introduced.

Employees of the Ann Arbor Gas Company served customers from this "commodious" gaslit office at 211 East Huron until 1913. A much-expanded business office was then maintained at this location through the 1970s.

the Washtenaw Gas Company to the American Light and Traction Company, later renamed the American Natural Gas Company, a holding company owning the gas utilities in Detroit, Grand Rapids, and Muskegon. These four utilities combined in 1938 to form the Michigan Consolidated Gas Company.

The real revolution in the gas business began in 1939 with the introduction of natural gas, which was cheaper than manufactured gas and gave almost twice the heat value per cubic foot. MichCon built a pipeline to tap into the supply line that ran to Detroit from the Texas Panhandle. Rates were lowered, and gas became even more competitive with coal and oil as a heating fuel.

By 1948 MichCon had opened an office in Chelsea and had leased the city-owned propane gas company in Ypsilanti, later buying the firm and switching to natural gas. In 1956 residents of Saline, Milan, and Milford also began enjoying MichCon service.

To meet the growing demand for gas heating, MichCon's parent company at the time, American Natural Gas, organized a pipeline company in 1949 to link the district directly to sources in Texas and Oklahoma. The firm soon needed additional sources of

supply, so a second pipeline company was organized to bring gas to southeastern Michigan from Louisiana. This pipeline was operational in the Ann Arbor area by the summer of 1956. Since 1982 MichCon's parent company has been the Primark Corporation.

Recently MichCon's meter-reading operation converted from hand-marked meter cards to hand-held computers. Meter reader microprocessors now contain a tape storing information about each customers' typical gas usage. The new system compares the latest readings with previous ones, reducing error and bill preparation time. MichCon also has begun the switch to a remote meter-reading system that eliminates the need for meter readers to enter homes and buildings.

In October 1987 MichCon introduced the latest technology in mobile communications. Called Mercury, the new system uses a computer-generated burst of tones to send information faster than radio transmission. It also allows a two-way, immediate flow of information between field service employees and customer service representatives and dispatchers. An automatic call-ahead to customers feature is being added to the system.

Today 150 MichCon employees serve Washtenaw County customers

from three locations. The Broadway Station service center in Ann Arbor handles service needs inside customer homes and businesses and also houses a small public affairs staff. The Michigan Avenue center in Ypsilanti takes care of outdoor gas mains and services, and a customer business office is located on Washtenaw Avenue between the two cities.

For more than 130 years the Michigan Consolidated Gas Company has enjoyed steady and continuous growth. And, from its forerunner companies up to today, MichCon has given Washtenaw County a bright past and will be a part of a warmer future.

With the company's new computer-based Mercury system, MichCon field service and dispatch center employees utilize instant two-way communication to reduce paperwork and provide faster service for customers.

GENERAL MOTORS-WILLOW RUN

The largest U.S. corporation in the world? According to a 1980 survey conducted by *Fortune* magazine, the answer is General Motors, with worldwide sales in 1985 totaling $96.3717 billion.

Despite the global magnitude of these numbers, the greatest portion of General Motors' automobile manufacturing is located within the United States. At present GM has more than 200 operations in 30 states and 125 cities. Two of these facilities, Hydramatic Division Willow Run Plant and the Buick-Oldsmobile-Cadillac Willow Run Assembly Plant, are in Washtenaw County, situated on 446 acres made famous during World War II when the area was commonly referred to as Willow Run.

It is a rare industrial complex with a unique place among "factories." Timing, a sense of destiny, preparedness, and its vast size all have played a role in its importance in manufacturing history in the United States.

Its beginnings were tranquil enough. Named after the quiet, blue stream that flowed from the Huron River, the fertile land, consisting of several hundred acres, was purchased by Henry Ford in 1939 and developed into a campground for boys who learned to raise crops from that land. It was called "Camp Willow Run," and the children who lived there were the sons of World War I veterans.

World War II brought an abrupt end to this pastoral site, however. Upon careful analysis, the government determined that the U.S. automobile industry was the one best suited to convert to the manufacture of military aircraft; thus Ford Motor Company and the U.S. Army Air Force entered into a joint-venture agreement for its production. In 1941 the camp was closed down, and by 1942 the huge manufacturing complex that President Franklin D. Roosevelt labeled "the arsenal of democracy" emerged in its place. Designed by the famous American architect, Albert Kahn, the first phase, an 80-acre plant, went up in record time to house parts for the production of B-24 "Liberator" Bombers. Ultimately, there was enough concrete in the construction of runways and taxi stops to build a two-lane highway 120 miles long. The plant itself was large enough to house stockpiles, at any given time, to build 1,000 B-24 Liberator Bombers, each containing 1.225 million loose parts and 400,000 rivets. During peak months of production between 1942 and 1945, the plant employed more than 42,000 women and men. A wartime movie character, "Rosie the Riveter," became the symbol of all the American women working on these wartime assembly lines like those at Willow Run. By June 1945, when the last plane took to the air, Willow Run had produced 8,685

Just 12 weeks after the disastrous fire at Hydra-matic's Livonia plant in 1953, the first transmission came off the converted Willow Run plant's assembly line. Operation Hydra-matic remains an unequaled example of industrial efficiency, cooperation, and teamwork.

The more than 10,000 employees at the Hydra-matic Willow Run plant produced 1.4-million automatic transmissions in 1987.

B-24s. Each one was towed to the runway, tested, and flown off to Air Corps bases around the country.

By the war's end Americans were anxious for a return to normalcy. Most of the women who entered the work force to help the war effort left it to resume homemaking skills. The population swelled with returning veterans and new babies, and the demand for manufactured consumer goods, ranging from waffle irons and washing machines to automobiles, was intense. Automobile manufacture had some catching up to do.

In 1947 Ford sold the gargantuan bomber plant to Kaiser-Frazer for production of its snappy "Henry-J" automobile. In those expansionistic years after World War II, economics and emergency both had a hand in Willow Run's future. Five years after establishing its administrative offices at Willow Run, Kaiser-Frazer sought to trim its operating costs. General Motors, on

the other hand, needed a facility for the manufacture of Hydra-matic automatic transmissions.

Hydra-matic Division

Hydra-matic was organized as the Detroit Transmission Division in 1939 in Detroit, Michigan, to produce the Hydra-matic drive, the first fully automatic transmission for use in the 1940 Oldsmobile. In 1941 the Hydra-matic was introduced in the Cadillac passenger car.

The Hydra-matic transmission was the result of Alfred P. Sloan's search "to find a better and safer way to operate the automobile." In 1932, under the direction of Sloan, then the chairman of General Motors, extensive research and development led to what

ranks among the most important engineering developments in the history of the automobile—the Hydra-matic.

During World War II a military model of the Hydra-matic transmission was developed. One version had the capability of handling light trucks and other versions were used in armored cars and amphibious vehicles. The Buick Hellcat and the tank destroyer also required heavy-duty use of the Hydra-matic.

After World War II Hydra-matic became optional equipment in Pontiac passenger cars, GMC trucks and buses, Chevrolet trucks, as well as Lincoln, Nash, Hudson, Rolls Royce, and Willys automobiles.

The demand for the Hydra-matic was high, which necessitated the need to expand in order to meet customer demand. Therefore, construction of the first unit of a new plant in Livonia commenced in 1948. In 1951 the Hydra-matic transmission was produced for military trucks for the Korean conflict. By the end of July 1953 all automotive transmission production had been moved to the Livonia facility. Then tragedy struck. On

The Buick, Oldsmobile, and Cadillac division gives employment to approximately 5,000 in the Washtenaw area.

lease agreement with Kaiser-Frazer Corporation, who then owned the famous Willow Run bomber plant at Willow Run (Ypsilanti, Michigan). Less than four weeks after the fire, Hydra-matic people began moving into the Willow Run plant and a major rearrangement program was immediately put into high gear. To accommodate mass-production manufacturing operations, virtually an entire new plant, except for the outside walls and roof, had to be built inside the bomber plant.

On November 4, 1953, just 12 weeks after the fire, Hydra-matic transmissions were being manufactured and delivered at Willow Run. Shortly after Willow Run's production began in November, Curtice, then General Motors president, announced that the corporation had purchased the Willow Run property and that it was to be Hydra-matic Division's permanent home.

GM's "rush-order" relocation has settled into a long-term living arrangement. Willow Run has been Hydramatic's headquarters site for 35 years. Milestones at the site have been numerous. In 1966, Hydra-matic organized a new Defense Division for production of 6,110 twenty-millimeter aircraft cannons and nearly 500,000 M16A1 rifles for the Vietnam conflict. The first U.S metric three-speed automatic transmission, model 200-THM, was introduced in 1975; two additions to the plant (increasing its size to 4.8 million square feet) have made it one of the largest plants in the world under one roof; and in 1980 it was dedicated as a state historical site by Governor

August 12, 1953, the automotive industry suffered a destructive blow. The Livonia plant was destroyed by fire. As a result, more than 3,300 precision machines, powered by 25,000 motors, were destroyed or extensively damaged. Thus, a recovery program dubbed "Operation Hydra-matic," commenced. This program represented an example of teamwork and cooperation from the employees of Hydra-matic, its suppliers, and other GM divisions, which in turn created a modern-day industrial miracle.

Approximately 10 days after the devastating fire, GM entered into a

William G. Milliken.

Hydra-matic Division has experienced tremendous growth through the years. Currently it consists of 11 plants in eight locations in three countries, totaling nearly 15 million square feet of facilities worldwide. It employs more than 30,000 people, and produces an average of 21,000 transmissions per day.

B-O-C Willow Run Assembly
Just across the road is GM's other Willow Run operation, the Buick-Oldsmobile-Cadillac Willow Run Assembly plant (B-O-C). It joined Hydra-matic on this location in 1954, when GM moved its Chevrolet Truck assembly operations there.

Expansion, modernization, and a streamlining of organization took place at this plant within the next two years, and by 1960 the plant was designated to produce the Chevrolet Corvair. With its rear-engine, independent suspension system, and air-cooled engine, the Corvair was a revolutionary new design for American auto manufacturers and an enormously popular one. Assembled at the rate of 60 an hour, 145,000 Corvairs were manufactured at Willow Run in the first year of production, representing 60 percent of all the Corvairs produced nationwide. In its 10 years of production, 1.7 million Corvairs were manufactured and sold and it is still a favorite collector's item

for car buffs. As a bit of nostalgia and pride-in workmanship, a project initiated at B-O-C Willow Run in 1982-1983 restored a 1964 Corvair to its original status, using today's technology. Five employees who had worked on the original Corvairs in 1960 worked on this project.

The year 1968 brought social change as well as new manufacturing events to B-O-C; women returned to the work force, and the Chevy Nova was introduced. These were banner years, for 1960 saw Willow Run with a record production of 250,000 cars, and in 1970 it turned out 315,000 units. There were reorganizational changes within management ranks, too, for Willow Run's assembly operations now came under the auspices of a new division named the General Motors Assembly Division, forged out of a union between the Fisher Body and Chevrolet divisions. Other new GM models went into production in the years immediately after: Pontiac Ventura (1970), Oldsmobile Omega (1972), and the Buick Skylark (1977).

New technology became increasingly important for American automobile companies by the end of the 1970s. The oil crisis in the Middle East had made Americans think more seriously about our interdependence on other nations. Natural resources were not inexhaustible, and other nations were going to be able to test

the United States' industrial muscle in new ways.

The plant encountered a major renovation in 1985 to begin production of the all new Oldsmobile Delta 88. The following year, production commenced for the 1987 model Pontiac Bonneville. Today the plant consists of approximately 2.3 million square feet of floor space, produces more than 1,000 vehicles per day, and has an employment of approximately 5,000.

GM and the Future
Currently the General Motors Ypsilanti Operations, along with the United Auto Workers leadership, is strongly committed to work proactively together to ensure a sound and competitive future. A new era of teamwork and technology, resulting in greater trust and mutual respect, has begun. A strong commitment has been made to product integrity, technological leadership, and employee involvement to assure General Motors' position of industry leadership today and tomorrow.

BELOW LEFT: Workers add cables and controls to 1960 Chevrolets moving down the Willow Run plant's assembly line.

In its 1985 modernization the Buick-Oldsmobile-Cadillac body shop at Willow Run added 175 robots—but also took on more workers for production of H-body Oldsmobile Delta 88s and Pontiac Bonnevilles.

SCHLUMBERGER TECHNOLOGY—
CAD/CAM DIVISION

Increasing numbers of U.S. and international manufacturers look to Schlumberger Technology—CAD/CAM Division, a pioneer in computer software, to shorten the product cycle and increase manufacturing flexibility and efficiency. The CAD/CAM Division, with world headquarters in Ann Arbor, was created by the 1985 merger of two Schlumberger Ltd. operating units—Manufacturing Data Systems Inc. (MDSI) and Applicon, both founded independently in 1969.

MDSI was founded in Ann Arbor in 1969 by Kenneth Stephanz and three associates, Charles Hutchins, Urbanes Van Bemden, and Bruce Nourse. All four had professional backgrounds in manufacturing and computer programming. MDSI originally developed a high-level computer language, called COMPACT II, that made it easy to produce tapes for numerically controlled (N/C) machine tools. COMPACT II used familiar words and simple statements to define part shapes, select tools, and direct the machine. The computer translated these commands into code and prepared an N/C machine tape to make a specific part. COMPACT II became an industry standard. MDSI started out with 2,500 square feet of space on the second floor of a building on Packard, and soon expanded to the basement "dungeon." Eventually the company grew to 100 employees and moved to 320 North Main. In 1976 MDSI moved to its own new building at 4251 Plymouth Road. By 1981 MDSI had added two large, modern facilities for a total of 200,000 square feet of office space in the beautiful 78-acre, country-type setting.

That same year MDSI was acquired by Schlumberger Ltd., a global company based in New York. Schlumberger Ltd. focuses on the development of tools for the acquisition, analysis, and simulation of data for many different industries.

Applicon, founded in 1969, was one of the original entrants in the computer-aided design/computer-assisted manufacturing (CAD/CAM) industry—a dynamic, developing market in the 1970s. Starting with $400,000 venture capital, three Ph.D.s from the Massachusetts Institute of Technology's Lincoln Laboratories, Gary Hornbuckle, Fontaine Richardson, and Dick Spann, developed Applicon's first product: computer software for CAD applications that ran on timeshare computers. CAD and CAM revolutionized the drafting and designing functions in many industries, but at first required advanced computers and terminals.

In the early 1970s Applicon developed programming for a CAD/CAM system that could be used on a customer's own mainframe computer, requiring only the purchase of peripheral equipment. By the mid-1970s Applicon was producing a turnkey hardware and software system that was complete and ready to start upon delivery. Schlumberger Ltd. acquired the Burlington, Massachusetts-based Applicon in 1982.

In 1985 Schlumberger merged MDSI's CAM strengths with Applicon's CAD/CAM expertise under the name of Applicon. The company employs 1,100 people worldwide, including 225 in Ann Arbor. Recently a transition from the name Applicon to Schlumberger Technology—CAD/CAM Division began. One major new software product, Bravo III, integrates CAD, CAM, and CAE (computer-aided engineering) systems to design, analyze, and manufacture machinery and electronics for world markets.

Applicon's 4790 work station, built on a MicrovAx II CPU with a large, high-resolution screen, supports all Bravo III software.

The headquarters of Schlumberger Technology's CAD/CAM Division, created by the 1985 merger of two Schlumberger Limited operating units—Manufacturing Data Systems Inc. (MDSI) and Applicon—includes three buildings on the 78-acre site in Ann Arbor.

CUSHING-MALLOY, INC.

Cushing-Malloy's tradition of quality printing and book manufacturing is substantiated by the number of new titles and repeat contracts it receives each year. The firm's 40-year reputation for excellence is due to low turnover among management and staff, plus a companywide commitment to quality and value.

The second-oldest printing business in Ann Arbor has been in Cushing family hands since it was founded in 1948 by B.E. Cushing and his partner, James Malloy, who left the firm in 1960. Cushing's son, Tom, began working in the plant after school 35 years ago. Following B.E. Cushing's death in 1972, Tom and his wife, Edna, became the principal stockholders, and Tom serves as chairman of the board. His cousin, James Cushing, who has spent 25 years with the firm, is president of Cushing-Malloy.

Family or not, Cushing-Malloy people tend to stay on. Vice-presidents Lynn Richards, Tom Weber, and Bob Wagner together have 72 years invested in the company. The

Cushing-Malloy has been a major contributor to the printing industry of Ann Arbor since 1948, and has been satisfying customers with honesty, reliability, and economy.

95-member staff of today has worked there an average of 16 years, and many are second- and even third-generation employees. The accumulated experience and continuity mean quality service for Cushing-Malloy customers.

In the early years Cushing-Malloy printed religious books, short-run textbooks, and many out-of-print titles. It has kept these specialties, but expanded to include printing contracts with scholarly journals, professional societies, and universities. The firm prints the many volumes of The University of Michigan's *Middle English Dictionary*, and an ongoing series of history books on the American West for two large midwestern universities. Cushing-Malloy has printed 1,500 to 2,000 new and reprint titles each year in recent years. One title may run anywhere from 500 to 30,000 copies.

The company's lithography printing process transfers photograhic negatives of the pages to aluminum plates, which are put onto one or more of several printing presses in the plant. Keeping up to date with the printing revolution of the past two decades, Cushing-Malloy has modernized its plates, cameras, and presses. In 1988 a custom-made in-line binder from Germany, which will be able to gather,

bind, and cut 7,000 books per hour, will be installed.

"This is one company where management does daily quality control, checking individual runs off the presses, and redoing them if they're not up to our standard," Tom Cushing says. Concerned with saving customers money, the firm sometimes suggests a smaller press run than originally requested—since the negatives used in the printing process remain good for years and can be used when additional reprints are needed.

Cushing-Malloy has done printing jobs for customers in all 50 states and in many other countries as well. Much of its business comes from repeat orders or word-of-mouth referrals. The firm did not employ a salesman until five years ago.

The printing company has had many work-study high school students over the years, and contributes its services to several law enforcement and charitable organizations in the county.

In the words of president Jim Cushing, "Straightforward, progressive management and productive, committed employees have allowed us to deliver excellent value and quality, on schedule, over the past 40 years."

SPEAR & ASSOCIATES REALTORS, INC.

"When you sell real estate, you are really selling the community and its quality of life, not just a piece of property," says Phil Spear, president and founder of Spear & Associates Realtors, Inc. This philosophy has guided the growth of Spear & Associates from a four-person office in 1971 to one of the two largest real estate firms in Ann Arbor. Today the company has three offices, more than 50 agents, and 15 support staff, all carefully trained to treat potential buyers as guests and give them an overview of the communities in the county.

Spear & Associates prints and distributes three publications as a community service: the *Ann Arbor Area Handbook and Guide,* the *Washtenaw County Directory,* and an Ann Arbor-Ypsilanti street map. The *Handbook* was first put together in 1972, when many Bechtel employees were relocating to the area, and there was no handy source of information about local history, education, cultural activities, and recreational opportunities. Today 30,000 copies of the expanded, 100-page *Handbook* are distributed each year through the local chambers of commerce, universities, and local industries.

Phil Spear began his real estate career in 1962 as a partner in Ann Arbor Associates. Nine years later he founded Spear & Associates in a 350-square-foot office at 1945 Pauline Plaza. With one move in between, the growing business moved to its current 3,000-square-foot office complex at 1915 Pauline Plaza in 1978, and expanded again in 1988.

A second residential office was opened in 1984 at 2721 South State Street by Jim Anderson, now the vice-president and general manager of the firm. In 1985 the Commercial Division relocated to 217 East Huron Street, next door to the Ann Arbor Area Chamber of Commerce and the Hands-On Museum, two organizations that Spear & Associates actively supports.

More than 75 percent of Spear & Associates' business comes from referrals from satisfied clients. This repeat business is due to the company's success in matching buyers with properties, its reputation for integrity, and agents' knowledge and enthusiasm about the communities they serve. Nearly all of the firm's agents have earned advanced professional designations, and more than one-third have achieved the level of broker.

Spear & Associates offers a full range of real estate services: residential sales, multiple listing service, guaranteed home sales plan, commercial/industrial sales and leasing, property management, relocation services, plus extensive experience in working with local financial and business institutions.

A resident and local booster since 1945, Phil Spear has imbued the real estate company that bears his name with a dedication to "community first." His company's deep commitment to Ann Arbor and neighboring communities is reflected in its strong support of the Ann Arbor Area Chamber of Commerce, Washtenaw United Way, the Hands-On Museum, Ronald McDonald House, Mott Children's Hospital, and many other non-profit groups.

Community involvement also means helping university and business interviewees and new residents feel at home, and letting them know about the area's incredibly diverse choices and resources. Spear & Associates Realtors, Inc., has contributed a great deal to foster the quality of life and the growth of Washtenaw County—and continues this commitment.

ABOVE: Phil Spear founded the Spear & Associates Realtors, Inc., in 1971 in the Ann Arbor area. The firm has been so successful that it has grown to three offices with over 50 agents and 15 employed as a support staff.

The main office of Spear & Associates Realtors located at 1915 Pauline Plaza.

YPSILANTI PUBLIC SCHOOLS

Even before it became a village Ypsilanti residents considered their young people. This one room schoolhouse was built in 1929.

Around the close of the 19th century, these boys and girls at the Prospect School posed for this picture.

The community of Ypsilanti is proud of the Perry Child Development Center. This Head Start Program has proven a benefit to the entire community.

Ypsilanti's motto, Where Commerce and Education Meet, stresses the high value that the community places on learning. Today the Ypsilanti public school system runs an extensive, fully accredited, K-12 educational program for nearly 6,000 students in seven elementary schools, two middle schools, and one high school. Three-quarters of its 400-member instructional staff hold master's degrees. The district's richly diverse population is nourished by multicultural programs and other community services, including the seventh-largest adult education program in the state.

Education in Ypsilanti goes back to the 1820s, when Ypsilanti's first school was opened by Olive Gorton in her home on the west bank of the Huron River. Children on the east side of the river had to be rowed across. For rowing and teaching Gorton received two dollars per week. The first schoolhouse opened its doors in 1831. All grades were taught in one room, and students used hornbooks and slates. During the 1840s Ypsilanti residents became more aware of the need to educate all children. Michigan State Normal College (now Eastern Michigan University) opened in 1849, providing Ypsilanti schools with a ready source of teachers.

Around 1849 the old Tecumseh Hotel on Cross and Washington was converted into the Model School (later called Union Seminary), one of the first "graded" schools in Michigan. The high school offered novel courses: logic, philosophy, ethics, geography, English, classical and modern languages, art, and music at low cost.

Ypsilanti schools have been the focus of community life and have made steady progress, year by year. There was some upheaval during World War II, when children of workers at the Willow Run bomber plant swelled Ypsilanti's school population before a separate high school was opened in 1955.

In the fall of 1973 the present, architectural award-winning Ypsilanti High School on Packard Road was dedicated. District students also have the Regional Career Technical Center and a variety of extra-curricular and support programs available. The New Horizons Educational Center serves the needs of physically and otherwise health-impaired students.

District staff won a grant from the National Endowment for the Humanities to develop courses in local history, and Ypsilanti is now one of the few districts in the county to teach both state and local history. The school district also sponsors the Towner House Children's Museum in Ypsilanti's oldest standing building to provide hands-on learning about history.

Ypsilanti has a nationally respected preschool and kindergarten program in the Perry Child Development Center. Newly housed in a unique, award-winning building, the preschool program was begun by principal Charles E. Beatty in the early 1960s to give three-and-four-year-olds from disadvantaged homes the head start they need. A *New York Times* article (September 7, 1987) reported that "the preschoolers required less remedial education and services. Other dividends have mounted as the years pass."

Ypsilanti's schools have a history of consistent millage support from residents and personal support from parents, senior citizens, Eastern Michigan students, and community volunteers. The seven-member board of education works with the administration and the community to set policy that will lead Ypsilanti Public Schools successfully into the twenty-first century.

FORD MOTOR COMPANY

Ford Motor Company has deep roots and a long history in Washtenaw County. Henry Ford brought the automobile industry to the county in the early 1920s, and the firm has played a leading role in the area's growth ever since.

The father of modern industrial production, Henry Ford idealized the values of rural farm life. To slow down the migration of farm boys to the cities, Ford established "factories in the countryside." Ford's small factories became known as "paddle-wheel plants" because many were in converted water-powered gristmills. The experimental plants were kept small, producing no more than three automotive parts and using mainly hand tools plus a few power tools. They were also linked to Ford's values of economy and self-sufficiency; a company-owned farm in Manchester grew much of the food served in Ford plant cafeterias.

In just six years Ford constructed 13 small plants along southeastern Michigan's rivers and streams. Washtenaw County had a hydro-power station at Rawsonville, a factory in Ypsilanti on Ford Lake, and combination hydro plants and factories in Willow Run, Saline, Manchester, and Sharon Mills on the county's western border. By 1942 Ford had established 29 village industries throughout southeastern Michigan.

The plants provided well-paying jobs for rural residents and attracted workers to the area's smaller communities. While some of the original plants were never profitable and closed in the 1940s, others have a direct link with Ford operations in the county today.

Ford acquired the Saline hydro plant and factory in 1935. This paddle-wheel plant on the Saline River processed soybeans, producing meal and extracted oil used in plastics and paint. Ford led the industry in exploring the use of plastic in its cars. Saline's 37-acre, 1.6-million-square-foot plant

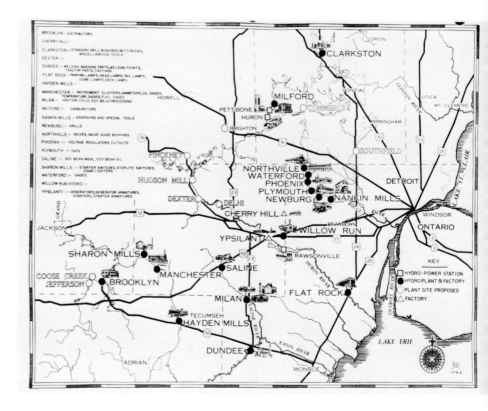

is the world's largest injection-molding facility under one roof. The plant supplies 90 percent of the speedometers, odometers, and fuel gauges used in Ford cars.

The Manchester hydro plant and factory, bought in 1936 by Ford Motor Company, built charge indicators, ammeters, front instrument panels, and related assemblies up to and during World War II. By 1946 the plant had nearly 300 employees. Nearby Sharon Mills hydro plant and factory included a windmill and granaries on its 2,100-acre site. Acquired in 1940, the plant produced stoplight and starter switches and cigar lighter assemblies, employing 53 workers until it closed in 1946.

Ypsilanti was the largest of Ford's Michigan paddle-wheel plants. Its Huron River site was acquired in 1931. In the middle of the Depression Henry Ford expanded employment in Ypsilanti. He constructed a new 63,000-square-foot factory and bought the adjacent City of Ypsilanti power-

Henry Ford constructed "paddle-wheel plants" along Michigan rivers and streams in the early 1920s. They were known as "factories in the countryside" and were productive until after the 1940s, when the company decided to concentrate on fewer facilities.

house, converting it to supply electricity from remote-controlled generators at Ford's Rawsonville Dam, four miles downstream.

Ford bought several other mill sites along the Huron River for proposed plant sites—at Hudson Mill, Dexter, and Delhi. In the 1930s Ford also purchased more than 300 acres along the Willow Run stream east of Ypsilanti, and in 1939 set up a farming camp for sons of World War I veterans. During World War II the land became the site of the nation's largest defense manufacturer: the Willow Run bomber plant.

The federal government bought adjacent land to expand the plant and build a runway for the bombers to take off. The first B-24 Liberator aircraft came off the Willow Run production lines in 1942. By 1944 the plant reached peak employment of 42,000, and by the end of the war had produced nearly 9,000 airplanes. The county's greatest influx of workers created Willow Run Village, a "city" of 15,000 just outside the plant grounds. Many bomber plant workers also lived in Wayne County. In 1940 work began on the Willow Run Expressway, a limited-access highway. Completed in 1944, the expressway led to the construction of I-94 and has had a major effect on the economic development of Washtenaw County.

During World War II all of Washtenaw County's Ford plants were converted to defense production. The Ypsilanti plant manufactured generators and starters for airplanes, armored cars, and tanks. A special department produced precision parts for the Pratt-Whitney aircraft engine. The Ypsilanti plant's wartime employment peaked at 1,400 workers in 1942. After the war the plant resumed production of auto generators and starters.

In the late 1950s and early 1960s the Ypsilanti plant recruited many workers from the rural South. By its 50th anniversary in 1982, the 976,000-square-foot plant had 1,800 employees producing starters, ignition coils, distributors, horns, struts, and other components.

The Ford Motor Company put renewed emphasis on quality and innovation, updating many of its manufacturing plants and methods. A major company reorganization in 1946 consolidated several plants, including Sharon Mills, and gave local plant managers greater responsibility for production quality and profitability.

Ford's Rawsonville hydro-plant station was donated to the city and township of Ypsilanti. An 810,000-square-foot facility was built in 1957. A year later 1,200 employees were producing metal products and

carburetors. The size of the plant nearly doubled in the late 1960s, as heater motors were added to the assembly lines. Today nearly 3,000 workers in a sophisticated 1.6-million-square-foot plant produce fuel-metering devices, alternators, small electric motors, and die-cast parts.

In the 1980s the Rawsonville plant became an industry model for its innovative programs to improve job security and the quality of the work environment. With union involvement, the firm pioneered a Pilot Employment Guarantee (PEG) Program in 1984 and implemented an Employee Involvement (EI) Process to improve the quality of Ford products and work life. The company's "Quality is Job #1," reflects a commitment to both Ford customers and Ford employees, nationally and locally.

Ford Motor Company continues to invest in its Washtenaw county production facilities to employ state-of-the-art technology and retain jobs. A three-year, $300-million program is now under way at the Rawsonville and Ypsilanti plants to retool for production of a new electronic ignition alternator and starter for Ford cars. The Saline plant is in the process of a $90-million redesign of Ford's front panel instrument cluster assembly.

Investments in new technology, sophisticated management practices, and a cooperative relationship with its work force have paid off for Ford Motor Company. The firm posted record profits in 1987, surpassing one billion dollars. Its Washtenaw County work force exceeds 8,500, making Ford one of the area's largest employers. The innovative spirit and economic growth that Henry Ford brought to Washtenaw County in the 1920s continues today in Ford's three Washtenaw County manufacturing centers.

ABOVE: The Willow Run bomber plant, east of Ypsilanti, was the site of the nation's largest defense manufacturer during World War II.

ABOVE: The Rawsonville plant is a sophisticated operation that has provided employees with security and opportunity.

RIGHT: The Saline plant, pictured here in the 1940s, has become a leader in the field of plastics.

AMERICAN BROACH & MACHINE COMPANY

The American Broach & Machine Company in Ann Arbor is one of the largest U.S. manufacturers of specialized metal-cutting tools and the machines that use them. Broaching is a machining method in which a series of cutting teeth pass inside or outside a metal workpiece, removing a portion of the stock with accuracy up to .0002 of an inch. Today broaching is widely used by industry for accurately finishing parts of all shapes and sizes, including the teeth inside pliers, the rifling in gun barrels, and splines in automotive gears.

American Broach & Machine was founded in 1919 by F.J. Lapointe, who came to the area from the East Coast to be near the automobile companies. Lapointe held many of the basic patents from which modern broaching techniques developed. The company's first plant was located on West Huron, just past the railroad bridge.

In 1937 the firm was purchased by the Sundstrand Corporation of Rockford, Illinois, and the machine division was moved to Rockford in 1958. Three years later the broaching

tool division was purchased by Harold Holly, Everett Vreeland, and a few other investors. In 1963 American Broach moved into the modern, attractive facility it still occupies at 4600 Jackson Road. The present ownership acquired the privately held company in 1977.

The firm's Ann Arbor plant designs and produces the tools used in broaching. In the late 1970s American Broach & Machine opened two other facilities—the one in Jackson County also manufactures tools, and the one in Wayne County produces broaching machines that use the tools. Some of these machines weigh up to 50,000 pounds and exceed 20 feet in height.

For nearly 70 years American Broach & Machine Company has maintained its tradition of experienced craftsmanship and high-quality products. Each broach is guaranteed for accuracy of dimension, finish, and quality of tool steel. Today the company's 50 engineers and craftsmen, many with many more than 25 years of experience, work with high-technology computers, computer-aided design and manufacturing systems, and computer numerical control equipment. These systems and machines permit the manufacture of products whose price and quality will stand up to increasing competition from overseas.

American Broach describes itself as a small company, with sales of roughly $4 million annually. Yet its customer list of 2,000 includes General Motors Corporation, Caterpillar, Ford Motor Company, Westinghouse, General Electric, and other automotive, appliance, hand tool, and electrical equipment manufacturers. Exports of American Broach's tools and machines to Canada, Mexico, China, Korea, Israel, Sweden, and elsewhere account for 25 percent of the firm's sales.

In spite of the decline of the U.S. machine tool industry during the past years, American Broach & Machine Company continues to compete, importing almost nothing and exporting its tools and machines worldwide. This historic Ann Arbor corporation with its stable, highly skilled work force has continually employed the most advanced technologies to remain viable in a hard-hit industry—keeping jobs in Washtenaw County during its seventh decade of manufacturing.

American Broach & Machine Company, located in Ann Arbor, designs and produces tools used in broaching, a machining process in which a series of cutting teeth pass inside or outside a metal piecework.

CNC broach machine with automatic tool changer allows for production broaching of various parts without operator intervention. CNC controls change cutting tools automatically when parts are changed.

ZANTOP INTERNATIONAL AIRLINES, INC.

Zantop International Airlines, Inc., a cargo air carrier with headquarters at Willow Run Airport, moves up to 1.5 million pounds of freight each day for the Big Three automakers, the U.S. Air Force, and hundreds of businesses and air freight forwarders. The company operates a fleet of 43 cargo aircraft. It has a maintenance facility in Macon, Georgia, as well as commercial flight facilities at 21 airports.

Zantop International Airlines was formed in 1972, but its beginnings go back to 1946, when Duane Zantop and his brothers, Lloyd, Elroy, and Howard—three of whom served in the Air Corps during World War II—opened the Zantop Flying Service in Jackson, Michigan, to offer pilot training under the G.I. Bill of Rights.

Soon afterward they formed Zantop Air Transport to move freight and passengers under a supplemental air carrier certificate, and moved the service to Detroit's Metro Airport. By 1966 Zantop Air Transport was the

world's largest supplemental air carrier, operating on a charter and contract basis. That year a New York group of investors bought the company, changed its name, and operated it out of Willow Run Airport and Oakland, California, until its demise in April 1972.

Meanwhile, there was a growing need for air cargo transport in the Washtenaw County and metropolitan Detroit area. "In May 1972 Zantop International Airlines was formed with a very modest capital investment, a few talented employees, and many understanding suppliers," president Duane Zantop says. To fill the need of local industry for air freight services, especially the Big Three automotive companies, Zantop International started with some 25 people and three aircraft. Today, with 1,700 employees, it is the fifth-largest privately owned service organization in metro Detroit, according to *Crain's Detroit Business*.

Currently approximately 25 percent of Zantop's business comes from the auto companies that depend on "prime-time" evening and night flights to transport engines, transmissions, and other parts urgently needed to keep production lines running.

A substantial part of the airline's business comes from air cargo service to 35 of the nation's leading industrial centers, plus worldwide char-

ter service through its commercial hub at Willow Run. Zantop's largest plane takes up to 90,000 pounds of freight.

Zantop International also provides daily domestic air cargo transportation for the U.S. Air Force under a government contract that calls for flying more than 3 million miles per year. The firm runs military airlifts to the United Kingdom, Europe, and the Middle East.

Zantop International's Willow Run facility includes offices, hangars, maintenance facilities, and storage on an adjacent 10-acre site. Management continues the family tradition. Founder and principal stockholder Duane Zantop works with his sons, Duane G., vice-president/materials; James, executive vice-president; David, director of cargo; son-in-law Edwin Freitag, assistant director of personnel; and other longtime staff members who have been with the firm since its inception.

As the largest of Willow Run's airlines, Zantop International fills a constantly growing need to move Washtenaw County businesses' critical shipments to U.S. or worldwide destinations within a few hours.

Special requirements for evening and nighttime freight airline services were the beginning of Zantop International Airlines in Willow Run in the early 1970s. Founder Duane Zantop continues a family tradition and works with sons Duane G., vice-president of materials; James, executive vice-president; David, director of cargo; and son-in-law Edwin Freitag, assistant director of personnel.

The increased need for such service allowed Zantop to expand from 25 people to 1,700 employees and cover an area throughout the United States, and the world.

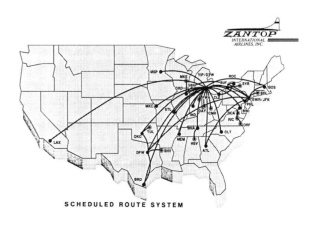

SCHEDULED ROUTE SYSTEM

YPSILANTI AREA CHAMBER OF COMMERCE

Three things a Board of Commerce can do for a community: "Create an atmosphere of enterprise in the community, teach the habit of giving, develop the habit of appreciating public service by the men and women of the community."

A yellowed and crumbling newspaper clipping from the June 8, 1920, *Daily Ypsilanti Press* carries that earnest entreaty—as valid today as it was on the occasion of the "great gathering of Ypsilanti people at a Civic Dinner . . . " to celebrate the Ypsilanti Board of Commerce.

Headlines in local and national newspaper articles since that time reflect the chamber's ongoing concern with identification of community problems and its active search for solutions: "Commerce Vote Favors School Site Purchase," "Homes, Banking, and Music are Evening Topics."

A Tacoma, Washington, newspaper offered its congratulations to the Ypsilanti Board of Commerce with a commendation that concluded, "The board's regular work embraces such unusual activities as directing an educational program for retail merchants to improve the town as a trading center, supervising a loan

association by which 50 deserving normal college students are enabled to remain in schools, and putting through a good city-zoning system."

Through peace and war the board has served its constituency: War Bond sales and salvage programs were initiated during World War II. In 1958 the Board of Commerce played an instrumental part in bringing about annexation of a 610-acre tract of land to the city—the first addition in 40 years. That same year the board officially changed its name to Ypsilanti Area Chamber of Commerce to include Ypsilanti Township A few years later the chamber's area of operation was further expanded to include Superior and Pittsfield townships.

Today the emphasis has not changed. Primary topics addressed by the current chamber of commerce are positive economic growth, the encouragement of tourism, and the coherent development of the down-

town area as a suitable and exciting location for both businesses and private residences. Ypsilanti shares in the national explosion of private entrepreneurship, and over the past three years $900,000 ($125,000 in public funding and $775,000 from private sources) has changed the environment of the central city core by supporting property rehabilitation. In addition, $200,000 in public improvements have increased parking and enhanced landscaping. While the city itself cannot spread, the potential for industrial and up-scale residential growth in the surrounding township is enormous.

The 1988 Ypsilanti Area Chamber of Commerce membership of approximately 600 men and women will continue to monitor and explore options and opportunities that will express the ongoing interests of residents and business people who share in the desire for a stable and interesting area in which to live and work.

WUOM RADIO

Twenty-four hours a day, seven days a week, Washtenaw County residents can turn to 91.7 FM and be entertained and informed by the many voices and sounds of WUOM. The University of Michigan radio station offers listeners a full schedule of classical music and information, including news, weather reports, and business updates, as well as features, discussions, interviews, lectures, jazz programs, broadcasts of University of Michigan events, concerts, and recitals.

The tradition of public service broadcasting at The University of Michigan goes back years before WUOM. As early as 1925 the University Broadcasting Service produced educational programs for distribution to commercial stations. WUOM officially went on the air on July 5, 1948, obtaining its license and its preferred call letters despite the FCC's initial objection that "WU" was hard to pronounce.

Broadcasting classical music has been a high priority of WUOM for

Fred Hindley, WUOM's public service director, began producing the station's news and public affairs programming as a refreshing addition to the traditional classical music and radio drama in the mid-1950s.

the past three decades; 75 percent of its broadcast day is devoted to music. In the early days music was either broadcast live or from records. Another early priority was radio drama, especially live broadcasts of dramatized histories. In the mid-1950s Fred Hindley built a news and public affairs organization to supplement music and drama programming, and this tradition continues today.

Over the years valuable early jazz record collections have been donated to the station by Phil Diamond and Carl Conlon, among many others. WUOM's early jazz library is now one of the most complete in the country, and director of broadcasting Hazen Schumacher's "Jazz Revisited" program attracts a large nationwide audience.

WUOM has benefited from new developments in audio technology. More reliable taping equipment allowed WUOM to record events and broadcast them at a later date. It also opened up a world of news to a once-confined studio operation. And by a sophisticated satellite interconnection system, WUOM, as a member of National Public Radio and an affiliate of American Public Radio, the WFMT Fine Arts Network, and other networks, now carries about 6.5 hours of national and international programming daily.

WUOM's purpose has remained unchanged during its 40-year history: to extend the cultural, academic, and informational resources of the university to the people of Michigan. The station extended its services to satellites in Grand Rapids (WVGR) in 1961 and Flint (WFUM) in 1985.

Resources utilized by the station include UM libraries and faculty members, who contribute their expertise. Experts in such diverse areas as politics of the Middle East, toxic

chemicals, and supreme court decisions share their knowledge with listeners.

Producers of classical music programs draw on a library of 30,000 LPs and compact discs, along with their collective experience. "WUOM has one of the best maintained and most easily accessed libraries of classical recordings in the country. This rich resource provides the backbone of our programming," says music director Stephen Skelley.

WUOM's studios are located in the university's LS&A building on State Street. Its 93,000-watt transmitter and antenna are on Peach Mountain, northwest of Ann Arbor. Contributions provide more than half of the operating budget; other funds come from the university, the Corporation for Public Broadcasting, and other foundations and underwriters.

Whether it's called educational radio or public radio or listener-supported radio, WUOM's quality and content make it radio at its best.

Nationally known for his "Jazz Revisited" program, Hazen Schumacher, director of broadcasting and media resources at The University of Michigan, has been with WUOM since 1950.

WIHT CHANNEL 31

Christopher Webb, general manager of WIHT Channel 31, looks like he belongs in front of the camera instead of behind the desk. He is enthusiastic and forceful as he talks about the future of the only independent Ann Arbor-based television station.

Actually, Ann Arbor has been called "a community that simply doesn't exist" in terms of the commercial television industry. Its location between Detroit's 1.6 million viewing households and Lansing's 213,000 households has meant that Ann Arbor as a potential market for independent television has never been tested.

But if Chris Webb has his way the next two years will see an audience for WIHT programming of some 500,000 viewers. There are many challenges ahead in meeting that goal, but the nature of this station has been to meet adversity with adaptation and ingenuity.

WIHT began as an In-home Theatre (IT) subscription television station on February 1, 1981, offering full-length movies with no commercial interruptions for 12 hours each day, the limit allowed by the Federal Communications Commission. But as cable TV became available and the popularity of home VCRs increased, subscription TV became less profitable. By November 1985 the station had become a full-time commercial independent station, offering classic movies and offbeat programming not provided by the major networks.

Still seeking a profitable programming mix, the 3,000-square-foot studio and control room on Varsity Drive was established in 1986 to provide technical facilities to do local and syndicated programming. Today Webb and a staff of 16 full-time employees keep the station on the air 24 hours a day. Half of these staff members man the

Christopher Webb, general manager, WIHT.

1,044-foot-high transmitter tower located four miles north of Chelsea. Homes in the western suburbs of Detroit, north to Lansing, west to Marshall, and south to Adrian can pick up the Channel 31 signal. The broadcast radius spans 65 miles and is the only full-power frequency licensed to Ann Arbor or Washtenaw County.

Webb and his staff recognize that programming represents their greatest challenge—the need to schedule programming that will attract viewers, which will in turn attract advertisers.

"Shop Around 31," a home-shopping program, was for a time the mainstay of station programming. Produced in four, one-hour segments, the show was broadcast approximately seven hours each day on Monday through Friday, and two hours during weekends. The show offered a range of products at prices at or lower than local discount stores. Show merchandise was procured by the station's owner, Tempo

Enterprises in Tulsa, Oklahoma.

Still seeking the most attractive approach to both viewers and advertisers, WIHT has recently moved away from the shopping format to combine locally produced public interest shows with nationally distributed programs, classic films, and news shows from a variety of sources.

One very successful step in the new direction resulted in the joint sponsorship with the League of Women Voters and subsequent airing of an hour-long televised debate between U.S. Representative Carl D. Pursell and his opponent, Dean Baker.

As new programming alternatives are sought, WIHT now airs a half-hour local events program called "The Heart of the Matter," hosted by a local radio personality. National Geographic Specials join news, outdoor, exercise, travel, and children's programming (also enjoyed by a large college student population) such as "Bullwinkle," "Zoobilee Zoo," and "Tennessee Tuxedo." Classic movies are local favorites, drawing on a large library of such favorites as John Wayne and Roy Rogers, as well as *A Star is Born, Dick Tracy,* and *Of Human Bondage.*

From its initial viewership of 17,000 households in 1985, Channel 31's current audience is 100,000 viewing households per week. Stressing intended reemphasis on local programming and encouraging interest from local businesses interested in buying commercial time, the goal of 500,000 viewers in the next two years is a distinct possibility, based on the potential 1.1 million households within the reach of the Chelsea transmitter.

"Ann Arbor is a community that has a story to tell, and a viewing population that is looking for what we have to offer," says Webb. "Independent stations like ours thrive on 'counter programming.' I feel strongly that the mix of commercial support and audience interest will come together in the near future to make WIHT a successful alternative to the national networks."

WIHT management staff (left to right): Jerry Samons, production manager; Mallory Longwerth, finance manager; Robert Thompson, chief engineer; Marge Wiechers, office manager; and Christopher Webb, general manager.

ANN ARBOR AREA CHAMBER OF COMMERCE

The Ann Arbor Area Chamber of Commerce has been drawing the communities of Washtenaw County together for more than 67 years. In 1921 the Retail Merchants' Association, as it was originally known, consisted of a group of local businesses that joined forces to attract farming residents from outlying areas to utilize downtown businesses. This early group of merchants grew into today's chamber, which boasts more than 1,200 member firms from the local business community.

The chamber of commerce's original goals have also expanded to reflect the growing needs of the business and residential community. Today the major emphasis of the chamber centers on increasing involvement in the downtown development plans, sponsoring fledgling businesses, and enhancing the quality of life for people living and doing business in the community.

In the early 1960s the chamber was instrumental in the development

The Ann Arbor Area Chamber of Commerce is proud of its success. The recent purchase of the chamber's downtown building at 211 East Huron reflects the established status the organization now holds in the city.

of the Greater Ann Arbor Research Park, home to some of the first high-technology firms in the area. With assistance from state and local agencies and The University of Michigan, this park was one of the first of its kind in the nation. Since that time the chamber of commerce has assisted in bringing a number of research and technological companies into the area, often called the Research Center of the Midwest.

In 1975 the development of the chamber-sponsored Convention and Visitors Bureau was made possible by the accommodation tax, specifically designated to support this citywide promotional agency. The bureau plays a vital marketing role in the community's economic development efforts, representing the city in a competitive marketplace. Promoting the Ann Arbor area as an ideal place to live, work, play, and visit has provided the impetus for positive growth and expansion.

The support and development of new businesses in the community has also been a continuing priority for the Ann Arbor Area Chamber of Commerce. This commitment was enhanced by the establishment of

the Chamber Innovation Center in 1984. The center assists budding entrepreneurs to turn their ideas and inventions into successful business ventures. Serving as an incubation environment, the center provides expertise and advice, management and marketing direction, as well as low-cost office space and basic services for the fledgling companies.

The Discover Ann Arbor program, Leadership Ann Arbor, the small business education seminars, and a variety of publications are some of the other ways in which the chamber of commerce contributes to the community.

The recent purchase of the chamber's downtown building at 211 East Huron reflects the established status the organization now holds in the city. As the needs of this growth-oriented area change, the Ann Arbor Area Chamber of Commerce prepares to encourage expansion and innovation while maintaining the quality of life that businesses and residents value so highly.

The Chamber Innovation Center was established to sustain and develop new business in the community.

WAAM RADIO

Community involvement, accessibility, and professionalism have always been the keys to successful operation of WAAM. For more than 40 years Washtenaw County's 5,000-watt AM radio station has specialized in giving voice to community news and interests. Twenty-four hours a day the station offers full, often live, coverage of local events—high school and college sports, election results, and school issues—as well as call-in shows, music, weather, and news.

In September 1947 two Ypsilanti residents, Fred Hopkins and Ray Augustus, saw the need for a local radio station that would keep on top of every facet of community life. Only the 1600 frequency was available when they started WHRV (Huron River Valley)—a position they capitalized on by calling it "the top spot on the dial." The station and transmitter were set up outside town on then-unpaved Packard Road between Carpenter and Golfside, with seven people on staff.

In 1955 the station was sold to Main Broadcasting. Owner Chuck Main of Detroit supported innovative ideas and ran the station as a group effort. Steve Filipiak ran the morning show. Ollie McLaughlin did the evening show, sometimes broadcasting from the station's lawn, and became the unofficial babysitter for 25,000 club-member listeners. And, of course, all major local high school and college sports events were broadcast live.

In 1958 Zanesville Publishing of Ohio bought the station, cut costs by hiring less-experienced staff, and sold out to Ann Arbor Radio three years later. Owner Frank Babcock wanted the station as much for professional as for investment purposes. Babcock, who had a national reputation for doing voice work for major corporate commercials, had definite ideas about quality

Yesterday, Today and Tomorrow:
Our Commitment is to You.

Radio 16 WAAM

broadcasting.

Renamed WAAM (Ann Arbor, Michigan), in 1961, with a new boxing glove logo, the station built a large, professional, and mobile staff. According to Wayne Adair, general manager from 1964 to 1972, "Sports were covered like a blanket. The news department alone had seven people, so police and fire departments could be covered in shifts. WAAM was on the scene of breaking news stories, civic events, and every local sports event in the community."

On a Friday the 13th in the fall of 1968, the station burned down in an early-morning fire. Nevertheless, WAAM staff broadcast a football game that afternoon with a borrowed transmitter and some help from WPAG in Ann Arbor. Radio WAAM broadcast from a trailer for several months until the station was rebuilt.

The station's roughest time was between 1971 and 1983, under

a series of out-of-state owners. Sinclair Broadcasting of Crawford, Indiana, owned WAAM for three years. WIMA Lima, Ohio, Broadcasting bought it in 1974 but went broke in fewer than three years. In 1978 the station was sold to WKBN of Youngstown, Ohio.

Since September 1983 WAAM has been owned by the Washtenaw County-based Whitehall Broadcasting Company, headed by Lloyd and Mabel Johnson. They brought in Clement "Skip" Diegel as general manager and attracted other professionals, including local dean of radio, Ted Heusel, from WPAG. News director Heusel delivers editorials on local events, and hosts a call-in show "for all of you out there in radio land." Today WAAM has more than 30 full- and part-time employees.

WAAM Radio has come through four eventful decades in fine shape— still broadcasting radio programming with a community focus at the top of the AM dial.

COMSHARE

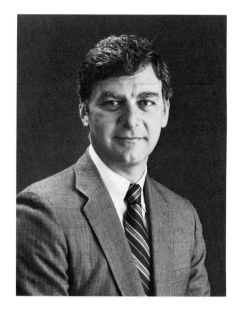

Comshare develops and markets software and services that give business professionals easy access to the computer—that "make the computer make sense." Since 1966 the Ann Arbor-based company has pioneered interactive computer time sharing, created data base management systems for many different industries, and developed state-of-the-art software for executive access to information.

Flexibility and entrepreneurship have contributed to Comshare's survival and success in the rapidly changing computer field. For many years after the first computer appeared on the scene in 1946, the huge machines remained expensive and difficult to use. Gaining access to a company computer, typically kept in the data-processing department's "glass house," was usually difficult. In the early 1960s many engineers and systems analysts asked people at the University of Michigan computer center for help in working out computer solutions to problems ranging from investment forecasts to rocket trajectories. Five locals then envisioned the need to create better and more interactive computer languages and programs. They saw the possibilities of establishing computer time-sharing services, then being pioneered at U.C.

Berkeley and elsewhere.

Comshare was founded in February 1966 by Robert Guise, Robert McDonald, George Perrett, Lawrence Boyd, and Richard L. Crandall. The company's first offices were located at 202 1/2 East Huron. Comshare set up its first computer in the lobby of the Huron Towers building on Fuller Road.

At that time the idea of time sharing appeared attractive and economical but making it easy for customers to interact with the computers posed major challenges. Comshare began creating its own programs and operating systems. By early 1967 Comshare had grown to 25 people and moved to a new location on Huron Parkway; by fall president Bob Guise had raised considerable venture capital locally.

However, the company soon realized that its potential market extended far beyond Washtenaw County. One Comshare engineer created a multiplexer that would compress many telephone calls over one channel. When a legal battle with a Pennsylvania telephone company, won by Comshare in 1967, opened an era of computer networking, Com-

share quickly set up communication centers in more than a dozen U.S. cities.

Between 1967 and 1969 capital and sales flowed in as scientists, engineers, and others took advantage of Comshare's time-sharing services and software. In October 1968 the firm went public and easily raised $5.5 million; stock values soared. With new headquarters at Pauline and Stadium, Comshare rapidly expanded to 220 employees and 15 sales offices by 1970.

Then the nation experienced a recession, stock markets fell, and the bloom was off high-technology ventures at a point when Comshare was most extended. Comshare stock plummeted, reaching an all-time low in August 1970. The management upheaval ended with 27-year-old Crandall becoming president. Comshare, which not long before had grown 10 percent a month, found its expenses far beyond its income. Staff was cut back to 150 by September 1971, when the company showed its first profit.

"Comshare was determined to survive, and set its focus in another direction. We targeted a whole class of computer users who had budgetary authority and also had unresolved problems," according to Crandall. "They were called 'management' and they

A view inside one of Comshare's data centers.

Software developers plan a product enhancement.

Comshare products are used by 3,200 customers.

needed a computer language of their own." In 1972 Comshare created a fourth-generation language that helped business users develop application prototypes, implementing them quickly and changing them easily. In 1974 Comshare introduced the Profiles system to personnel managers and the 4.1.1 systems for telephone companies. Throughout the 1970s the firm's growth was among the fastest in the industry.

In 1973 Comshare moved to the Wolverine Towers building at Eisenhower and State, where its headquarters remained, much expanded. By 1975 the company's staff had grown to 280 and about one-third of Comshare's revenues came from overseas markets. The firm first licensed soft-

ware to a Canadian affiliate in Toronto in 1969, and finally gained ownership of what is now a subsidiary headed by president Derek G. Price. In 1971 Comshare licensed software to Comshare International Ltd. in London, now a wholly owned subsidiary led by group vice-president and managing director of European operations Ian G. McMaught-Davis. In 1981, at the peak of its time-sharing operation, Comshare employed about 1,200 people.

In 1980-1981 Comshare made a strategic decision to sell its software applications separately from its time-sharing services. With businesses using more microcomputers networked to mainframes, companies still needed budgeting, business planning, and decision support applications, but the problem was how to make this information directly accessible to decision makers. In the early 1980s Comshare invested $40 million to develop several revolutionary products.

The first of Comshare's new generation of information management tools was the System W line. Released in 1983, the world's first distributed-decision support system integrated businesses' personal computers with in-house mainframes. System W software targeted business professionals' needs for modeling, decision support, budgeting, and strategic planning. In 1984 Comshare announced a precedent-setting marketing agreement with IBM.

Meanwhile, Comshare had been working for years on a new software product for executives. In May 1987 Comshare introduced a new graphic workstation product—the Commander Executive. Commander allows high-level executives to become proficient users in less than an hour. They can easily obtain a wide range of corporate reports, external reports,

and other documents.

Comshare continues to refine and expand other products such as Profiles PC, a microcomputer-based human resource management system, and Information Gateway Plus, a workstation software product for skilled computer users. With so many advanced proprietary products, it is little wonder that "software overtook time-sharing services as Comshare's primary source of its over $70 million revenues in 1987, and is projected to bring in over two-thirds of sales in 1988," according to T. Wallace Wrathall, group vice-president and chief financial officer.

Businesses can use Comshare's proprietary software on their in-house mainframe, mini- and microcomputers, or by way of Comshare's international communications network and data centers. Comshare's client list includes 3,200 medium- to large-size industrial corporations, financial institutions, utilities, and government agencies in North America and Europe. Many have shared a partnership with Comshare for 15 years and longer.

"While the type of customer Comshare serves has not varied over the years, clients' needs have changed dramatically," Crandall explains. "Over our history we've broadened our user base, serving business analysts, mid-level managers, and now top-level executives. Comshare's products have expanded too—from interactive problem solving, to decision support software, to 'customizable' executives' productivity tools. But one thing remains a Comshare hallmark: a commitment to customer satisfaction by putting the computer under the direct control of the user."

Now in its third decade of delivering top-quality information management systems and services, Comshare is working on products to meet the future needs of businesses around the world.

BURLINGTON EXECUTIVE CENTERS

Burlington Executive Centers in Ann Arbor was one of the first companies to offer a shared office resources environment in Washtenaw County. Jon McClory, an Eastern Michigan University graduate, and Laura Dykstra, a graduate of The University of Michigan, met while working on another project in the area. Both agreed there was an unmet need in the local market for this unique concept.

The partners began in 1983 with a few offices and a small support staff. By 1985 the company moved to larger quarters in the Burlington Office Center II at 315 East Eisenhower. McClory and Dykstra also opened Burlington Executive Centers in West Bloomfield (1984), Lansing (1985), and Northville (1987).

According to president McClory, the Ann Arbor Burlington Executive Center provides more than 25 fully furnished offices and suites, including a reception area, conference room, and all office and communication services. "Within 30 minutes of walking in the door, you can have a first-class, functioning office," states McClory.

Tenants have included *Fortune* 500 executives who are spending a short time in the area, new businesses not ready to invest in a long-term lease, and professionals who do not need a full-time support staff of their own. Vice-president Dykstra says that tenants can save 20 to 70 percent on overhead costs by leasing Burlington's Class A office accommodations and services rather than leasing traditional office space, furnishing it, and paying rent, personnel, utilities, and maintenance.

Burlington Executive Centers also offers flexibility in its lease periods. Tenants may choose full-time, half-time, or part-time office packages. While the average lease is for a one-year period, tenants may rent by the day or even by the hour.

Close to Briarwood and I94, the Burlington Executive Center in Ann Arbor is located in an architecturally impressive building with a large central atrium. Third-floor offices and suites are tastefully furnished. Businesses each have their own telephone number, and receptionists answer telephones with the company name. Telephone services include long distance, TELEX, and FAX. Typing and word processing are available through the professional office staff.

Tenants in the Ann Arbor center have included Offerman and Company, financial advisers and stockbrokers; California-based LSI Logic, developer of integrated computer circuits; and Olson Engineering, consultant for foreign car manufacters on EPA standards. Family First Medical Centers started out there, and some individually owned insurance and financial advisory firms have maintained offices in the center since 1983.

Although McClory and Dykstra may have introduced the idea of a shared office resource environment to the local market, it has since been taken up by some other firms. "Burlington Executive Centers has planned and built in a full range of amenities and services that businesspeople expect from a first-class office environment; we go far beyond leasing space," McClory states.

Since 1983 the Burlington Executive Centers have served as the first or second home for some of the area's growing enterprises. Judging by the centers' expansion inside and outside Washtenaw County, the company has adroitly developed an innovative concept.

Burlington Executive Centers in Ann Arbor is located in the prestigious Burlington Office Center II.

Qualified personnel are provided to handle every business need, from telephone answering to word processing.

Fully equipped conference rooms are shared by Burlington clients.

PATRONS

The following individuals, companies, and organizations have made a valuable commitment to the quality of this publication. Windsor Publications and the Washtenaw County Historical Society gratefully acknowledge their participation in *Washtenaw County: An Illustrated History.*

American Broach & Machine Company*
Ann Arbor Area Board of REALTORS
Ann Arbor Area Chamber of Commerce*
Ann Arbor News*
Ann Arbor Transportation Authority*
Applied Dynamics International, Inc.*
Associated Spring-Barnes Group, Inc.*
Atwell-Hicks, Inc., Engineers & Surveyors
The Barfield Companies*
Beyer Memorial Hospital*
Braun-Brumfield, Inc.*
Burlington Executive Centers*
Chelsea Community Hospital*
City of Ann Arbor*
City of Ypsilanti*
Cleary College*
Comshare*
Control-o-mation, Inc.*
Cushing-Malloy, Inc.*
Dobson-McOmber Agency*
Domino's Pizza, Inc.*
Eberbach Corporation*
Environmental Research Institute of Michigan*
First of America Bank-Ann Arbor*
Ford Motor Company*
Gelman Sciences Inc.*
General Automotive Corporation*
General Motors Corporation/

Ypsilanti Operations*
Great Lakes Bancorp
Group Four, Inc., REALTORS
GT Products, Inc.*
J.P. Industries, Inc.*
Kerrytown Shops*
Catherine McAuley Health Center*
Manufacturers Bank*
Michigan Consolidated Gas Company*
National Sanitation Foundation*
O'Neal Construction, Inc.*
Parke-Davis Division*
Warner Lambert Company*
R&B Machine Tool Company*
Raycon Corporation*
Saline Community Hospital*
Schlumberger Technology-CAD/CAM Division*
Spear & Associates Realtors, Inc.*
Stark Funeral Service-Moore Memorial Chapel, Inc.*
University Lithoprinters, Inc.*
UMI (University Microfilms International)*
WAAM Radio*
Washtenaw Engineering Company*
Washtenaw Real Estate*
WIHT Channel 31*
WUOM Radio*
Ypsilanti Area Chamber of Commerce*
Ypsilanti Press*
Ypsilanti Public Schools*
The Ypsilanti Savings Bank*
Zantop International Airlines, Inc.*

*Partners in Progress of *Washtenaw County: An Illustrated History.* The histories of these companies and organizations appear in Chapter V, beginning on page 113.

BIBLIOGRAPHY

Adams, Charles Kendall. *Historical Sketch of the University of Michigan.* Ann Arbor, 1876.

Ancient and Modern Milan: A History of the City of Milan. Milan, 1976.

Ann Arbor Business Men's Association. *The City of Ann Arbor: Its Resources and Advantages.* Ann Arbor, 1887.

Art Work of Washtenaw County. Chicago, 1893.

Bald, Frederick Clever. *Michigan In Four Centuries.* Lansing, 1954.

Barnat, Rhonda. *A Capsule History of the Washtenaw County Farm.* Ann Arbor, 1976.

Beakes, Samuel Willard. *Past and Present of Washtenaw County.* Chicago, 1906.

Bidlack, Russell Eugene. "The Dixboro Ghost Skeleton in the Wall; or the Meaning of 'A.F.D.'" In *Washtenaw Impressions,* vol. 14, April 1963.

———. *John Allen and the Founding of Ann Arbor.* Ann Arbor, 1962.

———. "The Short and Troubled Lives of Elisha and Mary Ann Rumsey." Unpublished paper, 1985.

Bordin, Ruth. *A Pictorial History of the University of Michigan.* Ann Arbor, 1967.

Chapman, Alida. *Looking Back.* Delhi, 1976.

Chelsea 125th Anniversary, 1834-1959. Chelsea, 1959.

Christman, Adam Arthur. *Ann-Arbor: The Changing Scene.* Ann Arbor, 1983.

Cocks, J. Fraser III, ed. *Pictorial History of Ann Arbor.* Ann Arbor, 1974.

Colburn, Harvey C. *The Story of Ypsilanti.* Ypsilanti, 1923.

Combination Map of Washtenaw County. Everts & Stewart, publs. Chicago, 1874.

Connelly, Will. *Chelsea's First 150 Years.* Chelsea, 1984.

Crandell, Alger Buell. *Ann's Amazing Arbor: The Growth and Groans of a Great University Town.* Ann Arbor, 1965.

Dickinson, Zenas Clark. *Saline Valley Farms, A Cooperative Venture.* Ann Arbor, 1947.

Doll, Louis. *A History of the Newspapers of Ann Arbor.* Detroit, 1959.

———. *The History of Saint Thomas Parish.* Ann Arbor, 1941.

Duff, Lela. *Ann Arbor Yesterdays.* Ann Arbor, 1962.

Dunbar, Willis Frederick. *Michigan: A History of the Wolverine State.* Grand Rapids, 1970.

Farrand, Elizabeth Martha. *History of the University of Michigan.* Ann Arbor, 1885.

Ferris, Dennis. *Manchester Village: An Historical Architectural Survey of the Central Business District.* Ann Arbor, 1979.

Finney, Byron Alfred, ed. *Washtenaw County.* In George Fuller, ed., *Historic Michigan,* vol. 3. Dayton, Ohio, 1924.

Fletcher, Foster L. *Condensed History of the Ypsilanti Area.* Ypsilanti, 1980.

Freeman, Carol Willits. *Of Dixboro: Lest We Forget.* Dixboro, 1979.

Hennings, Thomas P. *From the Marshgrasses: A History of Saint Patrick's Parish.* Ann Arbor, 1981.

———. *Looking Back: The History of Northfield Township and the Whitmore Lake Area.* Ann Arbor, 1985.

Hinsdale, Burke Aaron. *History of the University of Michigan.* Ann Arbor, 1906.

Historical Records Survey. *Michigan, Inventory of the Archives of Washtenaw County.* N.p., 1938.

Historical Souvenir, Ypsilanti, Michigan. Ypsilanti, 1905.

History of Salem Township, Washtenaw County. Salem, 1976.

History of Washtenaw County, Michigan. Chicago, 1881.

Hubbard, Lucius Lee. *The University of Michigan: Its Origin, Growth, and Principles of Government.* Ann Arbor, 1923.

Isbell, Egbert R. *A History of Eastern Michigan University.* Ypsilanti, 1971.

Leverett, Frank. *Surface Geology and Agricultural Conditions of the Southern Peninsula of Michigan.* Lansing, 1912.

Marsh, Nicholas A. *Remembering Delhi Mills: Ninety Years of Forgotten History, 1827-1917.* Delhi, 1984.

Michigan: A Guide to the Wolverine State. Federal Writers Project. New York, 1941.

Millen, DeWitt Clinton. *Memories of 591 in the World War.* Ann Arbor, 1932.

Nevins, Allan. *Ford.* 3 vols. New York, 1954-1962.

Old West Side Association, Inc. *Old West Side Ann Arbor.* Ann Arbor, 1971.

Parker, James B. *A Brief History of Webster Township.* Dexter, 1983.

Peckham, Howard. *The Making of the University of Michigan.* Ann Arbor, 1967.

Peet, Bert W. *History of the First Presbyterian Church of Ypsilanti.* Ypsilanti, 1949.

Peninsular Paper Co. *Peninsular's Eightieth Anniversary.* Ypsilanti, 1947.

Pomerening, William K. *The Diary of a Doughboy.* Ann Arbor, 1931.

Portrait and Biographical Album of Washtenaw County, Michigan. Chicago, 1891.

Proctor, Hazel. *Old Ann Arbor Town, From Original Photographs.* Ann Arbor, 1981.

———. *Old Chelsea Village, From Original Photographs.* Ann Arbor, 1972.

———. *Old Dexter Village, From Original Photographs.* Ann Arbor, 1974.

———. *Old Manchester Village, From Original Photographs.* Ann Arbor, 1974.

———. *Old Saline Village, From Original Photographs.* Ann Arbor, 1975.

———. *Old Ypsilanti Town, From Original Photographs.* Ann Arbor, 1974.

Ryan, Virginia, and others. *Early Ann Arbor and Its People.* Ann Arbor, 1974.

Sagendorf, Kent. *Michigan, The Story of the University.* New York, 1948.

Saline Area Centennial. *A Century of Progress, 1866-1966.* Saline, 1966.

Saline Historical District Commission. *Saline Has a Past in Its Future.* Saline, 1976.

Schmid, Friedrich. *A Short Sketch of the Missionary Activity of the First Lutheran Pastor in Michigan.* N.p., 1932.

Schneider, Marie A., comp. *Manchester's First Hundred Years.* Manchester, 1967.

Scott, Irving Day. *Inland Lakes of Michigan.* Lansing, 1921.

Shaw, Wilfred Byron. *The University of Michigan Illustrated.* Ann Arbor, 1949.

Smith, Alan Carter. *Junius Emery Beal, 1860-1942, His Journalistic Career.* Ann Arbor, 1969.

Smith, Flora Eva (Bostwick). *Early Days in Dexter.* Dexter, 1941.

Spragg, Jennie Shipley. *My Families: Shipley and Woolsey.* Ypsilanti, 1981.

Standard Atlas of Washtenaw County, Michigan. George A. Ogle and Co. Chicago, 1895.

Stephenson, Orlando Worth. *Ann Arbor, The First Hundred Years.* Ann Arbor, 1927.

Sturgis, Samuel. *Memories of Old Ann Arbor Town, A Sesquicentennial Publication.* Ann Arbor, 1967.

Tobias, Thomas N. *The History of Ypsilanti: 150 Years.* Ypsilanti, 1973.

A Trail Through Time: A Brief History of the Dexter Area. Dexter, 1974.

Vander Werker, Nettie Idell Schepeler. *History of Earliest Ann Arbor.* Ann Arbor, 1919.

Vaughn, Harold M. *A Ten Year Sketch of Saline Valley Farms.* Saline, 1942.

Walton, Genevieve Marie Julia. *History of St. Luke's Parish, Ypsilanti.* From *Michigan Churchman,* April 1916.

Whitaker, Catherine. *A Tradition of Mercy.* Ann Arbor, 1983.

NEWSPAPERS AND SERIALS

Ann Arbor Observer

Ann Arbor News (under its various names)

Dexter Leader

Manchester Enterprise (July 5, 1871 to July 15, 1954)

Michigan History (1917-1977)

Michigan Manual (1879-present)

Michigan Pioneer and Historical Collections (1874-1924)

Washtenaw Impressions (an occasional publication of the Washtenaw Historical Society, 1943-present)

Ypsilanti Commercial and True Democrat (March 1864 to February 2, 1899)

Ypsilanti Press

NOTE ON MANUSCRIPT SOURCES

The manuscript resources for Washtenaw County are varied and almost unlimited in scope. They include personal papers, church records, photographs, papers of business firms, and institutional records. The bulk of these are housed in the Bentley Historical Library at the University of Michigan, but significant manuscript collections are also to be found in the Ypsilanti Historical Society, the Manchester Library, the Dexter Public Library, the Dexter Historical Museum, the Chelsea Public Library, and the Saline Public Library. The archives of the University of Michigan are part of the Bentley Library's collections, and the archives of Michigan Normal School (later Eastern Michigan University) are to be found in the special collections of the Eastern Michigan University Library. Both Concordia College and Washtenaw Community College have preserved and organized their own archives. A longer, fully annotated version of this text, in manuscript form, has been deposited in the Bentley Historical Library of the University of Michigan.

INDEX

Partners in Progress Index

American Broach & Machine Company, 176

Ann Arbor Area Chamber of Commerce, 182

Ann Arbor News, 130-131

Ann Arbor Transportation Authority, 129

Applied Dynamics International, Inc., 117

Associated Spring-Barnes Group, Inc., 134-135

Barfield Companies, The, 140-141

Beyer Memorial Hospital, 158-159

Braun-Brumfield, Inc., 118

Burlington Executive Centers, 186

Chelsea Community Hospital, 157

City of Ann Arbor, 144-145

City of Ypsilanti, 127

Cleary College, 119

Comshare, 184-185

Control-o-mation, Inc., 156

Cushing-Malloy, Inc., 171

Dobson-McOmber Agency, 116

Domino's Pizza, Inc., 163

Eberbach Corporation, 138

Environmental Research Institute of Michigan, 120-121

First of America Bank-Ann Arbor, 147

Ford Motor Company, 174-175

Gelman Sciences Inc., 115

General Automotive Corporation, 132-133

General Motors Corporation/Ypsilanti Operations, 166-169

GT Products, Inc., 153

Industries, Inc., J.P., 124-125

Kerrytown Shops, 122

McAuley Health Center, Catherine, 126

Manufacturers Bank, 148-149

Michigan Consolidated Gas Company, 164-165

National Sanitation Foundation, 137

O'Neal Construction, Inc., 123

Parke-Davis Division, Warner-Lambert Company, 150

R&B Machine Tool Company, 142-143

Raycon Corporation, 152

Saline Community Hospital, 151

Schlumberger Technology-CAD/CAM Division, 170

Spear & Associates Realtors, Inc., 172

Stark Funeral Service-Moore Memorial Chapel, Inc., 154-155

University Lithoprinters, Inc., 136

UMI (University Microfilms International), 139

WAAM Radio, 183

Washtenaw County Historical Society, 114

Washtenaw Engineering Company, 128

Washtenaw Real Estate, 146

WIHT Channel 31, 180-181

WUOM Radio, 179

Ypsilanti Area Chamber of Commerce, 178

Ypsilanti Press, 160-161

Ypsilanti Public Schools, 173

Ypsilanti Savings Bank, The, 162

Zantop International Airlines, Inc., 177

General Index

Italicized numbers indicate illustrations

A

Adams, Charles Kendall, 62
African Methodist Episcopal Church, 39
Agriculture, 8, 77-79, 86
Algonquin, 13, 22
Allen, Ann, 20, 22
Allen, James, 18, 54
Allen, John, 8, 12, 18-20, 22, 24, 41, 54, 65
Allen, Sarah, 20
Alley, Genevieve, 89
Allied Alley Fiesta, 71
Allison, Andrew, 66
Allmendinger, Daniel F., 37
Allmendinger, David F., 62, 63
American Broach, 65, 75
American Foundries Company, 85
American Legion Club, *98*
American party. *See* Know-Nothing party
American Revolution, 16, 22
Anderson, Dame Judith, 92
Andrews House, 26
Angell, James Burrill, 8, *32*, 33, 36, 57
Angell, Robert Cooley, 32
Angell Hall, 74
Ann Arbor, 8, 12, 18-20, 22, 24-26, 32,
    35-37, 45, 49, 58, 66, 74, 88, 90, 92,
    98; churches in, 42, 43; during Great
    Depression, 75, 77; during World War I,
    70, 72; first schools in, 30, 31; industry
    in, 62-65, 85, 86; music in, 60-62;
    origin of name, 22; public utilities in,
    53, 54, 56, 57; railroad in, 27, 47; transpor-
    tation in, 50-52
Ann Arbor *Argus,* 65
Ann Arbor Art Fair, 90
Ann Arbor Bank, 92
Ann Arbor Choral Union, 61, 62
Ann Arbor Gas Light Company, 56
Ann Arbor Land Company, 32
Ann Arbor News, 65, 85
Ann Arbor Railroad, 47, 51, 57
Ann Arbor *Times,* 65
Anti-Masonic party, 41, 45, 65
Armistice Day, 72
Army Specialized Training Programs (ASTP),
    81, 82
Arts Theater, 92
Automobiles, 72-74

B

Bach, Anna, 67
Baird, Carillon, 110
Baltic (H.M.S.), 71
Bancroft, George, 33
Bank of Superior, 25
Bank of the United States, 25
Bank of Washtenaw, 25
Baptist church, 42, 43
Barton Hills, 74
Base Lake, 12, 22, 74
Beal, Junius, 51

Beal Block, *66*
Bethlehem Church, 63
Beyer Hospital, 75
Bishop, Sarah, 66
Black Action Mobilization (BAM), 91
Black Economic Development League
    (BEDL), 93
Black Hawk, 26
Black Hawk War, 26
Black Manifesto, 92
Booth, Edwin, 46
Bower, Emma, 67
Boyden, Luther, 45
Bridgewater, 22, 51
Briggs, Walter Owen, 77
Burton Tower, *110*

C

Cady, Calvin O., 61, 62
Cass, Lewis, 18, 20
Catherine Street hospitals, *58*
Catholic church, 37-39, 42-44, 92
Champion, Salmon, 25
Chapin, Lucy, 25
Chase, Alvin Wood, 63
Chase, Leonard, 39
Chelsea, 52; in Civil War, 41; industry in, 64,
    65, 72, 86; public utilities in, 54, 56; rail-
    road in, 47, 51
Chelsea *Herald,* 66
Chelsea Manufacturing Company, 64
Chelsea Milling Company, 85
Chelsea Products, 85
Chelsea Screw Works, 72, 85
Chelsea *Standard,* 66
Chicago Road, 18, 26, 52
Civil War, 24, 25, 30, 37, 39-42, 45, 47, 66,
    72, 77
Clark, Mary, 30
Clark Perforating Company, 85
Cleary, Patrick Roger, 60, 61
Cleary Business School (originally Cleary Col-
    lege), 61, 88
Clements Library. *See* William L. Clements
    Library
Climax Molybdenum, 85
Cobblestone Farm, 44
Colburn, Henry, 64
Community Development Center, 93
Concordia College, *87*, 88
Conductron, 85
Congregational church, 42, 47
Convention of Assent, 26
Cook, William W., 110
Cornell, Katherine, 92
Cornwell, Clark, 56
Cornwell, Cornelius, 63, 64
Cornwell's Ypsilanti Paper Company, 57, 75

D

de Chambre, Romaine, 18
Democratic party, 41, 42, 77
Depot Town, *101*
Depression. *See* Great Depression

Dexter, Samuel, 8, 18, 19, 22, 24, 41, 43, 65,
    94
Dexter, 12, 20, 22, 24, 45, 50, 54; fire depart-
    ment in, 52, 53; first schools in, 30; in
    Civil War, 41; public utilities in, 56; rail-
    road in, 47, 51
Dexter mansion, *23*
Dexter Road, 52
Detroit, 8, 13, 16, 18, 19, 22, 27, 36, 37, 42,
    47, 51, 52, 56, 72, 74, 85, 86, 92
Detroit and St. Joseph Railroad, 27
Detroit Edison, 56
Detroit, Hillsdale, and Indiana Railroad, 51
Detroit, Ypsilanti, and Ann Arbor Street Rail-
    way Company, 51
Dix, John, 19, 22
Dixboro, 19, 22
Dr. Chase's Recipe Book, 63
Domino's Farm, *107*
Double A Products, 85
Douglas, Silas H., 56
Dramatic Arts Center, 92
Dresselhouse and Davidter's shop, *37*

E

Earhart farm, 88
Eastern Michigan University, 8, 88, 92. *See
    also* Michigan Normal School
Eberbach, Christian, 62
Eberbach, Ottmar, 62
Eberbach and Company, 62
Edwards Brothers, 63
Elbel, Louis, 60
Erie Canal, 39
Estabrook, Joseph, 30, *36*

F

Federal Mogul, 85
Federal Screw Works, 72
Felch, Alpheus, 8, 35
Filmore, Calvin, 43
Fire department, 52, 53
First National Bank, 64, 75
First Presbyterian Church, 93
Fletcher, Franklin, 67
Ford, Henry, 75, 79
Ford Motor Company, 75
Forsythe, Lee, 26
Foster, Samuel, 22
Foster Station, 22
Free Hospital Association, 66
Freeman, Amariah, 45
Freeman, Fred, *43*
Freemasonry, 41, 45, 92
"Free soil," 39
Free Speech movement, 92
Frieze, Henry Simmons, 44, 61, 62

G

Gaetner, G.F., 62
General Motors, 85
German Evangelical Reform Church, 42
Germans (in Washtenaw County), 36-39, 43,
    61, 62, 70, 71, 91

Gerry, Ruth, 66
G.I. Bill of Rights, 86
Gilbert Park, *20*
Glazier, Frank P., 54, 56, 64, 65
Glazier Stove Works, 64
Godfroy, Gabriel, 18
Goodrich, Chauncy, 24
Goodrich, Morell, 26
Goodrich House, 24, 26
Gordon Hall, 43
Gothic Revival architecture, *47*
Grand River, 12, 22
Gray, Harold Studley, 78, 79
Great Depression, 69, 75-79, 82
Great Sauk Trail, 16, 19, 52
Greek Orthodox church, 92
Greek Revival architecture, *23,* 24, 42, 43, *44*
Greenman, Emerson, 22
Guthrie, Tyrone, 92

H
Harwood, William, 16, 30
Hatch, Jennie, 75
Hayes, Helen, 92
Heritage project, 68
Heusel, Samuel, *36*
Hewitt Hall, 45
Hill Auditorium, 60, 71
H.M.S. Pinafore, 45, *46*
Hobbs, William, 96
Hoover, Herbert, 77
Hoover Ball and Bearing Company, 65, 70, 75, 85
Hoover Elementary Science Laboratory, 77
Hospitals, 35
Hull, William, 13, 16
Hunt, Henry, 18
Huron Hotel, *68,* 75
Huron River, 11-13, *14, 15,* 16, 19, 24, 56, 73-75, 87, 88
Huron River Bank of Ypsilanti, 25
Hutchinson, Shelley M., 64
Hutzel, Herman, 56

I
Independence Day, 21, 40, 47, 83
Indians, 25, 94; Chippewa, 13, 16; Fox, 26; Huron, 16; Ottawa, 13, 16; Potawatomi, *13,* 16, 21, 22; Sauk, 26
Industry, 62-65, 72, 82-86
Interfaith Coalition of Churches, 93
Interurban trolley, *50,* 51
Irish Catholics. *See* Catholic church
Isbell, Egbert, 81
Italianate architecture, 44

J
Jackson, Andrew, 25, 26
James River Company, 63, 64
Jefferson, Thomas, 22
Jiffy Mix factory, 85
Johnson, Henry, 39
Johnson, Nora, *38*

K
Kaiser-Frazer, 85
Kedron. *See* Chelsea
Kemnitz, Milt, 24
Kimble, Warren, 63
King-Seeley, 75, *84,* 85
Kirschgesner, Eugene, *43*
Kiwanis club, 20
Know-Nothing party, 39, 41

L
Ladies Library Association, 44, 45
Ladies Literary Club, 44
Lahr, Bert, 92
Law Quadrangle, 74, *110*
Lend-Lease Act, 79
Limpert, Iva, 75
Lincoln, Abraham, 41
Lincoln Laboratory School, 75, 86
Lucas, Robert, 26
Lusty, Mary Teresa Kelly, 38
Lutheran church, 42, 88
Lyon, Lucius, 18

M
McAndrew, Helen, 66
McClellan, George, 42
McCoy, George, 39
Mack Building, 72
McKinstry, Andrew, 18, 26
Manchester, 8, 24, 30, 37, 42, 57, 63, 65, 79; Germans in, 43; industry in, 85, 86; origin of name, 22; railroad in, 47, 51
Manchester Dandies, *43*
Manchester *Enterprise,* 66
Manchester Mill, *100*
Manchester Plastics, 85
Mann, Emanuel, 53
Mann, Jonathan Henry, 37
Maple Lane Farm, *48*
Marlowe, Julia, 46
Marvin, John, 47
Mason, Steven T., 26
Masons. *See* Freemasonry
Maumee Malleable Casting Company, 85
May Drama Festival, 92, 108
Maynard, William S., 32
Mercywood, 75
Methodist church, 42
Michigan Anti-Slavery Society, 39
Michigan Central Railroad, 47, 50, 51, 57
Michigan Consolidated Gas, 56
Michigan Equal Suffrage Association, 67
Michigan Freeman, 39
Michigan Molded Plastics, *82, 83,* 85
Michigan Portland Cement, 72
Michigan Normal School, 8, 16, 30, *34,* 51, 57, 58, 60, 66, 67, 74, 75, 86; beginnings, 35, 36; during Civil War, 41; during Great Depression, 77; during World War I, 72; during World War II, 81, 82; music at, 61, 62. *See also* Eastern Michigan University
Milan, 47, 50, 51, 79, 85

Milan *Leader,* 66
Miller, Albert, 61
Misses Clarks' School for Girls, 30, 31, 35
Morgan, William, 41
Morton, Robert, 39
Mosher, Eliza, 66
Munson, John, 81

N
National Security League, 96
National Youth Administration, 77
Native American Association of Ann Arbor, 39
Newberry Hall, 72
New Deal, 77
Newspapers, 65, 66
Nidmayer, Will, *43*
Nineteenth Amendment, 96
Nisle, August, *43*
Noble, Margaret, 20
Normal school. *See* Michigan Normal School
Norris, Mark, 39
Northwest Ordinance of 1787, 26, 29

O
Old Maude, 52
Old Sauk Trail. *See* Great Sauk Trail
Olney, Edward, 42
Ormandy, Eugene, *108*
Owen, Clara, 92
Owen, Henry, 92

P
Parke-Davis, 85
Parker Manufacturing, 65
Parsons, Roswell, family of, 30
Patee, Elias, 42
Patriotic Service League, 75
Pease, Frederick H., 61, 62
Pease Auditorium, 60, *61*
Peninsular Paper Company, 63, 64
Perry, Chester, 25
Perry House, 25
Pierce, John D., 8, 35
Pittsfield, 24, 51
Pokagon, Julia, 16
Political Equality Club, 67
Portage Lake, 12, 22, 74
Potawatomi. *See* Indians
Pray, George, 35
Pray-Harold building, 86, 92
Presbyterian church, 39, 42, 93
Prohibition, 66, 67, 72
Public Works Administration (PWA), 77

Q
Quakers, 38, 39
Quirk, Daniel, Jr., 64
Quirk, Daniel, Sr., 51, 64, 99

R
Railroads, 8, 27, 47, 50, 51
Raisin River, 12, 13, 21, 63, 65
Randall Physics Laboratory, 75

Rathbone, Basil, 92
Republican party, 37, 41, 42, 64, 77
Reserve Officer Training Corps (ROTC), 71, 72
Revolutionary War. *See* American Revolution
Rockwell Standard, 85
Romanesque architecture, *37,* 42, 61
Roosevelt, Franklin D., 77, 81
Roosevelt High School, *74,* 75
Rumsey, Elisha, 12, 18-20, 22, 24, 32
Rumsey, Mary Ann, 20, 22

S
St. Andrew's church, 42, *43,* 44
St. Francis of Assisi Catholic Church, 43
St. Joseph Trail, 16
St. Joseph's Catholic school, 38
St. Joseph's Mercy Hospital, 75
St. Luke's church, 42
St. Regis Paper Company, 85
St. Thomas the Apostle church, *37,* 43
Saline, 24, 26, 47, 50, 52; during Civil War, 41; during Great Depression, 78, 79; first schools in, 30; industry in, 85, 86; railroad in, 51
Saline River, 12, 21, 47, 50
Saline Valley Farms, 77, *78,* 79
Saturday Club, *45*
Schilling, Phillip, 37
Schmid, Rev. Frederick, 37
Second Baptist Church, 43
Sentinel (Ypsilanti newspaper), 65, 66
Seven Years War, 16
Signal Corps, 70
Signal of Liberty, 39
Sink, Charles, 62
Slavery, 38, 39, 41
Smith, Asa, 24
Smith, Cynthia, 66
Smith, Flora, 89
Society of Freemasons. *See* Freemasonry
Society of Friends. *See* Quakers
Solomos, Alexis, 92
Spafford, George, 66
Spanish influenza, 72
Spy of Shiloh, 45
Stanley, Albert, 62
Starkweather Hall, 60
Stewart, John, 16, 18
Stockwell Hall, 77
Stone School, *100*
Student Army Training Corps (SATC), 71, 72

Sutton, Benjamin, 39
Swabian Rhineland, 37

T
Tappan, Henry, 8, *32,* 33, 35, 36, 57
Taylor, Charles B., 23
Taylor, Millisent, 23
Teamsters Union, 79
Temperance, 45
Territorial Road, 52
Thayer, Charles, 31
Thomas, Charles, 92
Tickner, Frank, 75
Tiffin, Edward, 13
Toledo War, 26
Town, Thomas M., 42

U
Underground railroad, 38, 39, 41
Union Savings Bank, 42
Union School, *28*
University High School, 75
University Musical Society, 62
University of Michigan, 8, 22, 36, 51, 53, 56-58, 60, 63, 66, 67, 74, 75, 88, 90, 98, *108, 110;* beginnings, 30-33, 35; during Civil War, 41; during Great Depression, 77; during World War I, 70-72; during World War II, 81, 82; during Vietnam War, 92; map of, *97;* music at, 61, 62; racial conflicts at, 91-93
Uptown Saline Association, 85

V
Van Buren, Martin, 26
Van Depoele Light and Power Company, 56
Van Fossen, John B., 65
Veterans of Foreign Wars, 98
Victorian architecture, 43, 44
"Victors, The," *60*
Vietnam War, 92

W
Wabash Railroad, 47
"Walk-in-the-Water," *12,* 13
War of 1812, 13, 16
Washtenaw Community College, *87,* 88, 93
Washtenaw Guards, 27
Washtenaw, origin of name, 22
Washtenaw Post, 70
Waterman Gymnasium, 60
Wayne Company, 22

Webster, Daniel, 22
Welch, A.R., 64, 65
Welch, Adonijah Strong, 36
Welch Tourist, 65
Wenger, John, *51*
Wenger, Marie, *70*
Western Emigrant, 27, 41, 65
Whig party, 65
White, Orrin, 32
Whitmore, Oliver, 24
Whitmore Lake, 11, 12, 74
Whitney Opera House, 45
Wildcat banking, 25
Willard, Emma, 30
William L. Clements Library, 74, *108*
Williams, G. Mennen, 41
Willow Run bomber plant, *81,* 85
Willow Run Village, 85, 88
Wilson, Robert S., 43
Wilson, Woodrow, 70
Wolverine Building, 75
Wolverines, 111
Woman's Christian Temperance Union, 67
Woodruff, Benjamin, 18, 19, 21, 28, 47
Woodruff, Charles, 28, 30, 65
Woodruff, M.T., 66
Woodruff's Grove, 16-20, 42, 47, 66
Woodward, Augustus, 16, 18, 20, 22
World War I, 49, 52, 58, 60, 62, 65, 67, 69-72, 77, 81, 91, 96
World War II, 74, 75, 79-85, 86, 88, 90, 91, 103

Y
Yost Field House, 75
Ypsilanti, Demetrius, 22
Ypsilanti, 12, 18, 19, 24-26, 35, 39, 42, 45, 49, 55, 58, 66, 68, 83, 88, 90-92, 99, 101; centennial, *20;* during Civil War, 41; during Great Depression, 75-77; during World War I, 70-72; during World War II, 80; first schools in, 30; industry in, 63-65, 86; music in, 60-62; origin of name, 22; public utilities in, 53, 54, 56, 57; railroad in, 27, 47; transportation in, 50-52
Ypsilantian, 55, 66
Ypsilanti *Commercial,* 66
Ypsilanti Musical Union, 62
Ypsilanti Opera House, 46
Ypsilanti State Hospital, 75
Ypsilanti Union Seminary, 30
Ypsilanti Whist Club, 95